THE CRESSET LIBRARY

GENERAL EDITOR: JOHN HAYWARD

THE LIFE OF
GEORGE CRABBE

THE LIFE OF

GEORGE

CRABBE

BY HIS SON

WITH

AN INTRODUCTION BY

EDMUND BLUNDEN

LONDON

THE CRESSET PRESS

MCMXLVII

Published mcmxlvii in Great Britain
by the Cresset Press Ltd., 11 Fitzroy Square, London W.1
Printed by the Shenval Press, London and Hertford

Father and Son

IN THE annals of English poetry it is not the least remarkable thing that the physicians have been conspicuous: Conan Doyle himself was a lyrical writer of great directness, John Todhunter, M.D., possessed a true charm in verse, Sir Ronald Ross expressed his own scientific triumph in lively imaginative poems, Gordon Hake was not only Rossetti's friend but won the name of the Parable Poet, and everyone knows that Robert Bridges achieved a reputation in medical circles before he made the decision which carried him at length to the Laureateship. These are only a few modern instances; a glance into earlier literary history soon produces a great many more, and we see that here and there the list might be extended by the names of splendid poets who had more than a little inclination towards the world of the doctors of medicine. Coleridge found opportunity to accompany his brother round the hospital wards, and Shelley, in the words of an intimate friend, "visited the sick (at Great Marlow) in their beds, for he had gone the round of the hospitals on purpose to be able to practise on occasion."

This coalition of physician and poet, of which the Rev. George Crabbe, LL.B., was a strong representative, has been noticed frequently enough, but as yet seldom investigated with depth of thought except in the case of John Keats. No doubt the results of a critical survey would be uneven, and the poems of some of the physician-poets might disclose but little sign of the medical training or attitude possessed by the authors. Where does Campion the surgeon make himself known in Campion's lyrics, or what does Goldsmith's degree of M.B. do for "The Deserted Village"? The reader of Henry Vaughan's beloved book may easily picture that well-known Welsh doctor of three centuries ago on his wide journeys, but not so easily capture him in the actual exercise of his profession; Vaughan certainly shows now and then what remedies he derives from Nature, even from the violet which he employs for salves and syrups, and thence he comes at his theory of what is pure and vital. The studies and wonderings of the anatomist in German universities underlie "Death's Jest-Book" by T. L. Beddoes, and without them we lack the clue to that poet's strange intention in the work. The Robert Bridges of many a light song or sustained ode is not at all the obvious man for a Fellowship of the Royal College of Physicians; none the less, Bridges turns away from those poems to others, and to his ultimate great discourse on universal themes, as one speaking from the point of view of the skilled Aesculapian, and a physician of mankind.

George Crabbe, as his son's unpretentious biography of him shows, was never in sight of such professional distinction as Dr. Bridges quietly achieved while still a young man; he had not the natural endowments, and his training was haphazard and commonplace. All the same, medicine was the original object and labour of his youth; without it we should not have had the poetry which stands to his name. These tales and local reports, the domesday-book of some small parts of the England of his day, owe much to his necessary tours, calls and considerations; sitting down to disturb elegant culture with an anatomy of the passions and a selection of the queer complexities of life, Crabbe is unmistakably the general practitioner in country places. The number, variety, peculiarity and minute delineation of the private histories which he is moved to bring to light evince the opportunities, the attentive habits and the patient diagnosis of hidden cause which characterise that kind of visitor.

Nobody could be more favourably placed than the country doctor of any period for the discovering of such human histories as stand honestly engraved on the tablets of English literature by the fearless understanding of Crabbe. East Anglia is not a sentimental province, and Crabbe, an East Anglian, grew up with particular reason to acknowledge truth. It is the psychological art of the medical man who calls on patients usually suspicious and reticent to hear them fully, even where their news might seem loose and detached from the disease or mischief which has required him to cross the fields to the farmhouse; and they will speak to him as to one with higher powers than other men. "I *know* these Merriams," said a later doctor in Crabbe's county to me once, "I know them all." That is the essence of Crabbe's poems in contrast with most others. For a specimen of the strength which his position as the man of life and death developed in him we need look no further than to the unforgettable, terrible, but simply presented story of "Ellen Oxford." The old blind woman whose life of shocking miseries is there set out is obviously talking to the one possible confidant, the doctor; she recalls the illegitimate child, the realisation that her child is an idiot, the seduction of that pretty lunatic by an "unhealthy" brother, and all the rest, in the unforced and undissembling tone of one whose listener knows all there is in birth, death, lunacy and sex. To turn from the visions of life's stony tracks in Crabbe's book to the tales which even Wordsworth collects at the same period is to lose the last word in such writing. Crabbe had seen as in a white light what Wordsworth's rural walk could not unveil, and in particular he had isolated the factor of sex in its manifold action, a profound cause of lifelong dilemma, conflict, hope and despair.

With such reflections as these in my mind, not many years ago, I stood in the then remote village of Wickhambrook in Suffolk. The dispensary whence George Crabbe, as the apothecary's apprentice of the eighteenth century, had set forth with his bottles of medicine, was still serving its old purpose. The reigning doctor, who was aware of as many astonishing life-stories as ever Crabbe was, spoke with pride of the association with the poet. From the winding roads and the ploughed lands round Crabbe had surely collected on his many errands much of his knowledge of wild Nature inland. It is true that he said goodbye to the surgeon-apothecary of Wickhambrook when he was only seventeen years old, and the period of his service there would not by itself sustain the connection noticed above between Crabbe's profession and his poetical resources. But the biography drawn up by his son continues the evidence, and in due course we encounter not the shy and uncertain apprentice but Dr. Crabbe, his own master. The poet prevailed over the professional man; and yet the victory was doubtful. Crabbe is found at the age of forty, and for that matter at sixty, still in a measure "practising his original profession." The excellent son who bore his name allows that Crabbe was not gifted with those qualities which make a surgeon, but is pleased to cite a respectable opinion that the poet might have ranked high as a physician; and he points out in his uneffusive way a picturesque and useful distinction in his father's career, well known to the inhabitants of more than one parish through many years. It means that Crabbe never lacked the approach to life with which he began: "He grudged no personal fatigue to attend the sickbed of the peasant, in the double capacity of physician and priest."

Canon Deane, who did so much to keep Crabbe's best poetry in action in our own times, underlines the hints given by the poet's son upon the imperfections of Crabbe as a parson during part of his life. His long absence from his cure of souls in Leicestershire led to an incident which only an extremely candid son would relate; when Crabbe resigned the living, the villagers rang the bells for his successor before he had left his parsonage. But in respect of the poet's development, Crabbe's taking orders has another interest. As a priest he obtained new opportunities and another point of view for his observation of men and women and the ruling passions. His chaplaincy in a great house did much for his impressions of society and prestige, at some cost to his self-esteem, as his biographer allows us to know—the realisation that Vanity Fair has its ways of beguiling and wounding the sojourner. Even the failures which he incurred as a parish priest were contributory to his picture of the world, and passing beyond the tribulations of one compelled to endure contempt he realised the extent to which sectarian religion influences the commonwealth. He gained in tolerance even while he grew in stature; for the figure whom the son gradually describes is beyond doubt a commanding figure.

Crabbe, the clergyman, was not doomed to end his ministry in feelings of bitterness. The simplicity of his nature when he was met by hostility is mirrored in the preface to "Tales of the Hall", 1819: "It may appear to some that a minister of religion, in the decline of life, should have no leisure for such amusements as these, and for them I have no reply." The words of his friend Mr. Taylor at Trowbridge assure us that at last very few of his parishioners were inclined to dispute with him over his duties, principles or anything else; the man who is portrayed in this book was the man they all knew and accepted. So we accept his poems. They are majestically themselves. Crabbe for his part made no great show of seeing further into the councils of eternity than his neighbours. "We know that our duty is to submit, because there is enough we can see to make us rest in hope and comfort, though there be much that we cannot understand." And again, after the Fair, "When I saw four or five human beings, with painted faces and crazy gestures, trying to engage and entice the idle 'realist' = accepting contradiction

spectators to enter their showhouse, I felt the degradation; for it seemed like man reduced from his natural rank in the creation: and yet, probably, they would say: 'What can we do? We were brought up to it, and we must eat'." The reason why Thomas Hardy held Crabbe in honour comes out in such a place; the earlier realist also concluded that we do best in attempting no more than a good-natured recording of life's phenomena as they come. In the pulpit Crabbe did not contradict this while he "urged his flock to virtuous conduct, by placing a future award ever full in their view, instead of dwelling on the temporal motives rendered so prominent at that time by many of his brethren."

It is not only in the allusions to contemporary sects and schismatics that Crabbe's work as a clergyman makes its effect upon his poetry, nor in the reduction of the harsher and angrier style of depicting men and things with which he surprised the public first. His cassock haunts his later work in the tendency towards moralising his tales; he preaches the full hour and cannot keep his book of sermons and his poetical manuscripts separate. Capable as scarcely any man since Chaucer of telling a story with economy, he falls under the spell of his sacred office and produces his homilies at slow length; the custom, even if the prose novelists of an older day kept to it, dissipates his force. The story of "Edward Shore" comes to mind as a story weakened. Even there Crabbe is free from the drone of cant and of interdiction, but preamble is heavy and explanation protracted over Edward's fatal error of principle and over the very similar fantasy on the part of the friend whom Edward betrays.

More remarkable than this growth of exposition is the fact that Crabbe's position as a priest, when orthodoxy was at its most powerful point and ever prepared to smite the independent, never prevented the poet from fastening upon subjects in real life just as he chose and exhibiting them without the safeguard of a mystical background. The old psychologist was not to be suppressed by the theologian; the fascination of man as he is was not cancelled by the prospect of Heaven free from strife. George Crabbe, the younger, must be given praise for many things in his biography but not least for his signifying that the poet was never at war with life because of some ideal beyond its bounds. Not only did Crabbe remain the acute spectator of the things which happened to other people; he was very willing to have them happen to himself. Literary success and fame, we see, did not affect him as genuine experience. His reply to one of the authors of "Rejected Addresses" and his son's comment illustrate this detachment; so does his paragraph upon the critical essay in "The Spirit of the Age"—"I believe I felt something indignant: but my engraved seal dropped out of the socket and was lost, and I perceived this vexed me much more than the 'spirit' of Mr. Hazlitt." It was from other sources that Crabbe felt excitement and glory. When he was sixty and more he could fall in love; his son does not go into all the details, but we may know that in this respect, too, Crabbe was a harmless pluralist. "I am persuaded," the biographer says, "that but few men have, even in early life, tasted either of the happiness or the pain which attend the most exquisite of passions, in such extremes as my father experienced at this period of his life."

Readers of Crabbe's poetry will be slow to acquiesce in the notion that it is all of one kind, and that his ordinary preference of the rhyming couplet betrays a sameness of treatment and of inspiration. The recollections of the son contain scattered notices of the poet at work—in years when he would hardly have consented that even Charles James Fox should revise his verses. We are told that, like Wordsworth, he often composed as he was walking outdoors: "No one who observed him at these times could doubt that he enjoyed exquisite pleasure in composing. He had a degree of action whilst thus walking and versifying, which I hardly ever observed when he was preaching or reading." The process was intense, and Crabbe himself described it as hard work. We hear, too, that autumn seemed to him his best poetical season; that he wrote much at night; and that "there was something in the effect of a sudden fall of snow that appeared to stimulate him in a very extraordinary manner. It was during a great snowstorm that, shut up in his room, he wrote almost *currente calamo* his 'Sir Eustace Grey'." Such particulars the biographer provides for what they are worth in disclosing the poetical character of his father, but he gives another without guessing that it plays a part in the composition of the strange poem named and some others.

As in the instance of Coleridge, an anodyne was prescribed to Crabbe in an illness; he became an opium-taker, and his son says that his health was all the better for "a constant but slightly increasing dose." If the drug was the principal cause of the dream-poems of Coleridge, it was equally the key for Crabbe into a visionary world which, reported in verse of a curious inevitability, greatly alters the look of his poetry in a complete reckoning. "Sir Eustace Grey" is in and out of that world, now aflame with violent demons and now dreadfully calm:

" Upon that boundless plain, below,
   The setting sun's last rays were shed,
And gave a mild and sober glow
   Where all were still, asleep, or dead;
   Vast ruins in the midst were spread,
Pillars and pediments sublime,
   Where the grey moss had form'd a bed,
And clothed the crumbling spoils of time.

" There was I fix'd, I know not how,
     Condemn'd for untold years to stay:
Yet years were not—one dreadful *Now*
     Endured no change of night and day;
The same mild evening's sleeping ray
     Shone softly solemn and serene,
And all that time I gazed away
     The setting sun's sad rays were seen."

There the description of Crabbe as a "Pope in worsted stockings" is obviously inapplicable, and it is just as far from the
mark in respect of another mysterious lyrical ballad the origin
of which is described with loathing in Crabbe's journal for
July 21st, 1817. Coleridge's "Pains of Sleep" is of the same
breed and bosom as Crabbe's "World of Dreams." Once
more Crabbe is committed to a mad and mute desolation:

     "I sail the sea, I walk the land;
          In all the world I am alone:
     Silent I pace the sea-worn sand,
          Silent I view the princely throne:
     I listen heartless for the tone
     Of winds and waters, but in vain;
          Creation dies without a groan!
     And I without a hope remain."

In that region of images suddenly abnormal in their dis-
tinctness, then exchanged for others, the meaning of existence
is hideously wrong: all is bedevilled.

     " Within the basis of a tower
          I saw a plant—it graced the spot;
     There was within nor wind nor shower,
          And this had life that flowers have not.

I drew it forth—Ah, luckless lot!
It was the mandrake: and the sound
Of anguish deeply smother'd shot
Into my breast with pang profound."

Few of the many who possess Crabbe's works, I imagine,
have paused long over "The World of Dreams," though
Canon Deane included it in his little selection; and it would be
strange if the poet's son, who had not much of the dreamer
about him, had dwelt upon it, or tried to vary his pages with
critical theories on the paradoxes of his father's creations. He
was struck by one thing; the man who in his observation
lacked a thesis of the beautiful, and who lived without being
disturbed by a chaos of objects round him, was defective in
his writings in the important matter of "the conduct of the
whole." In other words, if he had ever felt himself qualified
to advise the parent whose greatness he seems everywhere to
apprehend rather than to have in full view, the younger Crabbe
would have urged the poet to new efforts in the words
written by Keats to Shelley: "Be more of an artist." The advice
would have been given without much expectation, for the
son believed the father to be pre-eminently of the scientific
type. "His powerful intellect did not seem to require the
ideas of sense to move it to enjoyment, but he could at all
times find luxury in the most dry and forbidding calculations."
Along some such lines as this, presumably, the biographer
would have explained the comparative indifference of his
father to the field of lyrical poetry which was open to him,
and wherein his contemporaries were seen planting and watering flowers of richest and highest grace. George Crabbe wrote
no sonnet of a single adoration, no ode with symphony of
thought and sound appropriate to one theme.

The son asserts that the deficiency in his father's poetry was related to his caring little for "painting, or music, or architecture, or for what a painter's eye considers as the beauties of landscape." The poems scarcely support that opinion, however they may fail in a strict test of proportion and management. Crabbe must have possessed his share of the aesthetic response, or whence did he find reasons for introducing into his novels in verse those famous seascapes and landscapes and occasionally interiors which make him something of a counterpart to the Norwich School in painting? If they are inspected as it were with a magnifying glass, they show that their maker was capable of the finest touches. No "Ode to Autumn" was ever written with more of sensibility in the stresses and the sequence of sounds, as well as the sustaining movement, than the description of the doomed lover at his window in "Delay Has Danger":

> " Early he rose, and look'd with many a sigh
> On the red light that fill'd the eastern sky:
> Oft had he stood before, alert and gay,
> To hail the glories of the new-born day;
> But now dejected, languid, listless, low,
> He saw the wind upon the water blow,
> And the cold stream curl'd onward as the gale
> From the pine-hill blew harshly down the dale;
> On the right side the youth a wood survey'd,
> With all its dark intensity of shade;
> Where the rough wind alone was heard to move,
> In this, the pause of Nature, and of love,
> When now the young are rear'd, and when the old,
> Lost to the tie, grow negligent and cold:
> Far to the left he saw the huts of men,
> Half hid in mist that hung upon the fen;
> Before him swallows, gathering for the sea,

Took their short flights, and twitter'd on the lea;
And near the bean-sheaf stood, the harvest done,
And slowly blacken'd in the sickly sun;
All these were sad in nature, or they took
Sadness from him, the likeness of his look,
And of his mind—he ponder'd for a while,
Then met his Fanny with a borrow'd smile."

Surely the most telling impression of the time and the place in all our verse; perhaps the most ably displayed scene in the poetry of landscape. Yet before the end Crabbe has turned away from that outward scene, and acknowledged that his thought had been as much upon the state of mind of his unfortunate hero—the psychological landscape. Elsewhere he is explicit upon the effect of mood acting upon the appearance of things; and "The Lover's Journey" begins with the declaration:

"It is the Soul that sees: the outward eyes
Present the object, but the Mind describes;
And thence delight, disgust, or cool indiff'rence rise."

A man who is of that opinion, most of the time, is likely to attempt studies of pure beauty or colour infrequently; neither Crabbe, nor Meredith, nor Hardy is inclined to represent what is lovely without the intertwining activity of the mind pursuing the plot, immense or local, of his book of life.

Crabbe is perfectly open in this energetic inclusiveness, and it may be he can persuade us in the end that his treatment of the beautiful, as an unfixed and passing current in the stream of our being, is as profound a work of art as any static rendering. What he does is well exemplified at the outset of "Delay

Has Danger," where nothing more than a morning excursion
is at the moment involved:

> "He rode to Ripley through that river gay,
> Where in the shallow stream the loaches play,
> And stony fragments stay the winding stream,
> And gilded pebbles at the bottom gleam,
> Giving their yellow surface to the sun,
> And making proud the waters as they run:
> It is a lovely place, and at the side
> Rises a mountain-rock in rugged pride;
> And in that rock are shapes of shells, and forms
> Of creatures in old worlds, of nameless worms
> Whose generations lived and died ere man,
> A worm of other class, to crawl began."

All our memories of the brooks in Anglia, making "washes"
across the sandy cartways, are brought to their brightest in
the first part of the passage, and we may well suppose that
another sort of fancy or personality would have gone on with
the delightfulness of that little river; but Crabbe the geologist
(and obviously the geologist cares nothing for the parson)
cannot be long excluded. Even so the contrast between the
fresh life of the stream and the tomb of the enormously remote
life that was here might be that of a regular ode on the occasion; it can be outlined in its beginning, middle and end,
harmonised in a philosophy. This is not Crabbe's way. He
is true to himself and he records his train of thought, ending
with his ambiguous definition—is it satirical, is it merely
scientific?—of the human being. And is this, in an artistic
consideration, a false note? Those who live with Crabbe as
he remains in his book will be less and less inclined to think so.

Without setting himself up as a champion Crabbe attacked

the prevailing notions of the beautiful and the ugly as soon as
he had grown mature in literature. His biographer must have
avoided the topic as too abstruse, except inasmuch as it was
connected with Crabbe's earliest surroundings. These in a
way overcame any theories of beauty in the abstract which
Crabbe knew or repeated; he might say that such and such a
scene was sordid, or dull, but it had him in thrall—it was a
picture, and he seized upon it in words with unique impartiality. For "Life, some think, is worthy of the Muse." A
saltern has at least one great English poet:

> " When tides were neap, and, in the sultry day
> Through the tall bounding mud-banks made their way,
> Which on each side rose swelling, and below
> The dark warm flood ran silently and slow;
> There anchoring, Peter chose from man to hide,
> There hang his head, and view the lazy tide
> In its hot slimy channel slowly glide;
> Where the small eels that left the deeper way
> For the warm shore, within the shallows play;
> Where gaping mussels, left upon the mud,
> Slope their slow passage to the fallen flood;
> Here dull and hopeless he'd lie down and trace
> How sidelong crabs had scrawl'd their crooked race,
> Or sadly listen to the tuneless cry
> Of fishing gull or clanging golden-eye;
> What time the sea-birds to the marsh would come,
> And the loud bittern, from the bull-rush home,
> Gave from the salt ditch side the bellowing boom."

The observer of the expressive means in traditional versification would applaud among other masterly details here the
third rhyme which Crabbe delivers at his choice; but the

larger sense of the poet's excellence replies to any questions about beauty that he has obeyed an admirable rule, and "gives Beauty all her right."

As a receptive witness of the external scene Crabbe was limited in later years by the strength of his first impressions, and his son readily refers to this inaction of his poetic mind when he was far inland. He might be writing in Wiltshire, his imagination generally travelled back to the East Coast; situations and crises in human life could take his fancy wherever they appeared, but for the settings he revisited his native haunts. Among those we must reckon after all the countryside towards Newmarket in which he had spent some years as the apothecary's apprentice; for one of the most vigorous and best varied of his "Posthumous Tales" was formed upon one of his visits to the mansion of the Duke of Rutland at Cheveley. Half a century and more had passed since that "happy day," but the pictures which the poem retains are of a singular brilliance. The poet's editors did well to print an alternative conclusion to this poem, in which Crabbe makes clear to us a cause why, the older he grew, the more willing he was to live in past time and enjoy the first impressions of which I spoke. The child whom the housekeeper had guided round the marvels of Cheveley, and who had thought

> "the lords of all these glorious things
> Are bless'd supremely".

had become the companion of those great ones, the participant of their daily life.

> "Well, thou hast tried it—thou hast closely seen
> What Greatness has without it, and within;
> Where now the joyful expectation?—fled!
> The strong anticipating spirit?—dead!"

This melancholy epitaph on early illusion and even the hollowness of achievement, taken with such things as "The World of Dreams" and the sharp bitterness which concludes so many of the Tales ("Crabbe's prodigals," Canon Deane notices, "have never a chance of return") betray the shadow within Crabbe's spirit. We shall never know him as he could know others. His most intimate companions did not know him fully; it was not that he wished to reserve anything or to appear other than he was. That he was a model of modesty at the height of his fame and a master of courtesy and pleasantness is undeniable. His conduct had the stamp of heroism, though his humorous smile and glance refused to have it called so. But in those words towards the final moment, "I thought it had been all over" (with such an emphasis on the all!) a story as bleak and forlorn as anything in his book appears to be summed up. Some appalments from the early years insisted on living with him in private as well as the happy days and the ever interesting host of characters good, bad and ridiculous.

The nearest approach to this seemingly simple, really complex man is afforded by the biography which, regarded as a small classic, is now republished. Even his son does not assume the air or claim the power of knowing George Crabbe throughout. The biography as we have it has suffered from the confident hand of a reviser, John Gibson Lockhart, who subjected the manuscript to those falsifications indicated by Sir Herbert Grierson in his own celebrated *Life of Scott*— juggling with document and date, polishing anecdote up. It was the age of free biographical behaviour—the aim was popular interest. Even so, this *Life of Crabbe* does not stand or fall by its statistical accuracy or otherwise, and those whose requirements lead them towards the exact account of every episode, and the correct text of every letter or extract from a memorandum book, are fortunate in being able to consult the late Professor Huchon's "George Crabbe and his Times."

The younger Crabbe was not a professional author, though he committed to the Press one or two essays in natural theology. Of his own capabilities as a poet, I know nothing more than what may be discerned in the following reply to an invitation from Edward Fitzgerald, who proposed to entertain a few friends at Boulge Cottage:

> "As sure as a gun
> I'll be in at the fun;
> For I'm the old Vicar
> As sticks to his liquor;
> And smokes a cigar,
> Like a jolly Jack Tar:
> I've no time for more,
> For the Post's at the door:
> But I'll be there by seven,
> And stay 'till eleven,
> For Boulge is my Heaven!"

Commenting upon this rhyme Bernard Barton, the Quaker poet who could himself unbend after closing his bank, wished to make it clear that its clerical author was no Bacchanalian, but it is apparent that he was a cheerful, good-natured man; and such he is while he puts together from fireside anecdotes and his own judgment of character and circumstance the biography of his father. If he cannot compass everything in that great subject, yet his book has a large range of his own—for he speaks of people and manners outside the stated theme with a zest worthy of the name which he bears. Without any trace of ambition in literature, he may be said to have made himself a place in its sunshine with passages not directly devoted to the family's man of genius—that first excursion into

Suffolk in 1790, for example. Charles Lamb is the prince of descriptions and studies of the sort, but the comparison does not make George Crabbe the Second look in the least unskilful. We could wish, in truth, that this unassuming parish priest *had* been stirred by more of literary ambition.

His work as biographer was undertaken in a style which probably guarded him and was meant to guard him from venturing into literary history and criticism, so far as they concerned the productions of George Crabbe. It was left for others to describe the relationships, for instance, of Crabbe's poem "The Village," which was written in time to be admired and touched up by a man well fitted to understand the newcomer—Samuel Johnson. With that poem

> "I paint the Cot
> As Truth will paint it, and as Bards will not—"

a striking chapter in English poetry and social criticism and controversy comes into sight; and the learned annotator of Crabbe's immature but disturbing essay in the realities of pastoral life in England would remember a number of "Villages." Crabbe himself named Stephen Duck, who humbly drew attention to the hardships of the farm labourer in Queen Anne's day; but since then Goldsmith had made a more eloquent and far-reaching protest in "The Deserted Village." Later on "The Favourite Village" by the Reverend James Hurdis resumed the Arcadian way of tinting the picture; "Our Village" by Miss Mitford did still more that way, in its poetically written prose; and in Crabbe's old age Ebenezer Elliott was penning those ardent manifestoes "The Splendid Village" and "The Village Patriarch" of which he avowed, "I am called, as I expected to be, an unsuccessful imitator of the pauper-poetry of Wordsworth... I might be truly called an unfortunate imitator of Crabbe, that most

British of poets; for he has long been bosomed with me; and if he had never lived, it is quite possible that I might never have written pauper-poetry." Elliott adds ironically, that because of a different plan of society, "the unhappy people of the United States of America cannot bear to read Crabbe."

A disquisition on matters like those would certainly have been welcome to Crabbe, the younger, even if he might inadvertently tear off a strip of it to light his cigar. But in preparing his father's biography he kept literature at as respectable a distance as he could in view of his father's eminence for literature. He was mainly attracted by the personality and vicissitudes of one whose insight into such humanities had been in some degree transmitted to him. To recapture even without explaining any habit, taste, casual experience of his father's was his pleasure; and from a word here and there we shall not be far wrong in seeing his brother John as of one mind with him in it. George Crabbe the Second had the happiness of finding in Edward Fitzgerald a lover of his father's poetry as hearty as himself, and a friend who valued friendship not less. Everything which we can now discover about this biographer justifies Fitzgerald's appreciation of him, and his grief when, in 1857, he died. Ten years earlier, Bernard Barton had written of his enthusiasm for Jenny Lind, though he wished she were not quite so lean: "Still harping on that Lindean wench! So is old Crabbe, who saw and heard her at Norwich, and for aught I know will carry her image enshrin'd in his heart with him to the grave, if it be not quenched in those clouds of smoke he emits every night."

EDMUND BLUNDEN

Contents

Preface to the First Edition

THE SUCCESS of some recent biographical works, evidently written by unpractised hands, suggested to me the possibility that my recollections of my father might be received with favour by the public. The rough draft of the following narrative was accordingly drawn up, and submitted to my father's friend, Mr. Thomas Moore, whom at that time I had never seen, and who, in returning it, was so kind as to assure me that he had read it with much interest, and conceived that, with a little correction, it might gratify the readers of Mr. Crabbe's Poetical Works. I afterwards transmitted it to his friend, Mr. Rogers, who expressed himself in terms equally flattering to an inexperienced writer; and who—as indeed, Mr. Moore had done before—gave me the most valuable species of assistance I could have received, by indicating certain passages that ought to be obliterated. Mr. Moore, Mr. Campbell, Mr. Lockhart, Mrs. Joanna Baillie, Mr. Duncan, Mr. Clark, and others of my father's friends have, moreover, taken the trouble to draw up brief summaries of their personal reminiscences of him, with which I have been kindly permitted to enrich this humble Memoir.

The letters and extracts of letters from Sir Walter Scott, Mr. Roger Wilbraham, Mr. Canning, Mrs. Leadbeater, and other eminent friends of Mr. Crabbe, now deceased, which are introduced in the following pages have been so used with the permission of their representatives; and I have to thank the Duke of Rutland, the Marquis of Lansdowne, Earl Grey, Lord Holland, the Right Hon. J. W. Croker, the Rev. Richard Turner, and the other living gentlemen, whose correspondence has been as serviceable to my labours as it was honourable to my father's character, for leave to avail myself of these valuable materials.

I cannot conclude, without expressing my sense of the important assistance which has been rendered to me, in finally correcting my work and arranging it for the press, by a friend high in the scale of literary distinction; who, however, does not permit me to mention his name on this occasion. On the assistance I have received from my brother, and another member of my own family, it would be impertinent to dwell.

PUCKLECHURCH, January 6, 1834.

CHAPTER I

1754—1775

Mr. Crabbe's Birth, Parentage and Early Education—His Apprenticeship to a Surgeon—His Attachment to Miss Elmy, afterwards his Wife—Publication of "Inebriety," a Poem.

AS ONE of the severest calamities of life, the loss of our first and dearest friends can be escaped by none whose own days are not prematurely cut short, the most pious affection must be contented to pray that the affliction may come on us gradually, and after we have formed new connections to sustain us, and, in part at least, fill up the void. In this view, the present writer has every reason to consider with humble thankfulness the period and circumstances of his father's departure. The growing decline of his bodily strength had been perceptible to all around him for several years. He himself had long set the example of looking forward with calmness to the hour of his dissolution; and if the firmness and resignation of a Christian's death-bed must doubly endear his memory to his children, they also afford indescribable consolation after the scene is closed. At an earlier period, Mr. Crabbe's death would have plunged his family in insupportable suffering: but when the blow fell, it had many alleviations.

With every softening circumstance, however, a considerable interval must pass, before the sons of such a parent can bear to dwell on the minor peculiarities of his image and character;—a much longer one, ere they can bring themselves to converse on light and ludicrous incidents connected with his memory. The tone of some passages in the ensuing narrative may appear at variance with these feelings; and it is therefore necessary for me to state here, that the design of drawing up some memoirs of my father's life, from his own fireside anecdotes, had occurred to me several years ago, and that a great part of what I now lay before the public had been committed to writing more than a twelvemonth before his decease. At the time when I was thus occupied, although his health was evidently decaying, there was nothing to forbid the hope that he might linger for years among us, in the enjoyment of such comforts as can smooth the gradual descent of old age to the tomb; and I pleased myself with the fond anticipation, that when I should have completed my manuscript, he himself might be its first critic, and take the trouble to correct it wherever I had fallen into any mistakes of importance. But he was at last carried off by a violent illness, of short duration—and thus ended for ever the most pleasing dream of my authorship.

I mention these things to caution the reader against construing into unfilial levity certain passages of this little work: but, at the same time, I feel that Mr. Crabbe himself would have wished his son, if he attempted to write his life at all, to do so, as far as might be possible, with the unbiassed fairness of one less intimately connected with him. To impartiality, certainly, I cannot pretend; but I hope partiality does not necessarily imply misrepresentation. I shall endeavour to speak of him as his manly and honest mind would have wished me to do. I shall place before the reader, not only his nobler qualities, but the weaknesses and infirmities which mingled with them—and of which he was more conscious than of the elevation of his genius. To trick out an ideal character for the public eye, by either the omission or the exaggeration of really characteristic traits, is an office which my respect for my father —even if there were nothing else—would render it impossible for me to attempt. I am sustained by the belief that his countrymen at large respect his memory too much to wish that his history should be turned into anything like a romance, and the hope that they will receive with indulgence a faithful narrative, even though it should be a homely one.

I have in vain endeavoured to trace his descent beyond his grandfather. Various branches of the name appear to have been settled, from a remote period, in Norfolk, and in different seafaring places on the coast of Suffolk; and it seems probable that the first who assumed it was a fisherman.[1] A pilot, by name Crabbe, of Walton, was consulted, as a man of remarkable experience, about the voyage of Edward the Third, previous to the battle of Cressy. The Crabbes of Norfolk have been, for many generations, in the station of farmers, or wealthy yeomen; and I doubt whether any of the race had ever risen much above this sphere of life; for though there is now in the possession of my uncle at Southwold an apparently ancient coat of arms—*gules*, three crab-fish, *or*—how or whence it came into the hands of his father we have no trace, and therefore I cannot attach much weight to such a shadowy token of *gentle* pretensions.

George Crabbe, the Poet's grandfather, was a burgess of Aldborough, who became, in his latter days, collector of the customs in that port, but must have died in narrow circumstances; since his son, named also *George*, and originally educated for trade, appears to have been, very early in life, the keeper of a parochial school in the porch of the church of Orford. From this place he removed to Norton, near Loddon, in Norfolk, where he united the humble offices of schoolmaster and parish clerk. He at length returned to Aldborough, where, after acting for many years as warehouse-keeper and

[1] "I cannot account for the vanity of that one of my ancestors who first (being dissatisfied with the four letters which composed the name of 'Crab,' the sour fruit, or 'Crab', the crusty fish) added his *be* by way of disguise. Alas! he gained nothing worth his trouble; but he has brought upon me, his descendant after I know not how many generations, a question beyond my abilities to answer."—*Mr. Crabbe to Mr. Chantrey, Dec.* 11, 1822.

deputy collector, he rose to be collector of the salt-duties, or Salt-master. He was a man of strong and vigorous talents, skilful in business of all sorts, distinguished in particular for an extraordinary faculty of calculation; and during many years of his life was the *factotum*, as the Poet expressed it, of Aldborough. Soon after his final settlement in his native town, he married a widow of the name of Loddock, a woman of the most amiable disposition, mild, patient, affectionate, and deeply religious in her turn of mind; and by her he had six children, all of whom, except one girl, lived to mature years.

GEORGE CRABBE, the Poet, was the eldest of the family; and was born at Aldborough, on the Christmas-eve of 1754.[2] His next brother, Robert, was bred to the business of a glazier, and is now living in retirement at Southwold. John Crabbe, the third son, served for some time in the Royal Navy, and became subsequently the captain of a Liverpool slave-ship. Returning from a successful voyage, he married the owner's daughter; and on his next excursion, he perished by an insurrection of the slaves. The negroes, having mastered the crew, set the whole of them adrift in an open boat; and neither Captain Crabbe nor any of his companions were ever again heard of. The fourth brother, William, also took to a seafaring life. Being made prisoner by the Spaniards, he was carried to Mexico, where he became a silversmith, married, and prospered, until his increasing riches attracted a charge of Protestantism; the consequence of which was much persecution. He at last was obliged to abandon Mexico, his property

---

[2] When my grandfather first settled in Aldborough, he lived in an old house in that range of buildings which the sea has now almost demolished. The chambers projected far over the ground-floor; and the windows were small, with diamond panes, almost impervious to the light. In this gloomy dwelling the Poet was born. The house, of which Mr. Bernard Barton has published a print as "the birth-place of Crabbe," was inhabited by the family during my father's boyhood.

and his family; and was discovered, in the year 1803, by an Aldborough sailor, on the coast of Honduras, where again he seems to have found some success in business. This sailor was the only person he had seen for many a year who could tell him anything of Aldborough and his family; and great was his perplexity when he was informed that his eldest brother, George, was a clergyman—the sailor, I dare say, had never himself heard of his being a poet. "This cannot be *our* George," said the wanderer—"he was a *doctor!*" This was the first, and it was also the last, tidings that ever reached my father of his brother William; and, upon the Aldborough sailor's story of his casual interview, it is obvious that the poet built his tale of "The Parting Hour," whose hero, Allen Booth, "yielded to the Spanish force," and—

> "no more
> Return'd exulting to his native shore."

Like William Crabbe,

> "There, hopeless ever to escape the land,
> *He* to a Spanish maiden gave his hand:
> In cottage shelter'd from the blaze of day
> He saw his happy infants round him play—
> Where summer shadows, made by lofty trees,
> Waved o'er his seat, and soothed his reveries."

But—

> " 'Whilst I was poor,' said Allen, 'none would care
> What my poor notions of religion were;
> I preached no foreign doctrine to my wife,
> And never mention'd Luther in my life;
> Their forms I follow'd, whether well or sick,
> And was a most obedient Catholick.
> But I had money—and these pastors found
> My notions vague, heretical, unsound.'

"Alas, poor Allen! through his wealth were seen
Crimes that by poverty conceal'd had been:
Faults that in dusty pictures rest unknown,
Are in an instant through the varnish shown.
They spared his forfeit life, but bade him fly;
Or for his crime and contumacy die.
Fly from all scenes, all objects of delight;
His wife, his children, weeping in his sight,
All urging him to flee—he fled, and cursed his flight.
He next related how he found a way,
Guideless and grieving, to Campeachy Bay:
There, in the woods, he wrought, and there among
Some labouring seamen heard his native tongue:

"Again he heard—he seized an offer'd hand—
'And when beheld you last our native land?'
He cried: 'and in what country? Quickly say.'
The seamen answer'd—strangers all were they—
One only at his native port had been;
He landing once the quay and church had seen." &c.

The youngest of this family, Mary, became the wife of Mr.
Sparkes, a builder in her native town, where she died in 1827.
Another sister, as has been mentioned, died in infancy; and I
find among my father's papers the following lines, referring
to the feelings with which, in the darkening evening of life,
he still recurred to that early distress:

"But it was misery stung me in the day
Death of an infant sister made his prey;
For then first met and moved my early fears
A father's terrors and a mother's tears.
Though greater anguish I have since endured,

Some heal'd in part, some never to be cured,
Yet was there something in that first-born ill
So new, so strange, that memory feels it still."

MS.

The second of these couplets has sad truth in every word.
The fears of the future poet were as real as the tears of his
mother, and the "terrors" of his father. The Salt-master was a
man of imperious temper and violent passions; but the darker
traits of his character had, at this period, showed themselves
only at rare intervals, and on extraordinary occasions. He had
been hitherto, on the whole, an exemplary husband and
father; and was passionately devoted to the little girl, whose
untimely death drew from him those gloomy and savage
tokens of misery which haunted, fifty years after, the memory
of his gentler son. He was a man of short stature, but very
robust and powerful; and he had a highly marked countenance, not unlike in lineaments, as my father used to say, to that
of Howard the philanthropist; but stamped with the trace of
passions which that illustrious man either knew not or had
subdued.

Aldborough (or, as it is more correctly written, Aldeburgh)
was in those days a poor and wretched place, with nothing of
the elegance and gaiety which have since sprung up about it,
in consequence of the resort of watering parties. The town lies
between a low hill or cliff, on which only the old church and
a few better houses were then situated, and the beach of the
German Ocean. It consisted of two parallel and unpaved
streets, running between mean and scrambling houses, the
abodes of seafaring men, pilots, and fishers. The range of
houses nearest to the sea had suffered so much from repeated
invasions of the waves, that only a few scattered tenements

appeared erect among the desolation.[3] I have often heard my father describe a tremendous spring-tide of, I think, the 1st of January, 1779, when eleven houses here were at once demolished; and he saw the breakers dash over the roofs, curl around the walls, and crush all to ruin. The beach consists of successive ridges—large rolled stones, then loose shingle, and, at the fall of the tide, a stripe of fine hard sand. Vessels of all sorts, from the large heavy trollboat to the yawl and prame, drawn up along the shore—fishermen preparing their tackle, or sorting their spoil—and nearer the gloomy old town-hall (the only indication of municipal dignity) a few groups of mariners, chiefly pilots, taking their quick short walk backwards and forwards, every eye watchful of a signal from the offing—such was the squalid scene that first opened on the author of "The Village."

Nor was the landscape in the vicinity of a more engaging aspect—open commons and sterile farms, the soil poor and sandy, the herbage bare and rushy, the trees "few and far between," and withered and stunted by the bleak breezes of the sea. The opening picture of "The Village" was copied, in every touch, from the scene of the Poet's nativity and boyish days:

"Lo! where the heath, with withering brake grown o'er,
　Lends the light turf that warms the neighbouring poor;
　From thence a length of burning sand appears,
　Where the thin harvest waves its wither'd ears;

---

[3] "From an accurate plan of the borough, which was taken in 1559, it appears that the church was then more than ten times its present distance from the shore; and also that there were Denes of some extent, similar to those at Yarmouth, between the town and the sea, which have long been swallowed up and lost. After very high tides, the remains of wells have been frequently discovered below high-water mark."—*Aldborough Described*, by the Rev. James Ford, p.4.

Rank weeds, that every art and care defy,
Reign o'er the land, and rob the blighted rye;
There thistles spread their prickly arms afar,
And to the ragged infants threaten war."

The "broad river," called the Ald, approaches the sea close
to Aldborough, within a few hundred yards, and then turning
abruptly continues to run for about ten miles parallel to the
beach—from which, for the most part, a dreary stripe of
marsh and waste alone divides it—until it at length finds its
embouchure at Orford. The scenery of this river has been
celebrated as lovely and delightful, in a poem called "Slaughden Vale," written by Mr. James Bird, a friend of my father's;
and old Camden talks of "the beautiful vale of Slaughden." I
confess, however, that though I have ever found an indescribable charm in the very weeds of the place, I never
could perceive its claims to beauty. Such as it is, it has furn-
ished Mr. Crabbe with many of his happiest and most
graphical descriptions: and the same may be said of the whole
line of coast from Orford to Dunwich, every feature of which
has somewhere or other been reproduced in his writings. The
quay of Slaughden, in particular, has been painted with all
the minuteness of a Dutch landscape:

"Here samphire banks and saltwort bound the flood,
There stakes and sea-weeds withering on the mud;
And higher up a ridge of all things base,
Which some strong tide has roll'd upon the place . . .
Yon is our quay! those smaller hoys from town
Its various wares for country use bring down." &c. &c.

The powerful effect with which Mr. Crabbe has depicted
the ocean itself, both in its calm and its tempestuous aspects,

may lead many to infer that, had he been born and educated in a region of mountains and forests, he might have represented them also as happily as he has done the slimy marshes and withered commons of the coast of Suffolk: but it is certain that he visited, and even resided in, some of the finest parts of our island in after-life, without appearing to take much delight in the grander features of inland scenery; and it may be doubted whether, under any circumstances, his mind would ever have found much of the excitement of delight elsewhere than in the study of human beings. And certainly, for one destined to distinction as a portrayer of character, few scenes could have been more favourable than that of his infancy and boyhood. He was cradled among the rough sons of the ocean—a daily witness of unbridled passions, and of manners remote from the sameness and artificial smoothness of polished society. At home, as has already been hinted, he was subject to the caprices of a stern and imperious, though not unkindly, nature; and, probably, few whom he could familiarly approach but had passed through some of those dark domestic tragedies in which his future strength was to be exhibited. The common people of Aldborough in those days are described as—

> ——"a wild, amphibious race,
> With sullen woe display'd in every face;
> Who far from civil arts and social fly,
> And scowl at strangers with suspicious eye."

Nor, although the family in which he was born happened to be somewhat above the mass in point of situation, was the remove so great as to be marked with any considerable difference in point of refinement. Masculine and robust frames, rude manners, stormy passions, laborious days, and, occasionally, boisterous nights of merriment—among such accompaniments was born and reared the Poet of the Poor.

His father, at this early period, was still, as I have already noticed, on the whole, domestic in his habits; and he used occasionally to read aloud to his family, in the evenings, passages from Milton, Young, or some other of our graver classics, with, as his son thought long afterwards, remarkable judgment, and with powerful effect: but his chosen intellectual pursuit was mathematical calculation. He mingled with these tastes not a little of the seafaring habits and propensities of the place. He possessed a share in a fishing-boat, in which he not unfrequently went to sea; and he had also a small sailing-boat, in which he delighted to navigate the river.

The first event which was deeply impressed on my father's memory was a voyage in this vessel. A party of amateur sailors was formed—the yacht-club of Aldborough—to try the new purchase; a jovial dinner prepared at Orford, and a merry return anticipated at night; and his fond mother obtained permission for George to be one of the company. Soon after sunrise, in a fine summer morning, they were seated in their respective vessels, and started in gallant trim, tacking and manoeuvring on the bosom of the flickering water as it winds gently towards its junction with the sea. The freshness of the early dawn, the anticipation of amusements at an unknown place, and no little exultation in his father's *crack* vessel, "made it," he said, "a morning of exquisite delight"; and, among the MSS. which he left, are the following verses on this early incident:

> "Sweet was the morning's breath, the inland tide,
> And our boat gliding, where alone could glide
> Small craft—and they oft touch'd on either side.
> It was my first-born joy—I heard them say,
> 'Let the child go; he will enjoy the day;

For children ever feel delighted when
They take their portion and enjoy with men.'
The linnet chirped upon the furze as well,
To my young sense, as sings the nightingale.
Without was Paradise—because within
Was a keen relish, without taint of sin."

But it appears that, as in other sublunary pleasures, the best part of this day's sport was the anticipation of the morning; for he adds—

"As the sun declined,
The good found early I no more could find.
The men drank much to whet the appetite,
And, growing heavy, drank to make them light;
Then drank to relish joy, then further to excite.
The lads play'd with the helm and oar,
And nervous women would be set on shore,
And 'civil dudgeon' grew, and peace would smile no more,
Till on the colder water faintly shone
The sloping light—the cheerful day was gone.
In life's advance, events like this I knew—
So they advanced, and so they ended too.
The promised joy, that like this morning rose,
Broke on the view—then clouded at its close." MS.

Though born and brought up almost within the washing of the surge, the future Poet had but few qualifications for a sailor. The Saltmaster often took his boys a-fishing with him; and sorely was his patience tried with the awkwardness of the eldest. "That boy," he would say, "must be a *fool*. John, and Bob, and Will, are all of some use about a boat; but what will that *thing* ever be good for?" This, however, was only the passion of the moment; for Mr. Crabbe perceived early the natural talents of his eldest son, and, as that son ever gratefully remembered, was at more expense with his education than his worldly circumstances could well afford.

My father was, indeed, in a great measure, self-educated. After he could read at all—and he was a great favourite with the old dame who taught him—he was unwearied in reading; and he devoured without restraint whatever came into his hands, but especially works of fiction—those little stories and ballads about ghosts, witches, and fairies, which were then almost exclusively the literature of youth, and which, whatever else might be thought of them, served, no doubt, to strike out the first sparks of imagination in the mind of many a youthful poet. Mr. Crabbe retained, to the close of life, a strong partiality for marvellous tales of even this humble class. In verse he delighted, from the earliest time that he could read. His father took in a periodical work, called "Martin's Philosophical Magazine," which contained, at the end of each number, a sheet of "occasional poetry." The Saltmaster irreverently cut out these sheets when he sent his magazines to be bound up at the end of the year; and the "Poet's Corner" became the property of George, who read its contents until he had most of them by heart. The boy ere long tried to imitate the pieces which he thus studied; and one of which, he used to say, particularly struck his childish fancy by this terrible concluding couplet—

> "The boat went down in flames of fire,
> Which made the people all admire."

Mild, obliging, and the most patient of listeners, he was a

great favourite with the old dames of the place. Like his own "Richard," many a friendly

> "matron woo'd him, quickly won,
> To fill the station of an absent son."

He admired the rude prints on their walls, rummaged their shelves for books or ballads, and read aloud to those whose eyes had failed them, by the winter evening's fire-side. Walking one day in the street, he chanced to displease a stout lad, who doubled his fist to beat him; but another boy interfered to claim benefit of clergy for the studious George. "You must not meddle with *him*," he said; "let *him* alone, for he ha' got l'arning."

His father observed this bookish turn, and though he had then no higher view of him in life than that he should follow his own example, and be employed in some inferior department of the revenue service, he resolved to give George the advantage of passing some time in a school at Bungay, on the borders of Norfolk, where it was hoped the activity of his mind would be disciplined into orderly diligence. I cannot say how soon this removal from the paternal roof took place; but it must have been very early, as the following anecdote will show:—The first night he spent at Bungay he retired to bed, he said, "with a heavy heart, thinking of his fond, indulgent mother." But the morning brought a new misery. The slender and delicate child had hitherto been dressed by his mother. Seeing the other boys begin to dress themselves, poor George, in great confusion, whispered to his bedfellow, "Master G——, can you put on your shirt?—for—for I'm afraid I cannot."

Soon after his arrival he had a very narrow escape. He and several of his schoolfellows were punished for playing at soldiers, by being put into a large dog-kennel, known by the terrible name of "the black hole." George was the first that entered: and, the place being crammed full with offenders, the atmosphere soon became pestilentially close. The poor boy in vain shrieked that he was about to be suffocated. At last, in despair, he bit the lad next to him violently in the hand. "Crabbe is dying—Crabbe is dying," roared the sufferer; and the sentinel at length opened the door, and allowed the boys to rush out into the air. My father said, "A minute more, and I must have died."

I am unable to give any more particulars of his residence at Bungay. When he was in his eleventh or twelfth year, it having now been determined that he should follow the profession of a surgeon, he was removed to a school of somewhat superior character, kept by Mr. Richard Haddon, a skilful mathematician, at Stowmarket, in the same county; and here, inheriting his father's talent and predilection for mathematical science, he made considerable progress in such pursuits. The Salt-master used often to send difficult questions to Mr. Haddon, and, to his great delight, the solution came not unfrequently from his son; and, although Haddon was neither a Porson nor a Parr, his young pupil laid, under his care, the foundations of a fair classical education also. Some girls used to come to the school in the evenings, to learn writing; and the tradition is, that Mr. Crabbe's first essay in verse was a stanza of doggerel, cautioning one of these little damsels against being too much elevated about a new set of blue ribbons to her straw bonnet.

After leaving this school, some time passed before a situation as surgeon's apprentice could be found for him; and, by his own confession, he has painted the manner in which most of this interval was spent, in those beautiful lines of his "Richard," which give, perhaps, as striking a picture of the

"inquisitive sympathy" and solitary musings of a youthful
poet as can elsewhere be pointed out:

> "I to the ocean gave
> My mind, and thoughts as restless as the wave.
> Where crowds assembled I was sure to run,
> Hear what was said, and muse on what was done.
> To me the wives of seamen loved to tell
> What storms endanger'd men esteem'd so well;
> No ships were wreck'd upon that fatal beach
> But I could give the luckless tale of each.
> In fact, I lived for many an idle year
> In fond pursuit of agitations dear:
> For ever seeking, ever pleased to find
> The food I sought, I thought not of its kind.
>
> "I loved to walk where none had walk'd before,
> About the rocks that ran along the shore;
> Or far beyond the sight of men to stray,
> And take my pleasure when I lost my way:
> For then 'twas mine to trace the hilly heath,
> And all the mossy moor that lies beneath.
> Here had I favourite stations, where I stood
> And heard the murmurs of the ocean-flood,
> With not a sound beside, except when flew
> Aloft the lapwing, or the grey curlew . . .
> When I no more my fancy could employ—
> I left in haste what I could not enjoy,
> And was my gentle mother's welcome boy."

The reader is not to suppose, however, that all his hours
were spent in this agreeable manner. His father employed him
in the warehouse on the quay of Slaughden, in labours which

he abhorred, though he in time became tolerably expert in them; such as piling up butter and cheese. He said long after, that he remembered with regret the fretfulness and indignation wherewith he submitted to these drudgeries, in which the Salt-master himself often shared. At length an advertisement, headed "Apprentice wanted," met his father's eye; and George was offered, and accepted to fill the vacant station at Wickham-Brook, a small village near Bury St. Edmunds. He left his home and his indulgent mother, under the care of two farmers, who were travelling across the country; with whom he parted within about ten miles of the residence of his future master, and proceeded, with feelings easily imagined in a low-spirited, gentle lad, to seek a strange, perhaps a severe, home. Fatigue also contributed to impart its melancholy; and the reception augmented these feelings to bitterness. Just as he reached the door, his master's daughters, having eyed him for a few moments, burst into a violent fit of laughter, exclaiming, "La! here's our new 'prentice." He never forgot the deep mortification of that moment; but justice to the ladies compels me to mention, that shortly before that period he had had his head shaved during some illness, and, instead of the ornamental curls that now embellish the shorn, he wore, by his own confession, a very ill-made scratch-wig. This happened when he was in his fourteenth year, in 1768.

Besides the duties of his profession, "our new 'prentice" was often employed in the drudgery of the farm—for his master had more occupations than one—and was made the bedfellow and companion of the ploughboy. How astonished would he have been, when carrying medicines on foot to Cheveley (a village at a considerable distance), could he have foreseen that, in a very few years, he should take his daily station in that same place at a duke's table! One day as he mixed with the herd of lads at the public-house, to see the

c

exhibitions of a conjurer, the magician, having worked many wonders, changed a white ball to black, exclaiming—"*Quique olim albus erat nunc est contrarius albo*—and I suppose none of you can tell me what that means." "Yes, I can," said George. "The d—l you can," replied he of the magic wand, eyeing his garb: "I suppose you picked up *your* Latin in a turnip-field." Not daunted by the laughter that followed, he gave the interpretation, and received from the seer a condescending compliment.

Whether my father complained of the large portion of agricultural tuition he received gratis, I know not; but, not being bound by indenture, he was removed, in the year 1771, to a more eligible situation, and concluded his apprenticeship with a Mr. Page, surgeon at Woodbridge, a market-town seventeen miles from Aldborough. Here he met with companions suitable to his mind and habits, and, although he never was fond of his destined profession, began to apply to it in earnest. I have often heard him speak with pleasure of a small society of young men, who met at an inn on certain evenings of the week to converse, over a frugal supper, on the subjects which they were severally studying. One of this rural club was a surgeon of the name of Levett, with whom he had had some very early acquaintance at Aldborough. This friend was at the time paying his addresses to a Miss Brereton, who afterwards married a Mr. Lewis, and published, under the name of Eugenia de Acton, several novels, which enjoyed a temporary popularity—"Vicissitudes of Genteel Life," "The Microcosm," "A Tale without a Title," &c. &c. Miss Brereton's residence was at Framlingham, and her great friend and companion was Miss Sarah Elmy, then domesticated in the neighbouring village of Parham, under the roof of an uncle, Mr. Tovell. Mr. Levett said carelessly one day: "Why, George, you shall go with me to Parham: there is a young lady there that would just suit you." My father accompanied him accordingly on his next "lover's journey," was introduced to Miss Brereton and her friend, and spent in their society a day which decided his matrimonial lot in life.[4]

He was at this time in his eighteenth year, and had already excited the attention of his companions by his attempts in versification—attempts to which it may be supposed his love now lent a new impulse, and supplied an inexhaustible theme. In an autobiographical sketch, published some years ago to accompany a portrait in the New Monthly Magazine, he says of himself, "He had, with youthful indiscretion, written for publications wherein Damons and Delias begin the correspondence that does not always end there, and where diffidence is nursed till it becomes presumption. There was then a Lady's Magazine, published by Mr. Wheble, in which our young candidate wrote for a prize on the subject of Hope,[5] and he had the misfortune to gain it; in consequence of which

---

[4] William Springall Levett died in 1774; and the following epitaph, written at the time by Mr. Crabbe, may be worth preserving:—

> "What! though no trophies peer above his dust,
> Nor sculptured conquests deck his sober bust;
> What! though no earthly thunders sound his name,
> Death gives him conquest, and our sorrows fame;
> One sigh reflection heaves, but shuns excess—
> More should we mourn him, did we love him less."
>
> *Green's History of Framlingham,* p. 163.

[5] After long search a copy of Wheble's Magazine for 1772 has been discovered, and it contains, besides the prize poem on Hope, four other pieces, signed "G. C., Woodbridge, Suffolk": "To Mira"; "The Atheist reclaimed"; "The Bee"; and "An Allegorical Fable". As might be supposed, there is hardly a line in any of these productions which I should be justified in reprinting. I shall, however, preserve the conclusion of the prize poem:—

> "But, above all, the POET owns thy powers—
> HOPE leads him on, and every fear devours;
> He writes, and, unsuccessful, writes again,
> Nor thinks the last laborious work in vain;
> New schemes he forms, and various plots he tries,
> To win the laurel, and possess the PRIZE."

he felt himself more elevated above the young men, his companions, who made no verses, than it is to be hoped he has done at any time since, when he has been able to compare and judge with a more moderate degree of self-approbation. He wrote upon every occasion, and without occasion; and, like greater men, and indeed like almost every young versifier, he planned tragedies and epic poems, and began to think of succeeding in the highest line of composition, before he had made one good and commendable effort in the lowest."

In fact, even before he quitted his first master at Wickham-Brook, he had filled a drawer with verses; and I have now a quarto volume before me, consisting chiefly of pieces written at Woodbridge, among which occur "The Judgment of the Muse, in the Metre of Spenser,"—"Life, a Poem,"—"An Address to the Muse, in the Manner of Sir Walter Raleigh,"—an ode or two, in which he evidently aims at the style of Cowley,—and a profusion of lyrics "To Mira"; the name under which it pleased him to celebrate Sarah Elmy. A parody on Shenstone's "My time, oh ye Muses," opens thus:

"My days, oh ye lovers, were happily sped,
Ere you or your whimsies got into my head;
I could laugh, I could sing, I could trifle and jest,
And my heart play'd a regular tune in my breast.
But now, lack-a-day! what a change for the worse,
'Tis as heavy as lead, yet as wild as a horse.

"My fingers, ere love had tormented my mind,
Could guide my pen gently to what I design'd.
I could make an enigma, a rebus, or riddle,
Or tell a short tale of a dog and a fiddle.

But since this vile Cupid has got in my brain,
I beg of the gods to assist in my strain.
And whatever my subject, the fancy still roves,
And sings of hearts, raptures, flames, sorrows, and loves."

The poet himself says, in "The Parting Hour"—

"Minutely trace man's life: year after year,
Through all his days, let all his deeds appear—
And then, though some may in that life be strange,
Yet there appears no vast nor sudden change:
The links that bind those various deeds are seen,
And no mysterious void is left between:"—

but, it must be allowed, that we want several links to connect
the author of "The Library" with the young lover of the
above verses, or of

"THE WISH

"My Mira, shepherds, is as fair
    As sylvan nymphs who haunt the vale,
As sylphs who dwell in purest air,
    As fays who skim the dusky dale,
As Venus was when Venus fled
From watery Triton's oozy bed.

"My Mira, shepherds, has a voice
    As soft as Syrinx in her grove,
As sweet as echo makes her choice,
    As mild as whispering virgin-love;
As gentle as the winding stream,
Or fancy's song when poets dream." &c. &c.

Before, however, he left Woodbridge, Mr. Crabbe not

only wrote, but found courage and means (the latter I know not how) to print and publish at Ipswich a short piece, entitled "Inebriety, a Poem," in which, however rude and unfinished as a whole, there are some couplets not deficient in point and terseness, and not a little to indicate that devotion to the style of Pope, which can be traced through all the maturer labours of his pen. The parallel passages from the Dunciad and the Essay on Man, quoted in the notes, are frequent; and to them he modestly enough alludes in "The Preface," from which, as an early specimen of his prose, it may be worth while to extract a paragraph:

"Presumption or meanness are both too often the only articles to be discovered in a preface. Whilst one author haughtily affects to despise the public attention, another timidly courts it. I would no more beg for than disdain applause, and therefore should advance nothing in favour of the following little Poem, did it appear a cruelty and disregard to send a first production naked into the world.

"The WORLD!—how presumptuous, and yet how trifling the sound. Every man, gentle reader, has a world of his own, and whether it consists of half a score or half a thousand friends, 'tis his, and he loves to boast of it. Into my world, therefore, I commit this, my Muse's earliest labour, nothing doubting the clemency of the climate, nor fearing the partiality of the censorious.

"Something by way of an apology for this trifle is, perhaps, necessary; especially for those parts wherein I have taken such great liberties with Mr. Pope. That gentleman, secure in immortal fame, would forgive me: forgive me, too, my friendly critic; I promise thee, thou wilt find the extracts from that Swan of Thames the best part of the performance."

I may also transcribe a few of the opening couplets, in which

we have the student of Pope, as well as of surgery, and not a
few germs of the future Crabbe:—

"When Winter stern his gloomy front uprears,
A sable void the barren earth appears;
The meads no more their former verdure boast,
Fast bound their streams, and all their beauty lost.
The herds, the flocks, in icy garments mourn,
And wildly murmur for the Spring's return;
The fallen branches, from the sapless tree,
With glittering fragments strow the glassy way;
From snow-topp'd hills the whirlwinds keenly blow,
Howl through the woods, and pierce the vales below;
Through the sharp air a flaky torrent flies,
Mocks the slow sight, and hides the gloomy skies;
The fleecy clouds their chilly bosoms bare,
And shed their substance on the floating air;
The floating air their downy substance glides
Through springing waters, and prevents their tides;
Seizes the rolling waves, and, as a God,
Charms their swift race, and stops the refluent flood.
The opening valves, which fill the venal road,
Then scarcely urge along the sanguine flood.
The labouring pulse a slower motion rules,
The tendons stiffen, and the spirit cools;
Each asks the aid of Nature's sister, Art,
To cheer the senses, and to warm the heart.
The gentle Fair on nervous tea relies,
Whilst gay good-nature sparkles in her eyes;
An inoffensive scandal fluttering round,
Too rough to tickle, and too light to wound;
*Champagne the courtier drinks, the spleen to chase,
The colonel Burgundy, and Port his grace.*"

(He was not yet a ducal chaplain.)

> "See Inebriety! her wand she waves,
> And, lo! her pale—and, lo! her purple slaves.
> Sots in embroidery, and sots in crape,
> Of every order, station, rank, and shape;
> The king, who nods upon his rattle-throne,
> The staggering peer, to midnight revel prone;
> The slow-tongued bishop, and the deacon sly,
> The humble pensioner, and gownsman dry;
> The proud, the mean, the selfish, and the great,
> Swell the dull throng, and stagger into state.
>
> "Lo! proud Flaminius, at the splendid board,
> The easy chaplain of an atheist lord,
> Quaffs the bright juice, with all the gust of sense,
> And clouds his brain in torpid elegance;
> In China vases, see! the sparkling ill;
> From gay decanters view the rosy rill;
> The neat-carved pipes in silver settle laid;
> The screw by mathematic cunning made;
> The whole a pompous and enticing scene,
> And grandly glaring for the surpliced swain:
> Ah, happy priest! whose God, like Egypt's, lies
> At once the Deity, and sacrifice."

He, indeed, seems to be particularly fond of "girding at" the cloth, which, in those early and thoughtless days, he had never dreamed he himself should wear and honour. It is only just to let the student of his maturer verses and formed character see in what way the careless apprentice could express himself, respecting a class of which he could then know nothing:

"The vicar at the table's front presides,
Whose presence a monastic life derides;
The reverend wig, in sideway order placed,
The reverend band, by rubric stains disgraced,
The leering eye, in wayward circles roll'd,
Mark him the Pastor of a jovial fold;
Whose various texts excite a loud applause,
Favouring bottle, and the Good Old Cause.
See the dull smile, which fearfully appears,
When gross Indecency her front uprears.
The joy conceal'd the fiercer burns within,
As masks afford the keenest gust to sin:
Imagination helps the reverend sire,
And spreads the sails of sub-divine desire—
But when the gay immoral joke goes round,
When Shame, and all her blushing train are drown'd,
Rather than hear his God blasphemed, he takes
The last loved glass, and then the board forsakes.
Not that religion prompts the sober thought,
But slavish custom has the practice taught:
Besides, this zealous son of warm devotion
Has a true Levite bias for promotion;
Vicars must with discretion go astray,
Whilst bishops may be d——d the nearest way."[6]

Such, in his twentieth year, was the poetry of Crabbe.
His Sarah encouraged him, by her approbation of his verses;
and her precept and example were of use to him in a minor
matter, but still of some importance to a young author. His
hand-writing had hitherto been feeble and bad; it now became

[6] "Inebriety," a Poem, in three Parts. Ipswich, printed and sold by C. Pun-
chard, Bookseller, in the Butter-Market, 1775. Price one shilling and six-
pence.

manly, clear, and not inelegant. Miss Elmy's passion for music induced him also to make some efforts in that direction; but Nature had given him a poor ear, and, after many a painful hour spent in trying to master "Grammachree" and "Over the water to Charlie," he laid aside his flute in despair.

To the period of his residence at Woodbridge, I suppose, may also be assigned the first growth of a more lasting passion —that for the study of botany which, from early life to his latest years, my father cultivated with fond zeal, both in books and in the fields.

CHAPTER II

1775—1780

Termination of Mr. Crabbe's Apprenticeship—Visit to London—He sets up for himself at Aldborough—Failure of his Plans there—He gives up his Business and proceeds to London as a literary Adventurer.

ABOUT THE end of the year 1775, when he had at length completed his term of apprenticeship, Mr. Crabbe returned to Aldborough, hoping to find the means of repairing to the metropolis, and there to complete his professional education. The Salt-master's affairs, however, were not in such order that he could at once gratify his son's inclination in this respect; neither could he afford to maintain him at home in idleness; and the young man, now accustomed to far different pursuits and habits, was obliged to return to the labours of the warehouse on Slaughden quay. His pride disdained this homely employment; his spirit rose against what he considered arbitrary conduct: he went sullen and angry to his work, and violent quarrels often ensued between him and his father. He frequently confessed in after-times that his behaviour in this affair was unjustifiable, and allowed that it was the old man's poverty, not his will, that consented to let him wear out any more of his days in such ignoble occupation.

I must add, however, that before he returned from Woodbridge, his father's habits had undergone a very unhappy change. In 1774 there was a contested election at Aldborough, and the Whig candidate, Mr. Charles Long, sought and found a very able and zealous partisan and agent in Mr. Crabbe. From that period his family dated the loss of domestic comfort, a rooted taste for the society of the tavern, and such an increase in the violence of his temper that his meek-spirited wife, now in poor health, dreaded to hear his returning footsteps. If the food prepared for his meal did not please his fancy, he would fling the dishes about the room, and all was misery and terror. George was the chief support of his afflicted mother—her friend and her physician. He saw that her complaint was dropsical, and, from the first, anticipated the fatal result which, after a few years of suffering, ensued. One of his favourite employments was to catch some small fish called "butts," the only thing for which she could muster a little appetite, for her nightly meal. He was in all things her dutiful comforter; and it may be supposed that, under such circumstances, he was not sometimes able to judge favourably of her husband's conduct, even where there might be nothing really blameworthy in it. To him, he acknowledged, his father had always been "substantially kind."

His leisure hours were spent in the study of botany, and other branches of natural history; and, perhaps, the ill success of "Inebriety" had no small share in withdrawing him, for a time, from the practice of versification. He appears, indeed, to have had, at this period, every disposition to pursue his profession with zeal. "The time," he says, in the sketch already quoted, "had come, when he was told, and believed, that he had more important concerns to engage him than verse; and therefore, for some years, though he occasionally found time to write lines upon 'Mira's Birthday' and 'Silvia's Lapdog,' though he composed enigmas and solved rebuses, he had some degree of forbearance, and did not believe that the knowledge of diseases, and the sciences of anatomy and physiology, were to be acquired by the perusal of Pope's Homer and a Treatise on the Art of Poetry."

His professional studies, in the meantime, continued to be interrupted by other things than the composition of trifles for a corner of Wheble's Magazine; and the mortifications he daily underwent may be guessed at from the following incident, which he used to relate, even in his old age, with deep feeling:—One of his Woodbridge acquaintances, now a smart young surgeon, came over to Aldborough, on purpose to see him; he was directed to the quay of Slaughden, and there discovered George Crabbe, piling up butter casks, in the dress of a common warehouseman. The visitor had the vanity and cruelty to despise the honest industry of his friend, and to say to him, in a stern, authoritative tone—"Follow me, sir." George followed him at a respectful distance, until they reached the inn, where he was treated with a long and angry lecture, inculcating pride and rebellion. He heard it in sad silence: his spirit was, indeed, subdued, but he refused to take any decided step in opposition to his parent's will, or rather, the hard necessities of his case. "My friends," said my father, in concluding this story, "had always an ascendancy over me." I may venture to add, that this was the consequence purely of the gentle warmth of his affections; for he was at heart as grave as affectionate. Never was there a more hopeless task than to rule him by intimidation.

After he had lingered at Aldborough for a considerable time, his father made an effort to send him to London, and he embarked in one of the trading sloops at Slaughden Quay, ostensibly to walk the hospitals, and attend medical lectures in customary form, but in reality with a purse too slenderly provided to enable him to do this; and, in short, with the purpose, as he said, of "picking up a little surgical knowledge as cheap as he could." He took up his quarters in the house of an Aldborough family, humble tradespeople, who resided somewhere in Whitechapel; and continued there for about eight or ten months, until his small resources were exhausted, when he returned once more to Suffolk, but little, I suspect, the better for the desultory sort of instruction that had alone been within his reach. Among other distresses of this time, he had, soon after he reached London, a narrow escape from being carried before the Lord Mayor as a resurrectionist. His landlady, having discovered that he had a dead child in his closet, for the purpose of dissection, took it into her head that it was no other than an infant whom she had had the misfortune to lose the week before. "Dr. Crabbe had dug up William; she was certain he had; and to the Mansionhouse he must go." Fortunately, the countenance of the child had not yet been touched with the knife. The "doctor" arrived when the tumult was at its height, and, opening the closet door, at once established his innocence of the charge.

On his return to Aldborough, he engaged himself as an assistant in the shop of a Mr. Maskill, who had lately commenced business there as a surgeon and apothecary—a stern and powerful man. Mr. Crabbe, the first time he had occasion to write his name, chanced to misspell it *Maskwell*; and this gave great offence. "D——n you, sir," he exclaimed, "do you take me for a proficient in deception? Mask-*ill*—Mask-*ill*; and so you shall find me." He assumed a despotic authority which the assistant could ill brook; and yet, conscious how imperfectly he was grounded in the commonest details of the profession, he was obliged to submit in silence to a new series of galling vexations. Nor was his situation at all improved, when, at the end of some miserable months, Mr. Maskill transferred his practice to another town, and he was encouraged to set up for himself in Aldborough.

He dearly loved liberty, and he was now his own master; and, above all, he could now more frequently visit Miss Elmy, at Parham; but the sense of a new responsibility pressed sorely and continually on his mind; and he never awoke without shuddering at the thought that some operation of real difficulty might be thrown in his way before night. Ready sharpness of mind and mechanical cleverness of hand are the first essentials in a surgeon; and he wanted them both, and knew his deficiencies far better than any one else did. He had, moreover, a clever and active opponent in the late Mr. Raymond; and the practice which fell to his share was the poorest the place afforded. His very passion for botany was in-jurious to him; for his ignorant patients, seeing him return from his walks with handfuls of weeds, decided that, as Dr. Crabbe got his medicines in the ditches, he could have little claim for payment. On the other hand, he had many poor relations; and some of these, old women, were daily visitors, to request "something from comfortable cousin George"; that is to say, doses of the most expensive tonics in his possession.

> "If once induced these cordial sips to try,
> All feel the ease, and few the danger fly;
> For while obtain'd, of drams they've all the force,
> And when denied, then drams are the resource."

Add to all this, that my poor father was a lover, separated from his mistress, and that his heart was in the land of imagina-tion—for he had now resumed his pen—and it is not wonderful that he soon began to despair altogether of succeeding in his profession.

Yet there was a short period when fortune seemed somewhat more favourable to him, even in Aldborough. In the summer of 1778, the Warwickshire militia were quartered in the town, and his emoluments were considerably improved in consequence. He had also the pleasure of finding his society greatly estimated by the officers, and formed a very strong friendship with one of them, Lieutenant Hayward, a highly promising young gentleman, who afterwards died in the East Indies. The Colonel—afterwards the celebrated field-marshal, Conway—took much notice of Mr. Crabbe; and among other marks of his attention, was the gift of some valuable Latin works on the favourite subject of Botany, which proved of advantage to him in more ways than one: for the possession of them induced him to take up more accurately than heretofore the study of the language in which they were composed; and the hours he now spent on Hudson's "Flora Anglica"[1] enabled him to enjoy Horace, and to pass with credit through certain examinations of an after-period. The winter following, the Warwick militia were replaced by the Norfolk; and Mr. Crabbe had the good fortune to be, for a time, their medical attendant also, and to profit, as before, by the society of educated gentlemen, who appreciated his worth, and were interested and pleased with his conversation.

This was a passing gleam of sunshine; but the chief con-

[1] In one of his early Note-books he has written:—

"Ah! blest be the days when with Mira I took
The learning of Love . . .
When we pluck'd the wild blossoms that blush'd in the grass,
And I taught my dear maid of their species and class;
For Conway, the friend of mankind, had decreed
That Hudson should show us the wealth of the mead."

Mr. Conway's character is familiar to every reader of his cousin Horace Walpole's Letters.

solation of all his distresses at this period, was the knowledge
that he had gained a faithful and affectionate heart at Parham,
and the virtuous and manly love which it was his nature to
feel, imparted a buoyancy to his spirits in the very midst of
his troubles. His taste and manners were different from those
of the family with whom Miss Elmy resided, and he was at
first barely tolerated. The uncle, Mr. Tovell, a wealthy yeoman of the highest class so denominated—a class ever jealous
of the privileges of literature—would now and then growl in
the hearing of his guest—"What good does their d——d
learning do them?" By degrees, his sterling worth made its
due impression: he was esteemed, then beloved by them all;
but still he had every now and then to put up with a rough
sneer about "the d——d learning."

Miss Elmy occasionally visited her mother at Beccles; and
here my father found a society more adapted to his acquirements. The family had, though in apparently humble circumstances, always been numbered among the gentry of the
place, and possessed education and manners that entitled them
to this distinction.[2] It was in his walks between Aldborough
and Beccles that Mr. Crabbe passed through the very scenery
described in the first part of "The Lover's Journey"; while
near Beccles, in another direction, he found the contrast of
rich vegetation introduced in the latter part of that tale; nor
have I any doubt that the *disappointment* of the story figures out
something that, on one of these visits, befell himself, and the
feelings with which he received it:—

> "Gone to a friend, she tells me.—I commend
> Her purpose;—means she to a *female friend?*" &c.

For truth compels me to say, that he was by no means free

[2] Miss Elmy's father was now no more. He had been a tanner at Beccles, but
failed in his business, and went to Guadaloupe, where he died some time before
Mr. Crabbe knew the family.

from the less amiable sign of a strong attachment—jealousy. The description of this self-torment, which occurs in the sixth book of "Tales of the Hall," could only have been produced by one who had undergone the pain himself; and the catastrophe which follows may be considered as a vivid representation of his happier hours at Beccles. Miss Elmy was then remarkably pretty; she had a lively disposition, and, having generally more than her share of attention in a mixed company, her behaviour might, without any coquettish inclination, occasion painful surmises in a sensitive lover, who could only at intervals join her circle.

In one of these visits to Beccles, my father was in the most imminent danger of losing his life. Having, on a sultry summer's day rowed his Sarah to a favourite fishing spot on the River Waveney, he left her busy with the rod and line, and withdrew to a retired place about a quarter of a mile off, to bathe. Not being a swimmer, nor calculating his depth, he plunged at once into danger, for his foot slid on the soft mud towards the centre of the stream. He made a rush for the bank, lost his footing, and the flood boiled over his head; he struggled, but in vain; and his own words paint his situation:

"An undefined sensation stopp'd my breath;
Disorder'd views and threat'ning signs of death
Met in one moment, and a terror gave
—I cannot paint it—to the moving grave:
My thoughts were all distressing, hurried, mix'd,
On all things fixing, not a moment fix'd.
Brother, I have not—man has not—the power
To paint the horrors of that life-long hour;
Hour!—but of time I knew not—when I found
Hope, youth, life, love, and all they promised, drown'd."
                                    —*Tales of the Hall.*

My father could never clearly remember how he was saved. He at last found himself grasping some weeds, and by their aid reached the bank.

Mr. and Mrs. Crabbe, cordially approving their son's choice, invited Miss Elmy to pass some time beneath their roof at Aldborough; and my father had the satisfaction to witness the kindness with which she was treated by both his parents, and the commencement of a strong attachment between her and his sister. During this visit[3] he was attacked by a very dangerous fever; and the attention of his affianced wife was unwearied. So much was his mind weakened by the violence and pertinacity of this disorder, that, on his dawning convalescence, he actually cried like a child, because he was considerately denied the food which his renovated stomach longed for. I have heard them laugh heartily at the tears he shed, because Sarah and his sister refused him a lobster on which he had set his affections. For a considerable time, he was unable to walk upright; but he was at length enabled to renew, with my mother, his favourite rambles—to search for fuci on the shore, or to botanise on the heath: and again he expresses his own feelings, in the following passage of "The Borough":

> "See! one relieved from anguish, and to-day
> Allow'd to walk, and look an hour away.
> Two months confined by fever, frenzy, pain,
> He comes abroad, and is himself again.
> He stops, as one unwilling to advance,
> Without another and another glance . . .
> With what a pure and simple joy he sees
> Those sheep and cattle browsing at their ease!

[3] At this period the whole family were still living together. Some time after my father and his sister had separate lodgings, at a Mr. Aldrich's.

Easy himself, there's nothing breathes or moves,
But he would cherish;—all that lives he loves."

On Miss Elmy's return to Parham, she was seized with the same or a kindred disorder, but still more violent and alarming; and none of her friends expected her recovery. My father was kindly invited to remain in the house. A fearful delirium succeeded: all hope appeared irrational; and then it was that he felt the bitterness of losing a fond and faithful heart. I remember being greatly affected, at a very early period, by hearing him describe the feelings with which he went into a small garden her uncle had given her, to water her flowers; intending, after her death, to take them to Aldborough, and keep them for ever. The disorder at last took a favourable turn.

But a calamity of the severest kind awaited her uncle and aunt. Their only child, a fine hale girl of fourteen, humoured by her mother, adored by her father, was cut off in a few days by an inflammatory sore throat. Her parents were bowed down to the earth; so sudden and unexpected was the blow. It made a permanent alteration at Parham. Mr. Tovell's health declined from that period, though he lived many years with a broken spirit. Mrs. Tovell, a busy, bustling character, who scorned the exhibition of what she termed "fine feelings," became for a time an altered woman, and, like Agag, "walked softly." I have heard my father describe his astonishment at learning, as he rode into the stable-yard, that Miss Tovell was *dead*. It seemed as if it must be a fiction, so essential did her life appear to her parents. He said he never recollected to have felt any dread equal to that of entering the house on this occasion; for my mother might now be considered as, in part at least, Mr. Tovell's heir, and he anticipated the reception he should meet with, and well knew what she must suffer from the first bitterness of minds too uncultivated to suppress their feelings. He found it as painful as he had foreboded. Mr. Tovell was seated in his arm-chair in stern silence; but the tears coursed each other over his manly face. His wife was weeping violently, her head reclining on the table. One or two female friends were there to offer consolation. After a long silence, Mr. Tovell observed: "She is now out of *everybody's* way, poor girl!" One of the females remarked that it was wrong, very wrong, to grieve, because she was gone to a better place. "How do I know where she is gone?" was the bitter reply; and then there was another long silence.

But, in the course of time, these gloomy feelings subsided. Mr. Crabbe was received as usual, nay, with increased kindness; for he had known their "dear Jane." But though the hospitality of the house was undiminished, and occasionally the sound of loud, joyous mirth was heard, yet the master was never himself again.

Whether my father's more frequent visits to Parham, growing dislike to his profession, or increasing attachment to poetical composition, contributed most to his ultimate abandonment of medicine, I do not profess to tell. I have said that his spirit was buoyed up by the inspiring influence of requited affection; but this necessarily led to other wishes, and to them the obstacles appeared insuperable. Miss Elmy was too prudent to marry where there seemed to be no chance of a competent livelihood; and he, instead of being in a position to maintain a family, could hardly, by labour which he abhorred, earn daily bread for himself. He was proud, too; and, although conscious that he had not deserved success in his profession, he was also conscious of possessing no ordinary abilities, and brooded with deep mortification on his failure. Meantime, he had perused with attention the works of the British poets and of his favourite Horace; and his desk had gradually been filled with verses which he justly esteemed more worthy of the public eye than "Inebriety." He indulged, in short, the dreams of a young poet:

"A little time, and he should burst to light,
And admiration of the world excite;
And every friend, now cool and apt to blame
His fond pursuit, would wonder at his fame,
'Fame shall be mine—then wealth shall I possess—
And beauty next an ardent lover bless.'"

The Patron.

He deliberated often and long—"resolved and re-resolved" —and again doubted; but, well aware as he was of the hazard he was about to encounter, he at last made up his mind. One gloomy day, towards the close of the year 1779, he had strolled to a bleak and cheerless part of the cliff above Aldborough, called "The Marsh Hill," brooding, as he went, over the humiliating necessities of his condition, and plucking every now and then, I have no doubt, the hundredth specimen of some common weed. He stopped opposite a shallow, muddy piece of water, as desolate and gloomy as his own mind, called the Leech-pond, and "it was while I gazed on it"— he said to my brother and me, one happy morning—"that I determined to go to London and venture all."

In one of his early note-books, under the date of December 31, 1779, I find the following entry. It is one upon which I shall offer no comment:

"A thousand years, most adored Creator, are, in thy sight, as one day. So contract, in my sight, my calamities!

"The year of sorrow and care, of poverty and disgrace, of disappointment and wrong, is now passing on to join the

Eternal. Now, O Lord! let, I beseech thee, my afflictions and prayers be remembered—let my faults and follies be forgotten!

"O thou, who art the Fountain of Happiness, give me better submission to thy decrees; better disposition to correct my flattering hopes; better courage to bear up under my state of oppression.

"The year past, O my God! let it not be to me again a torment—the year coming, if it is thy will, be it never such. Nevertheless, not as I will, but as thou wilt. Whether I live or whether I die, whether I be poor or whether I be prosperous, O my Saviour! may I be thine! Amen."

In the autobiographical sketch already quoted, my father thus continues his story: "Mr. Crabbe, after as full and perfect a survey of the good and evil before him as his prejudices, inclinations, and little knowledge of the world enabled him to take, finally resolved to abandon his profession. His health was not robust, his spirits were not equal; assistance he could expect none, and he was not so sanguine as to believe he could do without it. With the best verses he could write, and with very little more, he quitted the place of his birth; not without the most serious apprehensions of the consequence of such a step—apprehensions which were conquered, and barely conquered, by the more certain evil of the prospect before him, should he remain where he was.

"When he thus fled from a gloomy prospect to one as uncertain, he had not heard of a youthful adventurer, whose fate it is probable would, in some degree, have affected his spirits, if it had not caused an alteration in his purpose. Of Chatterton, his extraordinary abilities, his enterprising spirit, his writing in periodical publications, his daring project, and his melancholy fate, he had yet learned nothing; otherwise it may be supposed that a warning of such a kind would have had no small

influence upon a mind rather vexed with the present than expecting much from the future, and not sufficiently happy and
at ease to draw consolation from vanity—much less from a
comparison in which vanity would have found no trifling
mortification."[4]

When his father was at length informed that he felt it to
be of no use to struggle longer against the difficulties of his
situation, the old man severely reproached him with the expenses the family had incurred, in order to afford him an
opening into a walk of life higher than their own; but when
he, in return, candidly explained how imperfectly he had ever
been prepared for the exercise of his profession, the Salt-
master in part admitted the validity of his representation, and
no further opposed his resolution.

But the means of carrying this resolution into effect were
still to seek. His friends were all as poor as himself; and he
knew not where to apply for assistance. In this dilemma, he at
length addressed a letter to the late Mr. Dudley North,
brother to the candidate for Aldborough, requesting the loan
of a small sum; "and a very extraordinary letter it was,"
said Mr. North to his petitioner some years afterwards: "I
did not hesitate for a moment."

The sum advanced by Mr. North, in compliance with his
request, was *five pounds;* and after settling his affairs at Aldborough, and embarking himself and his whole worldly substance on board a sloop at Slaughden, to seek his fortune in
the Great City, he found himself master of a box of clothes, a
small case of surgical instruments, and three pounds in money.

---

[4] "Talking," says my brother John, "of the difficulties of his early years,
when, with a declining practice, riding from one cottage to another, and glad
to relieve his mind by fixing it on the herbs that grew on the wayside, he often
made the assertion, which I could never agree to, that it was necessity that
drove him to be an author;—and more than once he quoted the line—

'Some fall so hard that they rebound again.'"

.   During the voyage he lived with the sailors of the vessel, and partook of their fare.

In looking back to the trifling incidents which I have related in this chapter, I feel how inadequate is the conception they will convey of feelings so deep and a mind so exuberant. These were the only circumstances that I heard him or others mention relative to that early period; but how different would have been the description, had he himself recorded the strongest of his early impressions! Joining much of his father's violence with a keen susceptibility of mortification, his mind must have been at times torn by tumultuous passions; always tempered, however, by the exceeding kindness of his heart. There can scarcely be a more severe trial than for one conscious of general superiority to find himself an object of contempt, for some real and palpable defects. With a mind infinitely above his circumstances, he was yet incompetent to his duties, both in talent and knowledge; and he felt that the opinion of the public, in this respect, was but too just. Nor were those the only trials he had to endure; but the strong and painful feelings to which he was subjected in the very outset of life, however distressing *then*, were unquestionably favourable to his education as a poet, and his moral character as a man.

The following lines, from a manuscript volume, appear to have been composed after he had, on this occasion, bidden farewell to Miss Elmy:

"The hour arrived! I sigh'd and said,
How soon the happiest hours are fled:
On wings of down they lately flew,
But then their moments pass'd with you;
And still with you could I but be,
On downy wings they'd always flee.

"Say, did you not, the way you went,
Feel the soft balm of gay content?
Say, did you not all pleasures find,
Of which you left so few behind?
I think you did: for well I know
My parting prayer would make it so.

"May she, I said, life's choicest goods partake,
Those, late in life, for nobler still forsake—
The bliss of one, th' esteem'd of many live,
With all that Friendship would, and all that Love
    can give!"

I shall conclude this chapter with the stronger verses in
which he, some months after, expressed the gloomier side of
his feelings on quitting his native place—the very verses, he
had reason to believe, which first satisfied Burke that he was a
true poet:

"Here wand'ring long, amid these frowning fields
I sought the simple life that Nature yields;
Rapine, and wrong, and fear usurp'd her place,
And a bold, artful, surly, savage race,
Who, only skill'd to take the finny tribe,
The yearly dinner, or septennial bribe,
Wait on the shore, and, as the waves run high,
On the tost vessel bend their eager eye,
Which, to their coast directs its vent'rous way,
Theirs or the ocean's miserable prey.

"As on their neighbouring beach yon swallows stand,
And wait for favouring winds to leave the land,
While still for flight the ready wing is spread—
So waited I the favouring hour, and fled;

Fled from those shores where guilt and rapine reign,
And cried, Ah! hapless they who still remain—
Who still remain to hear the ocean roar,
Whose greedy waves devour the lessening shore,
Till some fierce tide, with more imperious sway,
Sweeps the low hut and all it holds away;
When the sad tenant weeps from door to door,
And begs a poor protection from the poor."

The Village.

CHAPTER III

1780

Mr. Crabbe's Difficulties and Distresses in London—Publication of his Poem, "The Candidate"—His unsuccessful Applications to Lord North, Lord Shelburne, and other eminent Individuals—His "Journal to Mira."

ALTHOUGH THE chance of his being so successful in his metropolitan *début* as to find in his literary talents the means of subsistence must have appeared slender in the eyes of Mr. Crabbe's Suffolk friends, and although he himself was anything but sanguine in his anticipations—yet it must be acknowledged, that he arrived in London at a time not unfavourable for a new candidate in poetry. The field may be said to have lain open before him. The giants, Swift and Pope, had passed away, leaving each in his department examples never to be excelled; but the style of each had been so long imitated by inferior persons, that the world was not unlikely to welcome someone who should strike into a newer path. The strong and powerful satirist, Churchill, the classic Gray, and the inimitable Goldsmith, had also departed; and, more recently still, Chatterton had paid the bitter penalty of his imprudence, under circumstances which must surely have rather disposed the patrons of talent to watch the next oportunity that might offer itself of encouraging genius "by poverty depressed." The stupendous Johnson, unrivalled in general literature, had, from an early period, withdrawn himself from poetry. Cowper, destined to fill so large a space in the public eye, somewhat later, had not as yet appeared as an author;[1] and as for Burns, he was still unknown beyond the obscure circle of his fellow-villagers. The moment, therefore, might appear favourable for Mr. Crabbe's meditated appeal:[2] and yet, had he foreseen all the sorrows and disappointments which awaited him in his new career, it is probable he would either have remained in his native place, or, if he had gone to London at all, engaged himself to beat the mortar in some dispensary. Happily his hopes ultimately prevailed over his fears: his Sarah cheered him by her approbation of his bold adventure; and his mind soared and exulted when he suddenly felt himself freed from the drudgery and anxieties of his hated profession.

In his own little biographical sketch he says that, "on re-linquishing every hope of rising in his profession, he repaired to the metropolis, and resided in lodgings with a family in the

[1] Cowper's first publication was in 1782, when he was in the fiftieth year of his age.

[2] I find these lines in one of his note-books for 1780—

> "When summer's tribe, her rosy tribe, are fled,
> And drooping beauty mourns her blossoms shed,
> Some humbler sweet may cheer the pensive swain,
> And simpler beauties deck the withering plain.
> And thus when Verse her wint'ry prospect weeps,
> When Pope is gone, and mighty Milton sleeps,
> When Gray in lofty lines has ceased to soar,
> And gentle Goldsmith charms the town no more,
> An humbler Bard the widow'd Muse invites,
> Who led by hope and inclination writes:
> With half their art he tries the soul to move,
> And swell the softer strain with themes of love."

city; for reasons which he might not himself be able to assign, he was afraid of going to the west end of the town. He was placed, it is true, near to some friends of whose kindness he was assured, and was probably loth to lose that domestic and cheerful society which he doubly felt in a world of strangers."

The only acquaintance he had on entering London was a Mrs. Burcham, who had been in early youth a friend of Miss Elmy, and who was now the wife of a linen-draper in Cornhill. This worthy woman and her husband received him with cordial kindness; they invited him to make their house his home whenever he chose; and as often as he availed himself of this invitation, he was treated with that frank familiarity which cancels the appearance of obligation. It might be supposed that with such friends to lean upon, he would have been secure against actual distress; but his was, in some points, a proud spirit: he never disclosed to them the extent of his difficulties. Nothing but sheer starvation could ever have induced him to do so; and not even that, as long as there was a poor-house in the land to afford him refuge. All they knew was, that he had come to town a literary adventurer: but though ignorant of the exact nature of his designs, as well as of the extreme narrowness of his pecuniary resources, they often warned him of the fate of Chatterton—of whose genius and misfortunes, as we have seen, he had never heard while he remained in Suffolk.

To be near these friends, he took lodgings close to the Exchange, in the house of Mr. Vickery,[3] a hair-dresser, then or soon afterwards of great celebrity in his calling; and on the family's removing some months later to Bishopsgate-street, he accompanied them to their new residence. I may mention

[3] Mr. Vickery is still in life, a most respectable octogenarian. He laments that his memory retains little of Mr. Crabbe, except that he was "a quiet, amiable, genteel young man; much esteemed by the family for the regularity of all his conduct."

that, so little did he at first foresee the distress in which a shilling would be precious, that on taking up his quarters at Mr. Vickery's, he equipped himself with a fashionable tie-wig, which must have made a considerable hole in his three pounds. However, no sooner had he established himself here, than he applied, with the utmost diligence, to the pursuits for which he had sacrificed every other prospect. He had soon transcribed and corrected the poetical pieces he had brought with him from the country; and composed two dramas and a variety of prose essays, in imitation, some of Swift, others of Addison; and he was ere long in communication with various booksellers with a view to publication. "In this lodging," says the poet's own sketch, "he passed something more than one year, during which his chief study was to improve in versification, to read all such books as he could command, and to take as full and particular a view of mankind as his time and finances enabled him to do."

While residing in the City he often spent his evening at a small coffee-house near the Exchange, where, if prudence allowed only the most frugal refreshment, he had a more gratifying entertainment in the conversation of several young men, most of them teachers of mathematics, who, in his own words, "met after the studies and labours of the day, to commence other studies and labours of a lighter and more agreeable kind; and then it was," he continues, "that Mr. Crabbe experienced the inestimable relief which one mind may administer to another. He particularly acknowledges his obligations to Mr. Bonnycastle, the (late) Master of the Military Academy at Woolwich, for many hours of consolation, amusement, and instruction." With Mr. Bonnycastle he formed a close intimacy and attachment; and those who are acquainted with the character of that respected man will easily imagine the pleasure and advantage Mr. Crabbe must have

derived from his society. To eminence in his own vocation
he joined much general knowledge, considerable taste in the
fine arts,[4] colloquial talents of a high order, and a warm and
enlarged heart. Another of this little company was Mr.
Isaac Dalby, afterwards professor of mathematics in the
Military College at Marlow, and employed by the Ordnance
department on the trigonometrical survey of England and
Wales; and a third was the well-known mathematician,
Reuben Burrow, originally a merchant's clerk in the City,
who subsequently rose to high distinction in the service of
the East India Company, and died in 1791, while engaged in
the trigonometrical survey of Bengal.

These then obscure but eminently gifted and worthy men
were Mr. Crabbe's chosen companions, and to listen to their
instructive talk was the most refreshing relaxation of his manly
and vigorous mind: but bodily exercise was not less necessary
for a frame which, at that period, was anything but robust,
and he often walked with Mr. Bonnycastle, when he went to
the various schools in the suburbs, but still more frequently
strolled alone into the country, with a small edition of Ovid,
or Horace, or Catullus, in his pocket. Two or three of these
little volumes remained in his possession in latter days, and he
set a high value on them; for, said he, "they were the companions of my adversity." His favourite haunt was Hornsey-
wood, and there he often renewed his old occupation of
searching for plants and insects. On one occasion, he had
walked farther than usual into the country, and felt himself too
much exhausted to return to town. He could not afford to give
himself any refreshment at a public-house, much less to pay
for a lodging; so he stretched himself on a mow of hay,

---

[4] At one time, Mr. Bonnycastle was employed to revise and correct a
MS. of Cowper; but he and that poet did not agree in their tastes—Mr.
Bonnycastle being a staunch advocate for the finish and polish of Pope, while
the other had far different models in higher estimation.

beguiled the evening with Tibullus, and, when he could read no longer, slept there till the morning. Such was his habits and amusements; not do I believe that he ever saw the inside of a theatre, or of any public building, but a church or chapel, until the pressing difficulties of his situation had been overcome. When, many years afterwards, Mr. Bonnycastle was sending his son to London, he strongly enforced upon the young gentleman the early example of his friend, Mr. Crabbe, then enjoying the success of his second series of poems. "Crabbe," said he, "never suffered his attention to be diverted for a moment by the novelties with which he was surrounded at that trying period; but gave his whole mind to the pursuit by which he was then striving to live, and by which he in due time attained to competence and honour."

When my father had completed some short pieces in verse, he offered them for publication; but they were rejected. He says in his sketch, "he was not encouraged by the reception which his manuscripts experienced from those who are said to be not the worst judges of literary composition. He was, indeed, assured by a bookseller, who afterwards published for him, that he must not suppose that the refusal to purchase proceeded from a want of merit in the poems. Such, however, was his inference; and that thought had the effect which it ought—he took more pains, and tried new subjects. In one respect he was unfortunate: while preparing a more favourable piece for the inspection of a gentleman whom he had then in view, he hazarded the publication of an anonymous performance, and had the satisfaction of hearing, in due time, that something (not much, indeed—but a something was much) would arise from it; but while he gathered encouragement, and looked forward to more than mere encouragement from this essay, the publisher failed, and his hope of profit was as transitory as the fame of his nameless production."

This production[5] was "THE CANDIDATE, a Poetical Epistle to the Authors of the Monthly Review," which was published early in 1780, by H. Payne, opposite Marlborough House, Pall Mall; a thin quarto of 34 pages, and bearing on the title-page a motto from Horace: "Multa quidem nobis facimus mala sæpe poetæ," &c. It was a call on the attention, not an appeal from the verdict, of those whom he considered the most influential critics of the time; and it received, accordingly, a very cold and brief notice in their number for August; wherein, indeed, nothing is dwelt upon but some incorrectness of rhymes, and "that material defect, the want of a proper subject." Nor was the Gentleman's Magazine more courteous. "If," said Mr. Urban, "the authors addressed agree with us in their estimate, they will not give this *Candidate* much encouragement to stand a poll at Parnassus."

Whether "The Candidate" did not deserve rather a more encouraging reception, the public now has an opportunity of judging, as this long-forgotten poem, with some other early pieces, is included in the second volume of the poet's collected works.

The failure of Mr. Payne plunged the young poet into great perplexity. He was absolutely under the necessity of seeking some pecuniary aid; and he cast his eyes in succession on several of those eminent individuals who were then generally considered as liberal patrons of literature. Before he left Aldborough he had been advised to apply to the premier, Lord North; but he now applied to him in vain. A second application to Lord Shelburne met with no better success: and he often expressed in later times the feelings with which he contrasted his reception at this nobleman's door, in Berkeley-square, in

---

[5] There was no name in its title-page: the author, however, *hinted* his name:

"Our Mira's name in future times shall shine,
And shepherds—though the harshest—envy mine."—p. 21.

1780, with the courteous welcome which he received at a subsequent period in that same mansion, now Lansdowne House. He wrote also several times to the Lord Chancellor Thurlow; but with little better fortune. To the first letter, which enclosed a copy of verses, his Lordship returned for answer a cold, polite note, regretting that his avocations did not leave him leisure to read verse. The great talents and discriminating judgment of Thurlow made him feel this repulse with double bitterness; and he addressed to his Lordship some strong but not disrespectful lines, intimating that, in former times, the encouragement of literature had been considered as a duty appertaining to the illustrious station he held. Of this effusion the Chancellor took no notice whatever.

But I have it in my power to submit to the reader some fragments of a JOURNAL which my father kept during this distressing period for the perusal of his affianced wife. The manuscript was discovered lately in the possession of a sister of my mother's. My father had never mentioned the existence of any such treasure to his own family. It is headed "The Poet's Journal"; and I now transcribe it; interweaving, as it proceeds, a few observations, which occur to me as necessary to make it generally intelligible.

"THE POET'S JOURNAL

" 'Sunt lachrimæ rerum, et mentem mortalia tangunt.'

" 'He felt whate'er of sorrows wound the soul,
But view'd Misfortune on her fairest side.'

"*April* 21, 1780.—I DEDICATE to you, my dear Mira, this Journal, and I hope it will be some amusement. God only knows what is to be my lot; but I have, as far as I can, taken your old advice, and turned affliction's better part outward and am determined to reap as much consolation from my prospects as possible; so that, whatever befalls me, I will

E

endeavour to suppose it has its benefits, though I cannot immediately see them.

"*April* 24.—Took lodgings at a Mr. Vickery's, near the Exchange; rather too expensive, but very convenient—and here I, on reflection, thought it best to publish, if I could do it with advantage, some little piece, before I attempted to introduce my principal work. Accordingly, I set about a poem, which I called 'The Hero, an Epistle to Prince William Henry.'"

[I must here interrupt the Journal for a moment, to explain. The "principal work" alluded to in the above entry was a prose treatise, entitled "*A Plan for the Examination of our Moral and Religious Opinions,*" of which the first rough draft alone has been preserved; and to which, in one of his rhymed epistles to Mira, composed in this same April, 1780, my father thus alludes:

"Of substance I've thought, and the varied disputes
On the nature of man and the notions of brutes;
Of systems confuted, and systems explain'd,
Of science disputed and tenets maintain'd . . .
These, and such speculations on these kind of things,
Have robb'd my poor Muse of her plume and her wings;
Consumed the phlogiston you used to admire,
The spirit extracted, extinguish'd the fire;
Let out all the ether, so pure and refined,
And left but a mere *caput mortuum* behind."

With respect to the "Epistle to Prince William Henry"—now King William IV—I need only remind the reader that his Royal Highness had recently been serving with honour under Admiral Rodney, and was about to return to sea. The Poet, after many cautions against the flattery of courtiers,

&c. &c., thus concluded his Epistle. I copy from his note-book:

"Who thus aspiring sings? would'st thou explore;
A Bard replies, who ne'er assumed before—
One taught in hard affliction's school to bear
Life's ills, where every lesson costs a tear,
Who sees from thence, the proper point of view,
What the wise heed not, and the weak pursue.

*   *   *

"And now farewell, the drooping Muse exclaims.
She lothly leaves thee to the shock of war,
And fondly dwelling on her princely tar,
Wishes the noblest good her Harry's share,
Without her misery and without her care.
For, ah! unknown to thee, a rueful train,
Her hapless children, sigh, and sigh in vain;
A numerous band, denied the boon to die,
Half-starved, half-led by fits of charity.
Unknown to thee! and yet, perhaps, thy ear
Has chanced each sad, amusing tale to hear,
How some, like Budgell, madly sank for ease;[6]
How some, like Savage, sicken'd by degrees;
How a pale crew, like helpless Otway, shed
The proud big tear on song-extorted bread;
Or knew, like Goldsmith, some would stoop to choose
Contempt, and for the mortar quit the Muse.[7]

[6] Eustace Budgell drowned himself in the Thames in 1736: the miseries of Otway and Savage are familiar to every reader.

[7] Goldsmith, on his return to England, was so poor that it was with difficulty he was enabled to reach the metropolis with a few halfpence only in his pocket. He was an entire stranger, and without any recommendation. He offered himself to several apothecaries, in the character of a journeyman, but had the mortification to find every application without success. At length he was admitted into the house of a chemist. This example was often in my father's thoughts.

"One of this train—and of these wretches one—
Slave to the Muses, and to Misery son—
Now prays the Father of all Fates to shed,
On Henry, laurels; on his poet, bread!

"Unhappy art! decreed thine owner's curse;
Vile diagnostic of consumptive purse;
Still shall thy fatal force my soul perplex,
And every friend, and every brother vex!
Each fond companion!—No, I thank my God!
There rests my torment—there is hung the rod.
To friend, to fame, to family unknown.
Sour disappointments frown on me alone.
Who hates my song, and damns the poor design,
Shall wound no peace—shall grieve no heart but mine!

"Pardon, sweet Prince! the thoughts that will intrude,
For want is absent, and dejection rude,
Methinks I hear, amid the shouts of Fame,
Each jolly victor hail my Henry's name;
And, Heaven forbid that, in that jovial day,
One British bard should grieve when all are gay.
No! let him find his country has redress,
And bid adieu to every fond distress;
Or, touch'd too near, from joyful scenes retire,
Scorn to complain, and with one sigh expire!"

We now return to my father's Journal.]

"*April* 25.—Reading the 'Daily Advertiser' of the 22nd,
I found the following: 'Wanted an amanuensis, of grammatical education, and endued with a genius capable of
making improvements in the writings of a gentleman not well

versed in the English language.' Now, Vanity having no doubt
of my capacity, I sent immediately the following note to a
Mrs. Brooke, Coventry-street, Haymarket, the person at
whose house I was to inquire: 'A person having the advantage
of a grammatical education, and who supposes himself en-
dowed with a genius capable of making emendations to the
writings of any gentleman not perfectly acquainted with the
English language, would be very happy to act as an amanuensis, where the confinement was not too rigid,' &c. An
answer was returned verbally, by a porter, that the person
should call in a day or two.

"*April 27.*—Called on Mrs. Brooke, from whose husband
or servant in the shop I had the intelligence that the gentleman
was provided—twelve long miles walked away, loss of time,
and a little disappointment, thought I: now for my philosophy. Perhaps, then, I reflected, the 'gentleman' might not
have so very much of that character as I at first supposed:
he might be a sharper, and would not, or an author himself,
and consequently could not, pay me. He might have employed me seven hours in a day over law or politics, and treated
me at night with a Welsh rabbit and porter! It's all well; I
can at present buy porter myself, and am my own amanuensis.

"N.B. Sent my poem to Dodsley, and required him to
return it to-morrow if not approved, otherwise its author would
call upon him.

"*April 28.*—Judging it best to have two strings to the bow,
and fearing Mr. Dodsley's will snap, I have finished another
little work, from that awkward-titled piece 'The Foes of
Mankind'; have run it on to three hundred and fifty lines, and
given it a still more odd name, 'An Epistle from the Devil.'
To-morrow I hope to transcribe it fair, and send it by Monday.

"Mr. Dodsley's reply just received. 'Mr. Dodsley presents

his compliments to the gentleman who favoured him with the enclosed poem, which he has returned, as he apprehends the sale of it would probably not enable him to give any consideration. He does not mean by this to insinuate a want of merit in the poem, but rather a want of attention in the public.'

"Once more, my Mira, I'll try and write to Mr. Becket: if he fails me!—I know not how I shall ever get sufficient time to go through my principal design; but I've promised to keep up my spirits, and I will. God held me!

"*April* 28.—I thank Heaven my spirits are not at all affected by Dodsley's refusal. I have not been able to get the poem ready for Mr. Becket to-day, but will take some pains with it.

"I find myself under the disagreeable necessity of vending, or pawning, some of my more useless articles: accordingly have put into a paper such as cost about two or three guineas, and, being silver, have not greatly lessened in their value. The conscientious pawnbroker allowed me—'he *thought* he *might*'—half a guinea for them. I took it very readily, being determined to call for them very soon, and then, if I afterwards wanted, carry them to some less voracious animal of the kind.

"*May* 1.—Still in suspense; but still resigned. I think of sending Mr. Becket two or three little pieces, large enough for an eighteenpenny pamphlet: but, notwithstanding this, to set about the book I chiefly depend upon. My good broker's money reduced to five shillings and sixpence, and no immediate prospect of more. I have only to keep up my spirits as well as I can, and depend upon the protection of Providence, which has hitherto helped me in worse situations.

"Let me hope the last day of this month may be a more smiling one than the first. God only knows, and to Him I readily, and not unresignedly, leave it.

"*May* 3.—Mr. Becket has just had my copy. I have *made* about four hundred and fifty lines, and entitled them 'Poetical Epistles, with a Preface by the learned Martinus Scriblerus.' I do not say it is chance whether they take or not; it is as God pleases, whatever wits may say to the contrary.

"I this day met an old friend; poor Morley!—not very clean; ill, heavy, and dejected. The poor fellow has had Fortune's smiles and her frowns, and alas, for him! her smiles came first. May I hope a happy prognostic from this. No, I do not, cannot, will not depend upon Fortune.

"N.B. The purse a little recruited, by twenty-five shillings received for books. Now then, when the spirits are tolerable, we'll pursue our Work, and make hay while the sun shines, for it's plaguy apt to be clouded.

"*May* 6.—Having nearly finished my plan for one volume, I hope by next week to complete it, and then try my fortune in earnest. Mr. Becket, not yet called upon, has had a pretty long time to deliberate upon my 'Epistles.' If they will do, I shall continue them; London affording ample matter for the smiles as well as frowns of satire.

"Should I have time after my principal business is completed, I don't know whether I shall not write a Novel; those things used to sell, and perhaps will now—but of this hereafter. My spirits are marvellously good, considering I'm in the middle of the great city, and a stranger, too, without money—but sometimes we have unaccountable fears, and at other times unaccountable courage.

"*May* 10.—Mr. Becket says just what Mr. Dodsley wrote, 'twas a very pretty thing, 'but, sir, these little pieces the town do not regard: it has merit—perhaps some other may'—'It will be offered to no other, sir!'—'Well, sir, I am obliged to you, but,' &c.—and so these little affairs have their end. And are you not disheartened? My dearest Mira, not I! The wanting a letter from you to-day, and the knowing myself to be possessed but of sixpence-farthing in the world, are much more consequential things.

"I have got pretty forward in my book, and shall soon know its fate; if bad, these things will the better prepare me for it; if good, the contrasted fortune will be the more agreeable. We are helped, I'm persuaded, with spirits in our necessities. I did not, nor could, conceive that, with a very uncertain prospect before me, a very bleak one behind, and a *very* poor one around me, I should be so happy a fellow: I don't think there's a man in London worth but fourpence-halfpenny—for I've this moment sent seven farthings for a pint of porter—who is so resigned to his poverty. Hope, Vanity, and the Muse, will certainly contribute something towards a light heart; but Love and the god of Love only can throw a beam of gladness on a heavy one.

"I am now debating whether an Ode or a Song should have the next place in the collection; which being a matter of so great consequence, we'll bid our Mira goodnight.

"*May* 12.—Perhaps it is the most difficult thing in the world to tell how far a man's vanity will run away with his passions. I shall therefore not judge, at least not determine, how far my poetical talents may or may not merit applause. For the first time in my life that I recollect, I have written three or four stanzas that so far touched me in the reading them, as to take off the consideration that they were things of my own fancy. Now, if I ever do succeed, I will take particular notice if this passage is remarked; if not, I shall conclude 'twas mere self-love—but if so, 'twas the strangest, and, at the same time, strongest disguise she ever put on.

"You shall rarely find the same humour hold two days. I'm dull and heavy, nor can go on with my work. The head and heart are like children, who, being praised for their good behaviour, will overact themselves; and so is the case with me. Oh! Sally, how I want you!

"*May* 16.—O! my dear Mira, how you distress me: you inquire into my affairs, and love not to be denied—yet you must. To what purpose should I tell you the particulars of my gloomy situation; that I have parted with my money, sold my *wardrobe*, pawned my watch, am in debt to my landlord, and finally, at some loss how to eat a week longer? Yet you say, tell me all. Ah, my dear Sally, do not desire it; you must not yet be told these things. Appearance is what distresses me: I *must* have dress, and therefore am horribly fearful I shall accompany Fashion with fasting—but a fortnight more will tell me of a certainty.

"*May* 18.—A day of bustle—twenty shillings to pay a tailor, when the stock amounted to thirteen and threepence. Well —there were instruments to part with, that fetched no less than eight shillings more; but twenty-one shillings and three-pence would yet be so poor a superfluity, that the Muse would never visit till the purse was recruited; for, say men what they will, she does not love empty pockets nor poor living. Now, you must know, my watch was mortgaged for less than it ought; so I redeemed and repledged it, which has made me—the tailor paid and the day's expenses—at this instant worth (let me count my cash) ten shillings—a rare case, and most bountiful provision of fortune!

"Great God! I thank thee for these happy spirits: seldom they come, but coming, make large amends for preceding gloom.

"I wonder what these people, my Mira, think of me. Here's Vickery, his wife, two maids, and a shop full of men: the latter, consequently, neither know nor care who I am. A little pretty hawk-eyed girl, I've a great notion, thinks me a fool, for neglecting the devoirs a lodger is supposed to pay to an attendant in his house: I know but one way to remove the suspicion, and that in the end might tend to confirm it.

"Mrs. Vickery is a clear-sighted woman, who appears to me a good wife, mother, and friend. She thinks me a soft-tempered gentleman—I'm a gentleman here—not quite nice enough.

"Mr. Vickery is an honest fellow, hasty, and not over distinguishing. He looks upon me as a bookish young man, and so respects me—for he is bookish himself—as one who is not quite settled in the world, nor has much knowledge of it; and as a careless easy-tempered fellow, who never made an observation, nor is ever likely to do so.

"Having thus got my character in the family, my employment remains (I suppose) a secret, and I believe 'tis a debate whether I am copying briefs for an attorney, or songs for 'the lady whose picture was found on the pillow t'other day.'

"N.B. We remove to Bishopsgate-street in a day or two. Not an unlucky circumstance; as I shall then, concealing Vickery's name, let my father know only the number of my lodging.

"*May* 20.—The cash, by a sad temptation, greatly reduced. An unlucky book-stall presented to the eyes three volumes of Dryden's works, octavo, five shillings. Prudence, however, got the better of the devil, when she whispered me to bid three shillings and six-pence: after some hesitation, that prevailed with the woman, and I carried reluctantly home, I believe, a fair bargain, but a very ill-judged one.

"It's the vilest thing in the world to have but one coat. My only one has happened with a mischance, and how to manage it is some difficulty. A confounded stove's modish ornament caught its elbow, and rent it halfway. Pinioned to the side it came home, and I ran deploring to my loft. In the dilemma, it occurred to me to turn tailor myself; but how to get materials to work with puzzled me. At last I went running down in a hurry, with three or four sheets of paper in my hand, and begged for a needle, &c., to sew them together. This finished my job, and but that it is somewhat thicker, the elbow is a good one yet.

"These are foolish things, Mira, to write or speak, and we may laugh at them; but I'll be bound to say they are much more likely to make a man cry, where they *happen*—though I was too much of a philosopher for *that*, however, not one of those who preferred a ragged coat to a whole one.

"On Monday, I hope to finish my book entirely, and perhaps send it. God Almighty give it a better fate than the trifles tried before!

"Sometimes I think I cannot fail; and then, knowing how often I have thought so of fallible things, I am again desponding. Yet, within these three or four days, I've been remarkably high in spirits, and now am so, though I've somewhat exhausted them by writing upwards of thirty pages.

"I am happy in being in the best family you could conceive me to have been led to; people of real good character and good nature: whose circumstances are affluent above their station, and their manners affable beyond their circumstances. Had I taken a lodging at a different kind of house, I must have been greatly distressed; but now I shall, at all events, not be so before 'tis determined, one way or other, what I am to expect.

"I keep too little of the journal form here, for I always think I am writing to you for the evening's post; and, according to custom then, shall bid my dear Sally goodnight, and ask her prayers.

"*May* 21.—I give you, my dear Miss Elmy, a short abstract of a Sermon, preached this morning by my favourite clergy-

man, at St. Dunstan's.[8] There is nothing particular in it, but
had you heard the good man, reverend in appearance, and with
a hollow, slow voice, deliver it—a man who seems as if already half way to Heaven—you would have joined with me in
wondering, people call it dull and disagreeable to hear such dis-
courses, and run from them to societies where Deists fool-
ishly blaspheme, or to pantomimes and farces, where men seek
to deform the creatures God stamped his own image upon.
What, I wonder, can Mr. Williams,[9] as a free-thinker, or
Mr. Lee Lewis,[10] as a free-speaker, find so entertaining to
produce, that their congregations so far exceed those which
grace, and yet disgrace, our churches.

"TEXT.—'*For many are called, but few chosen.*'

"Observe, my brethren, that many are called—so many
that who can say he is not? Which of you is not called?
Where is the man who neither is, nor will be? such neither
is nor will be born. The call is universal; it is not confined to
this or that sect or country; to this or that class of people:
every man shares in this blessed invitation—every man is

[8] The Rev. Thomas Winstanley, of Trinity College, Cambridge, A.M.,
was appointed rector of St. Dunstan's in the East, in January, 1771,—succeeding the celebrated Dr. Jortin, author of the Life of Erasmus, &c. This eminently
respectable clergyman died in February, 1789.

[9] About this time, David Williams, originally a dissenting minister in
Glamorganshire, published "Lectures on the Universal Principles of Religion
and Morality," "Apology for professing the Religion of Nature," &c., and
attempted to establish a congregation, on the avowed principles of deism, in
Margaret-street, Cavendish-square: but this last plan soon failed. He died in
1816.

[10] Charles Lee Lewis, the celebrated comedian, was at this time amusing
the town with an evening entertainment of songs and recitations, in the style
of Dibdin.

called. Some by outward, some by inward means: to some, the happy news is proclaimed, to some it is whispered. Some have the word preached to their outward ears; some have it suggested, inwardly, in their hearts. None are omitted in this universal invitation; none shall say, 'I came not, for I was not called.' But take notice—when you have well considered the universality of the call—pondered it, admired, wondered, been lost in contemplation of the bounty; take notice how it is abused—'Few are chosen.' Few! but that, you will say, is in comparison, not in reality; a sad interpretation! degrading whilst it palliates, still it sounds a lesson to pride—still I repeat it, 'Few are chosen.' How doubly lessening! many, yea, all are called—are invited, are entreated, are pressed to the wedding. Many, yea, all—but a little remnant—heed not, love not, obey not the invitation. Many are called to the choice of eternal happiness, and yet few will make eternal happiness their choice.

"Brethren, what reasons may be assigned for these things? For the universality of the call? For the limitation of the choice? The reason why all are called, is this: that God is no respecter of persons. Shall any, in the last day, proclaim that the Judge of the whole earth did not right? Shall any plead a want of this call, as a reason why he came not? Shall any be eternally miserable, because he was refused the means of being happy? No not one. All require this mercy; all have this mercy granted them. From the first man to the last, all are sinners; from the first man to the last, all are invited to be clean; for, as in Adam all die, even so in Christ shall all be made alive.

"The reason why many are called, is, because the mercy of God is not confined, is unspeakable. The reason why so few are chosen, is, because man's depravity is so great, so extensive. The call is God's; the choice is ours—that we may be happy, is his, of his goodness; that we will not, is our own folly: He wills not that a sinner should die in his sins, but, sinners as we are, we had rather die than part with them. The reason why few are chosen doth not depend upon him who calls, but upon those who are called. Complain not that you want an invitation to heaven, but complain that you want the inclination to obey it. Say not that you cannot go, but that you will not part with the objects which prevent your going.

"Again: To what are we called? and who are those who obey the call? The last question is to us the most important. Those who accept the invitation are such as go like guests. Those who think themselves honoured in the summons will have on their wedding garment; they will put off the filthy robes of their own righteousness, and much more will they put aside the garments spotted with iniquity. They consider themselves as called to faith, to thanksgiving, to justification, to sanctification, and they will, therefore, go in the disposition and temper of men desirous of these immortal benefits; they know that he who had them not—and who, though but one, typifies all the rejected, all the not chosen—they know he was bound hand and foot, and thrust out for that reason: yet, mark you, my fellow sinners! this man went to the wedding, he enrolled himself amongst the guests, he was of the profession, a nominal Christian. How many are there now who are such, deaf to the true end of their calling! who love mercy, but not to use the means of attaining its blessing; who admire the robe of righteousness, but would wear it over the polluted weeds of depravity and hardness of heart.

"But to what are we called? To everlasting happiness! Consider, I implore you, whether it is worth the trouble of looking after. Do by it as by your worldly bargains, which surely do not offer more. Examine the truths it is founded upon; they will bear examination. Try its merits; they will stand the trial. You would grieve to see thousands of saints in the kingdom of God, and you yourselves shut out; and yet, shut out you will be into everlasting darkness, unless you rightly obey the call which you have heard. It is not enough to be called; for that all are. It is not enough to obey the call, for he did so in part who was rejected from the wedding; but to join the practice of religion to the profession of it, is truly to accept the invitation, and will, through our Lord Jesus Christ, entitle you to the mercy to which we are called, even the pleasures which are at the right hand of God the Father Almighty, to whom," &c.

"The foregoing, as near as I remember, was the substance of the good Doctor's discourse. I have doubtless not done him justice in the expressions; those it was impossible for me to retain; but I have preserved, in a great measure, the manner, pathos, and argument. Nor was the sermon much longer, though it took a long time to preach, for here we do not find a discourse run off as if they were the best teachers who say most upon a subject; here they dwell upon a sentence, and often repeat it, till it shall hardly fail of making an impression.

"I have this night been drawing out my letter to Lord North. I have diligently read it over, and believe it far the most consequential piece I ever executed, whether in prose or poetry. Its success will soon prove whether it is in the power of my talents to obtain me favour.

"To-morrow, my beloved Sally, I shall transcribe it for you and his Lordship; and if I could suppose you both had the same opinion of its writer, my business were done. You will perceive there is art in it, though art quite consistent with truth—for such is actually the case with me. My last shilling became eight-pence yesterday. The simplicity of the style is, I hope, not lost in endeavouring at the pathetic; and if his

Lordship is indeed a literary man, I am not without hope that it may be a means of obtaining for me a better fortune than hitherto has befallen us.

"*May* 22.—I have just now finished my book, and, if I may so say, consecrated it, by begging of Him, who alone can direct all things, to give me success in it, or patience under any disappointment I may meet with from its wanting that. I have good hope from my letter, which I shall probably copy for you to-morrow, for I find I can't to-day. This afternoon I propose to set out for Westminster, and I hope shall not meet with much difficulty in getting the book delivered to his Lordship——

"—I am now returned from Downing Street, Lord North's place of residence. Every thing at this time becomes consequential. I plagued myself lest I should err in little things— often the causes of a person's doing wrong. The direction of the letter, and the place to call at, puzzled me; I forgot his Lordship's name, and had no Court Calendar. See how trifles perplex us! However, my book is safely delivered, and I shall call again on Wednesday, when I hope to be told something.

"I know not how totally to banish hope, and yet can't encourage it. What a day will to-morrow be to me! a day of bread and expectation. Ah, dear Mira, my hopes are flying; I see now my attempt in its darkest side—twice, nay, three times unsuccessful in a month I have been here—once in my application to the person advertising, and twice in the refusal of booksellers. God help me, my Sally, I have but a cowardly heart, yet I bear up as well as I can; and if I had another shilling would get something to-night to keep these gloomy thoughts at bay, but must save what I have, in hopes of having a letter to pay for to-morrow. How, let me suppose, shall I be received? The very worst I can possibly guess will be to have my book returned by the servant, and no message; next to this a civil refusal. More than these I dare not dwell upon; and yet these alone are uncomfortable things.

"O! what pains do we take, what anxiety do we feel, in our pursuit of worldly good—how reproachful a comparison does it make to our more important business! When was I thus solicitous for the truly valuable riches? O my GOD! forgive a creature who is frailty itself—who is lost in his own vileness and littleness: who would be happy, and knows not the means. My GOD, direct me!

"*May* 23.—Here follows, my dearest Sally, a copy of my letter. I am in tolerable spirits this morning, but my whole night has been spent in waking and sleeping visions, in ideas of the coming good or evil; names, by the way, we learn early to misplace. Sometimes I have dwelt upon all my old views and romantic expectations; have run from disappointment to disappointment; and such as the past has been, so, said I, shall be the future. Then my vanity has told fairer things, and magnified my little talents, till I supposed they must be thought worthy of notice. So that from fear to flattery, and from hope to anxiety, I passed a varied and unquiet night. To-day I am at least more composed, and will give you the letter promised."

*   *   *

[Some leaves are here torn out.]

*   *   *

"Like some poor bark on the rough ocean tost,
My rudder broken, and my compass lost,
My sails the coarsest, and too thin to last,
Pelted by rains, and bare to many a blast,

F

My anchor, Hope, scarce fix'd enough to stay
Where the strong current Grief sweeps all away.
I sail along, unknowing how to steer,
Where quicksands lie and frowning rocks appear.
Life's ocean teems with foes to my frail bark,
The rapid sword-fish, and the rav'ning shark,
Where torpid things crawl forth in splendid shell,
And knaves and fools and sycophants live well.
What have I left in such tempestuous sea?
No Tritons shield, no Naiads shelter me!
A gloomy Muse, in Mira's absence, hears
My plaintive prayer, and sheds consoling tears—
Some fairer prospect, though at distance, brings,
Soothes me with song, and flatters as she sings."

*   *   *

"*June 5.*—Heaven and its Host witness to me that my soul is conscious of its own demerit. I deserve nothing. I do nothing but what is worthy reproof. I expect nothing from what is nearest in my thoughts or actions to virtue. All fall short of it; much, very much, flies from it.

"I make no comparison with the children of men. It matters not to me who is vile or who is virtuous. What I am is all to me; and I am nothing but in my dependence.

"O! Thou, who searchest all hearts, who givest, and who hast given, more than I deserve, or can deserve—who withholdest punishment, and proclaimest pardon—form my desires, that Thou mayest approve them, and approving gratify. My present, O! forgive and pity, and as it seemeth good to Thee, so be it done unto me."

"*June 6.*—I will now, my dearest Mira, give you my letter to Lord Shelburne, but cannot recollect an exact copy, as I altered much of it, and I believe, in point of expression, for the better. I want not, I know, your best wishes; those and her prayers my Mira gives me. God will give us peace, my love, in his time: pray chiefly that we may acquiesce in his righteous determinations.

"*To the Right Honourable the Earl of Shelburne.*

"Ah! SHELBURNE, blest with all that's good or great,
T'adorn a rich, or save a sinking state,
If public Ills engross not all thy care,
Let private Woe assail a patriot's ear,
Pity confined, but not less warm, impart,
And unresisted win thy noble heart:
Nor deem I rob thy soul of Britain's share,
Because I hope to have some interest there;
Still wilt thou shine on all a fostering sun,
Though with more fav'ring beams enlight'ning one—
As Heaven will oft make some more amply blest,
Yet still in general bounty feeds the rest.
Oh hear the Virtue thou reverest plead;
She'll swell thy breast, and there applaud the deed.
She bids thy thoughts one hour from greatness stray,
And leads thee on to fame a shorter way;
Where, if no withering laurel's thy reward,
There's shouting Conscience, and a grateful Bard;
A bard untrained in all but misery's school,
Who never bribed a knave or praised a fool—
'Tis Glory prompts, and as thou read'st attend,
She dictates pity, and becomes my friend;
She bids each cold and dull reflection flee,
And yields her Shelburne to distress and me!

"Forgive, my Lord, a free and, perhaps, unusual address; misfortune has in it, I hope, some excuse for presumption. Your Lordship will not, cannot, be greatly displeased with an unfortunate man, whose wants are the most urgent; who wants a friend to assist him, and bread.

"I will not tire your Lordship with a recital of the various circumstances which have led to this situation. It would be too long a tale; though there are parts in it which, I will venture to assure your Lordship, would not only affect your compassion, but, I hope, engage your approbation. It is too dull a view of the progression from pleasing, though moderate expectation, to unavoidable penury.

"Your Lordship will pardon me the relation of a late and unsuccessful attempt to become useful to myself and the community I live in. Starving as an apothecary, in a little venal borough in Suffolk, it was there suggested to me that Lord North, the present minister, was a man of that liberal disposition, that I might hope success from a representation of my particular circumstances to him. This I have done, and laid before his Lordship, I confess a dull, but a faithful account of my misfortunes. My request had bounds the most moderate. I asked him not to feed upon the spoils of my country, but by an honest diligence and industry to earn the bread I needed. The most pressing part of my prayer entreated of his Lordship his speedy determination, as my little stock of money was exhausted, and I was reduced to live in misery and on credit.

"Why I complain of his Lordship is not that he denied this, though an humble and moderate petition, but for his cruel and unkind delay. My Lord, you will pardon me a resentment expressed in one of the little pieces I have taken the liberty of enclosing, when your Lordship considers the inhumanity I was treated with: my repeated prayers for my sentence were put off by a delay; and at length a lingering refusal, brought me by an insolent domestic, determined my suit, and my opinion of his Lordship's private virtues.

"My Lord, I now turn to your Lordship, and entreat to be heard. I am ignorant what to ask, but feel forcibly my wants —Patronage and Bread. I have no other claim on your Lordship than my necessities, but they are great, unless my Muse, and she has, I am afraid, as few charms; nor is it a time for such to flourish: in serener days, my Lord, I have produced some poetical compositions the public might approve, and your Lordship not disdain to patronise. I would not, my Lord, be vain farther than necessity warrants, and I pray your Lordship to pardon me this. May I not hope it will occur to you how I may be useful? My heart is humbled to all but villainy, and would live, if honestly, in any situation. Your Lordship has my fortune in your power, and I will, with respect and submission, await your determination. I am, my Lord, &c. &c."

"—You see, my dear Mira, to what our situation here may reduce us. Yet am I not conscious of losing the dignity becoming a man: some respect is due to the superiority of station; and that I will always pay, but I cannot flatter or fawn, nor shall my humblest request be so presented. If respect will not do, adulation shall not; but I hope it will; as I'm sure he must have a poor idea of greatness, who delights in a supple knee bending to him, or a tongue voluble in paltry praise, which conscience says is totally undeserved. One of the poetical pieces I sent to Lord Shelburne you have no copy of, and I will therefore give it you here.

"*An Epistle to a Friend.*

"Why, true, thou say'st the fools at Court denied,
Growl vengeance—and then take the other side:
The unfed flatterer borrows satire's power,
As sweets unshelter'd run to vapid sour.

But thou, the counsel to my closest thought,
Beheld'st it ne'er in fulsome stanzas wrought.
The Muse I caught ne'er fawn'd on venal souls,
Whom suppliants angle, and poor praise controls;
She, yet unskill'd in all but fancy's dream,
Sang to the woods, and Mira was her theme.
But when she sees a titled nothing stand
The ready cipher of a trembling land—
Not of that simple kind that placed alone
Are useless, harmless things, and threaten none—
But those which, join'd to figures, well express
A strengthen'd tribe that amplify distress,
Grow in proportion to their number great,
And help each other in the ranks of state;
When this and more the pensive Muses see,
They leave the vales and willing nymphs to thee;
To Court on wings of agile anger speed,
And paint to freedom's sons each guileful deed.
Hence rascals teach the virtues they detest,
And fright base action from sin's wavering breast;
For though the knave may scorn the Muse's arts,
Her sting may haply pierce more timid hearts.
Some, though they wish it, are not steel'd enough,
Nor is each would-be villain conscience-proof.

"And what, my friend, is left my song besides?
No school-day wealth that roll'd in silver tides,
No dreams of hope that won my early will,
Nor love, that pain'd in temporary thrill;
No gold to deck my pleasure-scorn'd abode,
No friend to whisper peace—to give me food—
Poor to the World I'd yet not live in vain,
But show its lords their hearts, and my disdain.

"Yet shall not Satire all my song engage
In indiscriminate and idle rage;
True praise, where Virtue prompts, shall gild each line,
And long—if Vanity deceives not—shine.
For though in harsher strains, the strains of woe,
And unadorn'd, my heart-felt murmurs flow,
Yet time shall be when this thine humbled friend
Shall to more lofty heights his notes extend.
A Man—for other title were too poor—
Such as 'twere almost virtue to adore,
He shall the ill that loads my heart exhale,
As the sun vapours from the dew-pressed vale;
Himself uninjuring shall new warmth infuse,
And call to blossom every want-nipp'd Muse.
Then shall my grateful strains his ear rejoice,
His name harmonious thrill'd on Mira's voice;
Round the reviving bays new sweets shall spring,
And SHELBURNE's fame through laughing valleys ring.

"Pay me, dear, for this long morning's work, with your patience, and, if you can, your approbation. I suppose we shall have nothing more of this riot in the city, and I hope now to entertain you with better things. God knows, and we will be happy that it is not the work of accident. Something will happen, and perhaps now. Angels guide and bless you!"

"June 8.—Yesterday, my own business being decided, I was at Westminster at about three o'clock in the afternoon, and saw the members go to the House. The mob stopped many persons, but let all whom I saw pass, excepting Lord Sandwich, whom they treated roughly, broke his coach windows, cut his face, and turned him back. A guard of horse and foot were immediately sent for, who did no particular service, the mob increasing and defeating them.

"I left Westminster when all the members, that were permitted, had entered the House and came home. In my way I met a resolute band of vile-looking fellows, ragged, dirty, and insolent, armed with clubs, going to join their companions. I since learned that there were eight or ten of these bodies in different parts of the City.

"About seven o'clock in the evening I went out again. At Westminster the mob were few, and those quiet, and decent in appearance. I crossed St. George's Fields, which were empty, and came home again by Blackfriars Bridge; and in going from thence to the Exchange, you pass the Old Bailey; and here it was that I saw the first scene of terror and riot ever presented to me. The new prison was a very large, strong, and beautiful building, having two wings, of which you can suppose the extent, when you consider their use; besides these, were the keeper's (Mr. Akerman's) house, a strong intermediate work, and likewise other parts, of which I can give you no description. Akerman had in his custody four prisoners, taken in the riot; these the mob went to his house and demanded. He begged he might send to the sheriff, but this was not permitted. How he escaped, or where he is gone, I know not; but just at the time I speak of they set fire to his house, broke in, and threw every piece of furniture they could find into the street, firing them also in an instant. The engines came, but were only suffered to preserve the private houses near the prison.

"As I was standing near the spot, there approached another body of men, I suppose 500, and Lord George Gordon in a coach, drawn by the mob towards Alderman Bull's, bowing as he passed along. He is a lively-looking young man in appearance, and nothing more, though just now the reigning hero.

"By eight o'clock, Akerman's house was in flames. I went close to it, and never saw any thing so dreadful. The prison was, as I said, a remarkably strong building; but, determined to force it, they broke the gates with crows and other instruments, and climbed up the outside of the cell part, which joins the two great wings of the building, where the felons were confined; and I stood where I plainly saw their operations. They broke the roof, tore away the rafters, and having got ladders they descended. Not Orpheus himself had more courage or better luck; flames all around them, and a body of soldiers expected, they defied and laughed at all opposition.

"The prisoners escaped. I stood and saw about twelve women and eight men ascend from their confinement to the open air, and they were conducted through the street in their chains. Three of these were to be hanged on Friday. You have no conception of the phrensy of the multitude. This being done, and Akerman's house now a mere shell of brickwork, they kept a store of flame there for other purposes. It became red-hot, and the doors and windows appeared like the entrance to so many volcanoes. With some difficulty they then fired the debtor's prison—broke the doors—and they, too, all made their escape.

"Tired of the scene, I went home, and returned again at eleven o'clock at night. I met large bodies of horse and foot soldiers coming to guard the Bank, and some houses of Roman Catholics near it. Newgate was at this time open to all; any one might get in, and, what was never the case before, any one might get out. I did both; for the people were now chiefly lookers on. The mischief was done, and the doers of it gone to another part of the town.

"But I must not omit what struck me most. About ten or twelve of the mob getting to the top of the debtors' prison, whilst it was burning, to halloo, they appeared rolled in black smoke mixed with sudden bursts of fire—like Milton's infernals, who were as familiar with flame as with each other. On comparing notes with my neighbours, I find I saw but a small part of the mischief. They say Lord Mansfield's house is now in flames."

*　　*　　*

[Some leaves are here torn out.]

*　　*　　*

"*June* 11.—Sunday.—As I'm afraid my ever dearest friend, my Mira, has not a preacher so affecting as my worthy rector, I shall not scruple to give his morning discourse in the way I have abstracted those before; and I know my dear Sally will pardon, will be pleased with, the trouble I give her."

*　　*　　*

With a short abstract of a sermon on the text "Awake, thou that sleepest." which I do not think it necessary to transcribe, the "Poet's Journal," as I have it, abruptly concludes. But my father kept, while resident in the City, another notebook, solely for himself, from which I consider it due to his memory—in order to complete the reader's impression of his character and conduct at this, the most melancholy period of his life—to make a very few extracts.

I

"O gracious Redeemer! fill me, I beseech thee, with Divine love; let me, O my Saviour! set my affections on thee and things above; take from me this over-carefulness and anxiety after the affairs of this mortal body, and deeply impress on my thoughts the care of my immortal soul. Let me love thee, blessed Lord! desire thee, and embrace thy cross when it is offered me. Set before me the value of eternal happiness, and the true worth of human expectations.

"O! detach my heart from self-pleasing, from vanity, and all the busy passions that draw me from thee. Fix it on thy love; let it be my joy to contemplate thy condescension and thy kindness to man; may gratitude to my Redeemer wean me from inclination for his foes; may it draw me from the objects of the world, the dreams of the senses, and all the power and temptation of the Devil and his angels.

"Remember me, Lord, at thy table; behold I desire to be with thee: O be thou with me! If thou art absent, I cannot receive comfort even there; if thou art with me, I cannot miss it. The treasures of eternal life are thine; O Lord! give me of those treasures; give me a foretaste of thy pleasures, that I may look more indifferently upon the earth and its enjoyments. Lord! where are thy old loving-kindnesses? Forgive me, most gracious Saviour; and restore me to thy favour. O give me the light of thy countenance, and I shall be whole. Amen!"

II

"O, my Lord God, I will plead my cause before thee, let me not be condemned; behold, I desire to be thine. O, cast me not away from thee. My sins are great, and often repeated. They are a burthen to me, I sink under them; Lord, save me, or I perish. Hold out thine hand; my faith trembles; Lord, save me ere I sink.

"I am afflicted in mind, in body, in estate; Oh! be thou my refuge! I look unto thee for help, from whence all help cometh; I cast off all dependence on the world or mine own endeavours: thou art my God, and I will trust in thee alone.

"O Lord Jesus Christ, who didst deliver us from darkness

and the shadow of death, illuminate, enlighten me; comfort me, O Lord, for I go mourning. O be thou with me, and I shall live. Behold, I trust in thee, Lord, forsake me not. Amen."

III

"I look back on myself—myself, an ample field of speculation for me. I see there the infant, the child, and all the rapid progress of human life; the swifter progress of sin and folly, that came with every new day, but did not like the day depart to return no more.

"If I die to-morrow—and it may be my lot—shall I not have cause to wish my death had happened at a former period? at a time when I felt strong hope and lively faith? and what inference will the wish lead me to draw—a wish for stronger hope and livelier faith, an ardent prayer and due repentance? If not, my wishes will be my torment. Never again, to be cheered with the comforts of divine grace, how sad! to be totally forsaken of it, how tremendous!

"But I speak of to-morrow, why may it not be to-day? why not now?—this instant, I ask my heart the question, it may cease to beat. The thunderbolt may be spent on my head. The thunderbolt, did I say? O the importance of a worm's destruction! A little artery may burst; a small vital chord drop its office; an invisible organ grow dormant in the brain, and all is over—all over with the clay, and with the immortal all to come.

"Of the ten thousand vital vessels, the minute, intricate network of tender-framed machinery, how long have they wrought without destroying the machine! How many parts necessary to being, how long held in motion! Our hours are miracles: shall we say that miracles cease, when, by being, we are marvellous? No, I should not think the summons wonderful; nor partial, for younger have been summoned; nor cruel, for I have abused mercy; nor tyrannical, for I am a creature, a vessel in the hands of the potter: neither am I without conviction that, if it be better for me to live another day, I shall not die this.

"But what of awe, of fear, in such a call? where is he who *then* thinks not—if he has permission to think—solemnly? God his Judge, and God his Redeemer; Terror visible, and Mercy slighted, are then to be heard: the moment at hand that brings heaven, or hell! where is an opiate for the soul that wakes *then*?

"O thou blessed Lord, who openedst the gate of life, let me live in true faith, in holy hope: and let not my end surprise me! Ten thousand thoughts disturb my soul: be, thou greatest and fairest among ten thousand, be thou with me, O my Saviour! Return! return! and bring me hope."

IV

"Amid the errors of the best, how shall my soul find safety? Even by thee, O Lord! Where is unlettered Hope to cast her anchor? Even in thy blessed Gospel! Serious examination, deep humility, earnest prayer, will obtain certainty.

"God is good. Christ is our only Mediator and Advocate. He suffered for our sins. By his stripes we are healed. As in Adam all die, so in Christ all are made alive. Whoso believeth shall be saved. But faith without works is dead. Yet it is the grace of God that worketh in us. Every good and every perfect work cometh from above. Man can do nothing of himself; but Christ is all in all; and, Whatsoever things ye shall ask in the name of Jesus, shall be granted. This is sufficient, this is plain; I ask no philosophic researches, no learned definitions; I want not to dispute, but to be saved. Lord! save me, or I perish. I only know my own vileness; I only know thy sufficiency; these are enough; witness Heaven and Earth, my trust is in God's mercy, through Jesus Christ, my blessed Redeemer. Amen!"

V

"My God, my God, I put my trust in thee; my troubles increase, my soul is dismayed, I am heavy and in distress; all day long I call upon thee; O be thou my helper in the needful time of trouble.

"Why art thou so far from me, O my Lord? why hidest thou thy face? I am cast down, I am in poverty and in affliction: be thou with me, O my God; let me not be wholly forsaken, O my Redeemer!

"Behold, I trust in thee, blessed Lord. Guide me, and govern me unto the end. O Lord, my salvation, be thou ever with me. Amen."

CHAPTER IV

1781

Mr. Crabbe's Letter to Burke and its Consequences—The Publication of "The Library"—He is domesticated at Beaconsfield—Takes Orders—Is appointed Curate at Aldborough.

IT IS to be regretted that Mr. Crabbe's Journal does not extend over more than three months of the miserable year that he spent in the City. During the whole of that time he experienced nothing but disappointments and repulses. His circumstances were now, indeed, fearfully critical: absolute want stared him in the face: a gaol seemed the only immediate refuge for his head; and the best he could hope for was, dismissing all his dreams of literary distinction, to find the means of daily bread in the capacity of a druggist's assistant. To borrow, without any prospect of repaying, was what his honesty shrunk from; to beg was misery, and promised, moreover, to be fruitless. A spirit less manly and less religious must have sunk altogether under such an accumulation of sorrows.

Mr. Crabbe made one effort more. In his "sketch," he says: "He did not so far mistake as to believe that any name can give lasting reputation to an undeserving work; but he was fully persuaded, that it must be some very meritorious and extraordinary performance, such as he had not the vanity to suppose himself capable of producing, that would become popular, without the introductory *probat* of some well-known and distinguished character. Thus thinking, and having now his first serious attempt nearly completed, afraid of venturing without a guide, doubtful whom to select, knowing many by reputation, none personally—he fixed, impelled by some propitious influence, in some happy moment, upon EDMUND BURKE—one of the first of Englishmen, and, in the capacity and energy of his mind, one of the greatest of human beings."

The letter which the young poet addressed to Burke must have been seen by Mr. Prior, when he composed his Life of the great statesman; but that work had been published for nine years before any of Mr. Crabbe's family were aware that a copy of it had been preserved; nor had they any exact knowledge of the extremity of distress which this remarkable letter describes, until the hand that penned it was in the grave. It is as follows:

"*To Edmund Burke, Esq.*

"SIR,—I am sensible that I need even your talents to apologise for the freedom I now take; but I have a plea which, however simply urged, will, with a mind like yours, Sir, procure me pardon: I am one of those outcasts on the world who are without a friend, without employment, and without bread.

"Pardon me a short preface. I had a partial father, who gave me a better education than his broken fortune would have allowed; and a better than was necessary, as he could give me that only. I was designed for the profession of physic; but not having wherewithal to complete the requisite studies, the design but served to convince me of a parent's affection, and the error it had occasioned. In April last I came to London, with three pounds, and flattered myself this would be sufficient to supply me with the common necessaries of life till my abilities should procure me more; of these I had the highest opinion, and a poetical vanity contributed to my delusion. I knew little of the world, and had read books only: I wrote, and fancied perfection in my compositions; when I wanted bread they promised me affluence, and soothed me with dreams of reputation, whilst my appearance subjected me to contempt.

"Time, reflection, and want, have shown me my mistake. I see my trifles in that which I think the true light; and whilst I deem them such, have yet the opinion that holds them superior to the common run of poetical publications.

"I had some knowledge of the late Mr. Nassau, the brother of Lord Rochford; in consequence of which I asked his Lordship's permission to inscribe my little work to him. Knowing it to be free from all political allusions and personal abuse, it was no very material point to me to whom it was dedicated. His Lordship thought it none to him, and obligingly consented to my request.

"I was told that a subscription would be the more profitable method for me, and therefore, endeavoured to circulate copies of the enclosed Proposals.

"I am afraid, Sir, I disgust you with this very dull narration, but believe me punished in the misery that occasions it. You will conclude that, during this time, I must have been at more expense than I could afford; indeed, the most parsimonious could not have avoided it. The printer deceived me, and my little business has had every delay. The people with whom I live perceive my situation, and find me to be indigent and without friends. About ten days since, I was compelled to give a note for seven pounds, to avoid an arrest for about double that sum which I owe. I wrote to every friend I had, but my friends are poor likewise; the time of payment approached, and I ventured to represent my case to Lord Rochford. I begged to be credited for this sum till I received it of my subscribers, which I believe will be within one month; but to this letter I had no reply, and I have probably offended by my importunity. Having used every honest means in vain, I yesterday confessed my inability, and obtained, with much entreaty, and as the greatest favour, a week's forbearance, when I am positively told, that I must pay the money, or prepare for a prison.

"You will guess the purpose of so long an introduction. I appeal to you, Sir, as a good and, let me add, a great man. I have no other pretensions to your favour than that I am an unhappy one. It is not easy to support the thoughts of confinement; and I am coward enough to dread such an end to my suspense.

"Can you, Sir, in any degree, aid me with propriety? Will you ask any demonstrations of my veracity? I have imposed upon myself, but I have been guilty of no other imposition. Let me, if possible, interest your compassion. I know those of rank and fortune are teased with frequent petitions, and are compelled to refuse the requests even of those whom they know to be in distress: it is, therefore, with a distant hope I ventured to solicit such favour; but you will forgive me, Sir, if you do not think proper to relieve. It is impossible that sentiments like yours can proceed from any but a humane and generous heart.

"I will call upon you, Sir, to-morrow, and if I have not the happiness to obtain credit with you, I must submit to my fate. My existence is a pain to myself, and every one near and dear to me are distressed in my distresses. My connections, once the source of happiness, now embitter the reverse of my fortune, and I have only to hope a speedy end to a life so unpromisingly begun: in which (though it ought not to be boasted of) I can reap some consolation from looking to the end of it. I am, Sir, with the greatest respect, your obedient and most humble servant,

"GEORGE CRABBE."

Mr. Burke was, at this period (1781), engaged in the hottest turmoils of parliamentary opposition, and his own pecuniary circumstances were by no means very affluent: yet he gave instant attention to this letter, and the verses which it enclosed. He immediately appointed an hour for my father to call upon him at his house in London; and the short interview that ensued, entirely, and for ever, changed the nature of his worldly fortunes. He was, in the common phrase, "a made man" from that hour. He went into Mr. Burke's room, a poor young adventurer, spurned by the opulent, and rejected by the publishers, his last shilling gone, and all but his last hope with it; he came out virtually secure of almost all the good fortune that, by successive steps, afterwards fell to his lot—his genius acknowledged by one whose verdict could not be questioned—his character and manners appreciated and approved by a noble and capacious heart, whose benevolence knew no limits but its power—that of a giant in intellect, who was, in feeling, an unsophisticated child—a bright example of the close affinity between superlative talents and the warmth of the generous affections. Mr. Crabbe had afterwards many other friends, kind, liberal, and powerful, who assisted him in his professional career; but it was one hand alone that rescued him when he was *sinking*. In reflecting upon the consequences of the letter to Burke—the happiness, the exultation, the inestimable benefits that resulted to my father, ascribing, indeed, my own existence to that great and good man's condescension and prompt kindness—I may be pardoned for dwelling upon that interview with feelings of gratitude which I should but in vain endeavour to express.

But sensible as I am of the importance of Mr. Burke's interference in my father's behalf, I would not imply that there was not ample desert to call it forth. Enlarged as was Mr. Burke's benevolence, had not the writings which were submitted to his inspection possessed the marks of real genius, the applicant would probably have been dismissed with a little pecuniary assistance. I must add that, even had his poems been evidently meritorious, it is not to be supposed that the author would have at once excited the strongest personal interest in such a mind, unless he had, during this interview, exhibited the traits of a pure and worthy character. Nay, had there appeared any offensive peculiarities of manner and address—either presumption or meanness—though the young poet might have received both kindness and patronage, can anyone dream that Mr. Burke would have at once taken up his cause with the zeal of a friend, domesticated him under his own roof, and treated him like a son? In mentioning his new *protégé*, a few days afterwards, to Reynolds, Burke said, "He has the mind and feelings of a gentleman." Sir Joshua told this, years later, to my grateful father himself. The autobiographical sketch thus continues the narrative of this providential turn in his affairs:

"To Mr. Burke, the young man, with timidity, indeed, but with the strong and buoyant expectation of inexperience, submitted a large quantity of miscellaneous compositions, on a variety of subjects, which he was soon taught to appreciate at their proper value; yet such was the feeling and tenderness of his judge, that in the very act of condemnation, something was found for praise. Mr. Crabbe had sometimes the satisfaction of hearing, when the verses were bad, that the thoughts deserved better; and that if he had the common faults of inexperienced writers, he had frequently the merit of thinking for himself. Among those compositions, were two poems of somewhat a superior kind—'The Library' and 'The Village': these were selected by Mr. Burke: and with the benefit of his judgment and the comfort of his encouraging and exhilarating predictions, Mr. Crabbe was desired to learn the duty of sitting in judgment upon his best efforts, and without mercy rejecting the rest. When all was done that his abilities permitted, and when Mr. Burke had patiently waited the progress of improvement in the man whom he conceived to be capable of it, he himself took 'The Library' to Mr. Dodsley, then of Pall-Mall, and gave many lines the advantage of his own reading and comments. Mr. Dodsley listened with all the respect due to the reader of the verses, and all the apparent desire to be pleased that could be wished by the writer; and he was as obliging in his reply as, in the very nature of things, a bookseller can be supposed to be towards a young candidate for poetical reputation: 'He had declined the venturing upon anything himself: there was no judging of the probability of success. The taste of the town was exceedingly capricious and uncertain. He paid the greatest respect to Mr. Burke's opinion that the verses were good, and he did in part think so himself: but he declined the hazard of publication; yet would do all he could for Mr.

Crabbe, and take care that his poem should have all the benefit he could give it.'

"The worthy man was mindful of his engagement: he became even solicitous for the success of the work; and no doubt its speedy circulation was in some degree caused by his exertions. This he did; and he did more—though by no means insensible of the value of money, he gave to the author his profits as a publisher and vender of the pamphlet; and Mr. Crabbe has seized every occasion which has offered to make acknowledgment for such disinterested conduct, at a period when it was more particularly acceptable and beneficial. The success of 'The Library' gave some reputation to the author, and was the occasion of his second poem, 'The Village,' which was corrected, and a considerable portion of it written, in the house of his excellent friend, whose own activity and energy of mind would not permit a young man under his protection to cease from labour, and whose judgment directed that labour to its most useful attainments.

"The exertions of this excellent friend in favour of a young writer were not confined to one mode of affording assistance. Mr. Crabbe was encouraged to lay open his views, past and present; to display whatever reading and acquirements he possessed: to explain the causes of his disappointments, and the cloudiness of his prospects; in short, he concealed nothing from a friend so able to guide inexperience, and so willing to pardon inadvertency. He was invited to Beaconsfield, the seat of his protector, and was there placed in a convenient apartment, supplied with books for his information and amusement, and made a member of a family whom it was honour as well as pleasure to become in any degree associated with. If Mr. Crabbe, noticed by such a man, and received into such a family, should have given way to some emotions of vanity, and supposed there must have been merit on one part, as well as benevolence on the other, he has no slight plea to offer for his frailty—especially as we conceive it may be added, that his vanity never at any time extinguished any portion of his gratitude; and that it has ever been his delight to think, as well as his pride to speak, of Mr. Burke as his father, guide, and friend: nor did that gentleman ever disallow the name to which his conduct gave sanction and propriety."

It was in the course of one of their walks amidst the classical shades of Beaconsfield, that Burke, after some conversation on general literature, suggested by a passage of the Georgics, which he had happened to quote on observing something that was going on in his favourite farm, passed to a more minute inquiry into my father's early days in Suffolk than he had before made, and drew from him the avowal that, with respect to future affairs, he felt a strong partiality for the church. "It is most fortunate," said Mr. Burke, "that your father exerted himself to send you to that second school; without a little Latin we should have made nothing of you: now, I think we shall succeed." The fund of general knowledge which my father gradually showed in these rambles, much surprised his patron. "Mr. Crabbe," he said early to Sir Joshua Reynolds, "appears to know something of everything." Burke himself was a strong advocate for storing the mind with multiform knowledge, rather than confining it to one narrow line of study; and he often remarked, that there was no profession in which diversity of information was more useful, and, indeed, necessary, than that of a clergyman. Having gone through the form—for it was surely little more—of making proper inquiries as to the impression left of Mr. Crabbe's character in his native place—Mr. Burke, though well aware of the difficulties of obtaining holy orders for any person not regularly educated, exerted himself to procure the assent, in this instance, of Dr. Yonge, the then Bishop of Norwich; and in this, backed by the favourable representations of Mr. Dudley North and Mr. Charles Long, he was eventually successful.

Meantime, nothing could be more cordial than the kindness with which my father was uniformly treated at Beaconsfield. Let no one say that ambition chills the heart to other feelings. This obscure young writer could contribute in nothing to the reputation of a statesman and orator, at the very apex of influence and renown; yet never had he been so affectionately received as when, a pennyless dependant, he first entered the hall of that beautiful mansion, and, during the whole of his stay, he was cheered by a constancy of kind and polite attention, such as I fear to describe, lest I should be suspected of fond exaggeration. As a trivial specimen of the conduct of the lady of the house, I may mention, that, one day, some company of rank that had been expected to dinner did not arrive, and the servants, in consequence, reserved for next day some costly dish that had been ordered. Mrs. Burke happened to ask for it; and the butler saying, "It has been kept back, as the company did not come"—she answered, "What! is not Mr. Crabbe here? let it be brought up immediately." It is not always that ladies enter so warmly into the feelings of their husbands on occasions of this sort. Mrs. Burke and her niece were afterwards indefatigable in promoting the sale of "The Library," both by letters and by personal application.

My father was introduced, while under this happy roof, to Mr. Fox, Sir Joshua Reynolds, and many others of Mr. Burke's distinguished friends, who, like himself, encouraged the young adventurer with approbation: and for Sir Joshua, in particular, he conceived a warm and grateful attachment, which subsequent experience only confirmed. When Mr. Burke's family returned to London for the winter, my father accompanied them; and, it being inconvenient for them to afford him an apartment at that time in their town house, he took lodgings in its neighbourhood. He, however, continued to dine commonly at Mr. Burke's table, and was introduced by him to several of the clubs of which he was a member, and gradually, I believe, to all those of his friends who took any interest in literature. But it was at Sir Joshua's table that he first had the honour of meeting Dr. Johnson; and I much regret that so little is in my power to tell of their intercourse. My father, however, said, that, at this first interview, he was particularly unfortunate: making some trite remark, or hazarding some injudicious question, he brought on himself a specimen of that castigation which the great literary bashaw was commonly so ready to administer. He remembered with half comic terror the Doctor's *growl*; but this did not diminish Mr. Crabbe's respect and veneration for the Doctor, nor did his *mal-à-propos*, on the other hand, prevent Johnson from giving him a most courteous reception, when, at Burke's suggestion, he some days afterwards called on him in Bolt Court. He then expressed no little interest in his visitor's success; and proved his sincerity by the attention with which he subsequently read and revised "The Village." Had I contemplated this narrative somewhat earlier, and led my father, with a view to it, to converse on the great men he met with at this time of his life, I might, no doubt, have obtained some curious information. But, in truth, he had neither the turn nor much of the talent for the retention of conversations; and even what he did remember, he was not always disposed to communicate. One maxim of Johnson's, however, had made a strong impression on him: "Never fear putting the strongest and best things you can think of into the mouth of your speaker, whatever may be his condition."[1]

When "The Library" was published, the opinion of Burke had its effect upon the conductors of the various periodical works of the time; the poet received commendatory *critiques* from the very gentlemen who had hitherto treated him with such contemptuous coldness; and though his name was not in the title-page, it was universally known.

Burke rejoiced in the success of his *protégé*; but, promising as the young author's prospects now appeared to be, the profits of so small a poem could not have been considerable; and his being accustomed to appear at such tables as those of Mr. Burke and Sir Joshua Reynolds, implied a certain degree of expense in articles of dress, so that, his modesty preventing him from stating his exact case to his ever-generous patron —while the patron on his part, having conferred such substantial benefits, had too much delicacy to make him feel dependent for alms—my father was at this time occasionally reduced to distress for an immediate supply of money. In an interval of something like his former misery—at all events, of painful perplexity—he received a note from the Lord Chancellor, politely inviting him to breakfast the next morning. His kind patron had spoken of him in favourable terms to the stern and formidable Thurlow, and his Lordship was now anxious to atone for his previous neglect. He received Mr. Crabbe with more than courtesy, and most condescendingly said, "The first poem you sent me, Sir, I ought to have noticed and I heartily forgive the second." They breakfasted together, and, at parting, his Lordship put a sealed paper into my father's hand, saying, "Accept this trifle, Sir, in the meantime, and rely on my embracing an early opportunity to serve

[1] I owe this to the recollection of my father's friend, Miss Hoare, of Hampstead.

you more substantially when I hear that you are in orders."
As soon as he had left the house he opened the letter, expecting
to find a present of ten, or perhaps twenty pounds: it contained
a bank note for a *hundred*; a supply which effectually relieved
him from all his present difficulties, while his new patron's
accompanying promise must have eased him of any apprehensions which might yet haunt his mind as to his future prospects
in the world.

I am enabled to state—though the information never came
from my father—that the first use he made of this good fortune was, to seek out and relieve some objects of real in-
digence—poor scholars like himself, whom he had known
when sharing their wretchedness in the City: and I must add,
that whenever he visited London in later years, he made it his
business to inquire after similar objects of charity, supposed
to be of respectable personal character, and to do by them as,
in his own hour of distress, he would have been done by.
But who knew better than he, that the metropolis has always
abundance of such objects, if any one would search for them?
or who—I may safely appeal to all that knew him—ever
sacrificed time and trouble in the cause of benevolence,
throughout every varying scene of his life, more freely than
Mr. Crabbe? No wonder it was his first thought, on finding
himself in possession of even a very slender fund, to testify
his thankfulness to that Being who had rescued himself from
the extreme of destitution, and to begin as early as possible to
pay the debt he owed to misfortune.

Mr. Crabbe, having passed a very creditable examination,
was admitted to deacon's orders, in London, on the 21st
December, by the Bishop of Norwich; who ordained him a
priest in August of the year following, in his own cathedral.
Being licensed as curate to the Rev. Mr. Bennett, rector of
Aldborough, he immediately bade a grateful adieu to his

illustrious patron and his other eminent benefactors—not forgetting his kind and hospitable friends in Cornhill—and went down to take up his residence once more in his native place.

The feelings with which he now returned to Aldborough may easily be imagined. He must have been more than man had he not exulted at the change. He left his home a deserter from his profession, with the imputation of having failed in it from wanting even common abilities for the discharge of its duties —in the estimation of the ruder natives, who had witnessed his manual awkwardness in the seafaring pursuits of the place, "a lubber," and "a fool," perhaps considered even by those who recognised something of his literary talent, as a harebrained visionary, never destined to settle to anything with steadiness and sober resolution; on all hands convicted certainly of the "crime of poverty," and dismissed from view as a destitute and hopeless outcast. He returned, a man of acknowledged talents; a successful author, patronised and befriended by some of the leading characters in the kingdom; and a clergyman with every prospect of preferment in the church. His father had the candour to admit, that he had underrated his poetical abilities, and that he had acted judiciously in trusting to the bent of nature, rather than persevering in an occupation for which he was, from the outset, peculiarly disqualified. The old man now gloried in the boldness of his adventure, and was proud of its success: he fondly transcribed "The Library" with his own hand; and, in short, reaped the reward of his own early exertions to give his son a better education than his circumstances could well afford.

On the state of mind with which the young clergyman now revisited Parham—on the beautiful and retributive conclusion thus afforded to the period of resignation and humble trust recorded in his "Journal to Mira"—I shall not attempt to comment. In the esteem of his ever encouraging and confiding friend there, he could not stand higher now than he had done when all the rest of the world despaired of or disowned him; but, with the hospitality and kindness he had long experienced from her relations, there was now mingled a respect to which he had previously been a stranger. He heard no more taunts about that "d——d learning."

On his first entrance, however, into his father's house, at this time, his joyous feelings had to undergo a painful revulsion. That affectionate parent, who would have lost all sense of sickness and suffering, had she witnessed his success, was no more: she had sunk under the dropsy, in his absence, with a fortitude of resignation closely resembling that of his own last hours. It happened that a friend and neighbour was slowly yielding at the same time to the same hopeless disorder, and every morning she used to desire her daughter to see if this sufferer's window was opened; saying, cheerfully, "she must make haste, or I shall be at rest before her." My father has alluded to his feelings on this occasion in the "Parish Register":

> "Arrived at home, how then he gazed around
> On every place where she no more was found;
> The seat at table she was wont to fill,
> The fireside chair, still set, but vacant still;
> The Sunday pew she fill'd with all her race,
> Each place of hers was now a sacred place."

And I find him recurring to the same theme in one of his manuscript pieces:

> "But oh! in after-years
> Were other deaths that call'd for other tears:
> No, that I dare not, that I cannot paint!
> The patient sufferer! the enduring saint!
> Holy and cheerful! but all words are faint!"

Mr. Crabbe's early religious impressions were, no doubt, strongly influenced by those of his mother; and she was, as I have already said, a deeply devout woman; but her seriousness was not of the kind that now almost exclusively receives that designation. Among persons of her class, at least, at that period, there was a general impression that the doctrinal creed ought rather to be considered the affair of the pastor than of the humble and unlearned members of his flock—that the former would be held responsible for the tenets he inculcated —the latter for the practical observance of those rules of conduct and temper which good men of all persuasions alike advocate and desire to exemplify. The controversial spirit, in a word, lighted up by Whitfield and Wesley, had not as yet reached the coast of Suffolk. Persons turned through misfortune, sickness, or any other exciting cause, to think with seriousness of securing their salvation, were used to say to themselves, "I must amend and correct whatever in my life and conversation does offend the eyes of my Heavenly Father; I must henceforth be diligent in my duties, search out and oppose the evil in my heart, and cultivate virtuous dispositions and devout affections." Not from their own strength, however, did they hope and expect such improvement: they sought it from and ascribed it to, "Him from whom all good counsels and works do proceed," and admitted, without hesitation, that their own best services could be made acceptable only through the merits of their Redeemer. Thus far such persons accorded with the more serious of a later period; but the subtle distinction between good works as necessary and yet not conditional to salvation, and others of a like kind, particularly prevalent afterwards, were not then familiar; nor was it at all common to believe, that Christians ought to renounce this world, in any other sense than that of renouncing its wickedness, or that they are called upon to shun anything but the excessive indulgence in amusements and recreations not in themselves palpably evil. Such was the religion of Mrs. Crabbe; and, doubtless, her mildness, humility, patient endurance of afflictions and sufferings, meek habits, and devout spirit, strongly recommended her example to her son, and impressed his young mind with a deep belief that the principles which led to such practice must be those of the Scriptures of God.

It is true that neither the precepts nor the example of his mother were able altogether to preserve Mr. Crabbe from the snares that beset, with peculiar strength, young men early removed from the paternal roof. The juvenile apprentice is, in many respects, too much his own master; and though my father, in his first service, escaped with no worse injury than the association with idle lads generally brings with it, yet, in his second apprenticeship, and afterwards, in the beginning of his own practice at Aldborough, he did not scruple to confess that he was not always proof against the temptations of a town. Where

"High in the street, o'erlooking all the place,
The rampant lion shows his kingly face"—

the Aldborough Boniface of the present day shows, I am told, with no little exultation, an old-fashioned room, the usual scene of convivial meetings, not always remarkable for "measured merriment," in which the young *doctor* had his share. It seems probable that the seriousness and purity of his early impressions had, for a season, been smothered: but they were never obliterated; and I believe I do not err in tracing to the severe illness which befell him not long after he had commenced as surgeon at Aldbrough, their revival and confirmation—a strong and a permanent change. On his recovery from an affliction, during which he had felt that life hung by a thread, he told his children that he made a solemn resolution against all deliberate evil; and those who observed him after that period all concur in stating his conduct and conversation to have been that of a regular, temperate, and religious young man.

When his sister and he kept house apart from the rest of the family, it was their invariable practice to read a portion of the Scriptures together every evening; and even while struggling with the difficulties of his medical occupation, poetry was not the only literary diversion he indulged in. His early note-books now before me, contain proofs that he was in the habit of composing sermons, in imitation of Tillotson, long before he could have had the least surmise that he was ever to be a preacher. Indeed, the "Journal to Mira" contains such evidence of the purity of his conduct, and of the habitual attention he paid to religious topics, that I need not enlarge further upon the subject. He certainly was not guilty of rushing into the service of the altar without having done his endeavour to discipline himself for a due discharge of its awful obligations, by cultivating the virtues of Christianity in his heart, and, in as far as his opportunities extended, making himself fit to minister to the spiritual necessities of others. But I am bound to add, that in a later period of life, and more especially during the last ten years of it, he became more consciouss of the importance of dwelling on the doctrines as well as the practice of Christianity, than he had been when he first took orders; and when a selection of his Sermons is placed, as I hope it ere long will be, before the public, it will be seen that he had gradually approached in substantial matters, though not exactly in certain peculiar ways of expression, to that respected body usually denominated Evangelical Christians of the Church of England; with whom, nevertheless, he was never classed by others, nor indeed, by himself.

And what, it will naturally be asked, was his reception by the people of Aldborough, when he re-appeared among them in this new character? "The prophet is not without honour, save in his own country": this Scriptural proverb was entirely exemplified here. The whisper ran through the town, that a man who had failed in one calling, was not very likely to make a great figure in a new one. Others revived, most unjustly, old stories, in which my father did not appear with quite clerical decorum: and others again bruited about a most groundless rumour that he had been, when in London, a preacher among the Methodists. For this last report there was, indeed, no foundation at all, except that an Aldborough sailor, happening one day to enter Mr. Wesley's chapel at Moorfields, had perceived my father, who had gone thither, like himself, from pure curiosity, standing on the steps of the pulpit; the place being so crowded that he could find no more convenient situation. But perhaps the most common, as well as unworthy, of all the rumours afloat, was, that he had been spoiled by the notice of fine folks in town, and would now be too proud to be bearable among his old equals. When I asked him how he felt when he entered the pulpit at Aldborough, for the first time, he answered, "I had been unkindly received in the place—I saw unfriendly countenances about me, and, I am sorry to say, I had too much indignation, though mingled, I hope, with better feelings, to care what they thought of me or my sermon." Perhaps, as he himself remarked, all this may have been well ordered for my father. Had there been nothing to operate as an antidote, the circumstances of his altered position in life might have tempted human infirmity, even in him, to a vain-glorious self-esteem.

He appears to have ere long signified some uneasiness of

feeling to the Lord Chancellor, whose very kind answer concluded in these words: "I can form no opinion of your present situation or prospects, still less upon the agreeableness of it; but you may imagine that I wish you well, and if you make yourself capable of preferment, that I shall try to find an early opportunity of serving you. I am, with great regard, dear Sir, your faithful friend and servant, THURLOW."

CHAPTER V

1782—1783

Mr. Crabbe's Appointment as domestic Chaplain to the Duke of Rutland—Removes to Belvoir Castle—Publication of "The Village."

MY FATHER continued to be curate at Aldborough for only a few months, during which his sister resumed the charge of his domestic affairs, in a small lodging apart from the rest of the family. His brother Robert, a man in many respects closely resembling himself, of strong faculties and amiable disposition, was now settled at Southwold; but the two brothers, much attached to each other's society, made a point of meeting one evening of each week at Blythborough, about half way between their places of residence. I need hardly add, that my father passed also a considerable part of his time under the same roof with Miss Elmy, who still prudently resisted every proposition of immediate marriage, being resolved not to take such a step until her lover should have reached some position less precarious than that of a mere curate.

Most persons who had done as much for one in my father's situation as Mr. Burke had already accomplished, would, no doubt, have been disposed to say, or to think, "Now, young man, help yourself": but it was far otherwise with Mr.

H

Crabbe's illustrious benefactor. He was anxious to see his *protégé* raised as high as his friendship could elevate him; and he soon was the means of placing him in a station such as has, in numerous instances, led to the first dignities of the church. My father received a letter from Mr. Burke, informing him that, in consequence of some conversation he had held with the Duke of Rutland, that nobleman would willingly receive him as his domestic chaplain at Belvoir Castle, so soon as he could get rid of his existing engagements at Aldborough. This was a very unusual occurrence, such situations in the mansions of that rank being commonly filled either by relations of the noble family itself, or by college acquaintances, or dependants recommended by political service and local attachment. But, in spite of political difference, the recommendation of Burke was all-powerful with the late Duke of Rutland, the son of the great Marquis of Granby; for this nobleman, though not what is usually called a literary man, had a strong partiality for letters, a refined taste for the arts, and felt that a young author of such genius as Burke had imputed to my father would be a valuable acquisition to the society of his mansion, where, like a genuine English peer of the old school, he spent the greater portion of his time in the exercise of boundless hospitality and benevolence. My father did not hesitate, of course, to accept the offered situation; and, having taken farewell for a season of his friends at Parham, he once more quitted Aldborough, but not now in the hold of a sloop, nor with those gloomy fears and trembling anticipations which had agitated his mind on a former occasion. He was now morally sure of being, within no long interval, placed in a situation that would enable him to have a house of his own and to settle to life in the enjoyment of at least a moderate competency.

What his hopes exactly amounted to when this change took

place, or what apprehensions chequered them when he approached Belvoir, or what were his impressions on his first reception there, are questions which I never ventured to ask of him. It would have been highly interesting, certainly, to have his remarks on what now befell him at the opening of so new a scene of life, recorded in another "Journal to Mira"; but none such has been discovered. He always seemed to shrink from going into oral details on the subject. The numberless allusions to the nature of a literary dependant's existence in a great lord's house, which occur in my father's writings, and especially in the tale of "The Patron," are, however, quite enough to lead any one who knew his character and feelings to the conclusion that, notwithstanding the kindness and condescension of the Duke and Duchess themselves—which were, I believe, uniform, and of which he always spoke with gratitude—the situation he filled at Belvoir was attended with many painful circumstances, and productive in his mind of some of the acutest sensations of wounded pride that have ever been traced by any pen.

The Duchess[1] was then the most celebrated beauty in England; and the fascinating grace of her manners made the due impression on my father. The Duke himself was a generous man, "cordial, frank, and free"; and highly popular with all classes. His establishments of racehorses, hunters, and hounds were extensive, because it was then held a part of such a nobleman's duty that they should be so; but these things were rather for the enjoyment of his friends than for his own. He was sufficiently interested in such recreations to join in them occasionally; but he would frequently dismiss a splendid party from his gates, and himself ride, accompanied only by Mr. Crabbe, to some sequestered part of his domain, to converse on

[1] Lady Mary-Isabella Somerset, daughter of the fourth Duke of Beaufort. She died in 1831.

literary topics, quote verses and criticise plays. Their Graces' children were at this period still in the nursery.

The immediate chiefs of the place, then, were all that my father could have desired to find them; but their guests, and, above all, perhaps, their servants, might not always treat him with equal respect. I must add, that although the state at the castle was by no means more strict than is usual in great establishments—and certainly not marked by the princely dignity and grandeur that have distinguished Belvoir in our own day—yet it could not but have been oppressive to a person of Mr. Crabbe's education and disposition. He might not, I can well believe, catch readily the manners appropriate to his station—his tact was not of that description—and, he ever had an ardent passion for personal liberty, inconsistent with enjoyment under the constraint of ceremony. With great pleasure, then, did he always hear of the preparations for removing to Cheveley, about the periods of the Newmarket races; for all there was freedom and ease; that house was small, the servants few, and the habits domestic. There was another occasion, also, on which ceremony was given to the winds—when the family resorted to Croxton Park (a small seat near Belvoir), to fish in the extensive ponds, &c. These times of relaxation contrasted delightfully with the etiquette at the castle. After more than usual ceremony, or more abundant conviviality, I have heard him speak of the relief and pleasure of wandering through the deep glades and secluded paths of the woods, catching beetles, moths, butterflies, and collecting mosses, lichens, or other botanical specimens; for this employment carried his imagination to those walks in which he had wandered so frequently with his best friend, his chosen companion; and he already longed for the period when he could call a country parsonage his own: nay, he was sometimes tempted to wish to exchange his station for a much more humble dwelling, and in this mood he once composed some verses, which I have heard him repeat, acknowledging they were not of the most brilliant description:

> "Oh! had I but a little hut,
>   That I might hide my head in;
> Where never guest might dare molest
>   Unwelcome or unbidden.
> I'd take the jokes of other folks,
>   And mine should then succeed 'em,
> Nor would I chide a little pride,
>   Or heed a little freedom." &c. &c.

Such lines might easily run from the pen from which came, in after-days—

> "Strive not too much for favour—seem at ease,
> And rather pleased thyself, than bent to please,
> Upon thy lord with decent care attend;
> Be not too near—thou canst not be a friend . . .

> "When ladies sing, or in thy presence play,
> Do not, dear John, in rapture melt away:
> 'Tis not thy part; there will be listeners round
> To cry divine, and doat upon the sound:
> Remember, too, that though the poor have ears,
> They take not in the music of the spheres."

I have heard my father mention but few occurrences in this period of his life; and if I had, the privacy of a family is not to be invaded because of its public station. But one incident I cannot forbear to mention, as it marked a trait in the Duke's mind peculiarly pleasing—his strong affection for his brother, Lord Robert Manners, who died of wounds received in leading his Majesty's ship Resolution against the enemy's line, in the West Indies, on the memorable 12th of April, 1782. Some short time previous to his Lordship's death, his hat, perforated with balls, was sent at the Duke's request to Belvoir Castle. The Duke first held it up with a shout of exultation and triumph—glorying in the bravery of his beloved brother; and then, as the thought of his danger flashed suddenly into his mind, sank on his chair in a burst of natural and irrepressible feeling.

Mr. Crabbe was particularly attached to the unfortunate Mr. Robert Thoroton, a relative of the family, who generally resided at the Castle. He was, it is true, a man of pleasure, and of the world, but distinguished by warm, frank-hearted kindness, and ever evinced a particular predilection to my father. He was remarked, even in the Belvoir hunt, for intrepid boldness, and once spurred his horse up the steep terraces to the castle-walls—a mad feat! Nor was he much less rash when, as my father one day (in an unusual fit of juvenile merriment) was pursuing him, he sprang over the boundary of the glacis —a steep and formidable precipice. He afterwards accompanied the Duke to Ireland and is mentioned in the singular work of Sir Jonah Barrington. After the Duke's death, he was involved in difficulties; and, under the maddening sufferings of an incurable disorder, he terminated his existence. Among the public characters of that time, the visitors at Belvoir who paid the most attention to Mr. Crabbe were the Duke of Queensberry, the Marquis of Lothian, Dr. Watson the celebrated Bishop of Llandaff, and Dr. Glynn.

A few months after Lord Robert's death, my father accompanied his Grace for a few days to London, and went with him to the studio of the royal academician Stothard, where he consoled his sorrow by giving directions for the painting of the beautiful picture from which the well-known print of the melancholy event is engraved. It seems to have been on this occasion that he received the following letter—

From Mr. Burke

"DEAR SIR,—I do not know by what unlucky accident you missed the note I left for you at my house. I wrote besides to you at Belvoir. If you had received these two short letters, you could not want an invitation to a place where everyone considers himself as infinitely honoured and pleased by your presence.

"Mrs. Burke desires her best compliments, and trusts that you will not let the holidays pass over without a visit from you. I have got the poem; but I have not yet opened it. I don't like the unhappy language you use about these matters. You do not easily please such a judgment as your own—that is natural; but where you are difficult, every one else will be charmed. I am, my dear sir, ever most effectionately yours,

"EDMUND BURKE."

By the time the family left Belvoir for the London season, my father had nearly completed for the press his poem of "The Village," the conclusion of which had been suggested by the untimely death of Lord Robert Manners. Through Sir Joshua Reynolds, he transmitted it to Dr. Johnson, whose kindness was such that he revised it carefully, and whose opinion of its merits were expressed in a note which, though it has often been printed, I must allow myself the gratification of transcribing here.

Dr. Johnson to Sir Joshua Reynolds

"March 4, 1783.

"SIR,—I have sent you back Mr. Crabbe's poem, which I read with great delight. It is original, vigorous, and elegant.

The alterations which I have made I do not require him to adopt; for my lines are, perhaps, not often better than his own; but he may take mine and his own together, and, perhaps, between them, produce something better than either. He is not to think his copy wantonly defaced: a wet sponge will wash all the red lines away, and leave the pages clean. His dedication will be least liked: it were better to contract it into a short sprightly address. I do not doubt of Mr. Crabbe's success. I am, sir, your most humble servant,

"SAMUEL JOHNSON."

Boswell says, "The sentiments of Mr. Crabbe's admirable poem, as to the false notions of rustic happiness and rustic virtue, were quite congenial with Dr. Johnson's own; and he took the trouble not only to suggest slight corrections and variations, but to furnish some lines, when he thought he could give the writer's meaning better than in the words of the manuscript. I shall give an instance, marking the original by Roman, and Johnson's substitution in *Italic* characters:

" 'In fairer scenes, where peaceful pleasures spring,
Tityrus the pride of Mantuan swains might sing;
But, charmed by him, or smitten with his views,
Shall modern poets court the Mantuan muse?
From Truth and Nature shall we widely stray,
Where Fancy leads, or Virgil led the way?'

" '*On Mincio's banks, in Caesar's bounteous reign,*
If Tityrus found the golden age again,
Must sleepy bards the flattering dream prolong,
Mechanick echoes of the Mantuan song?
From Truth and Nature shall we widely stray,
Where Virgil, not where Fancy leads the way?' "

"Here," says Boswell, "we find Dr. Johnson's poetical and critical powers undiminished. I must, however, observe, that the aids he gave to this poem, as to 'The Traveller' and 'Deserted Village' of Goldsmith, were so small, as by no means to impair the distinguished merit of the author."[1] Mr. Boswell ought to have added, that the six lines he quotes formed the only passage in the poem that was not *in substance* quite the author's own. The manuscript was also again submitted to the inspection of Mr. Burke; and he proposed one or two trivial alterations, which my father's grateful feelings induced him to adopt, although they did not appear to himself *improvements*. There were not wanting, I have heard, *friends* in Suffolk, who, when "The Village" came out, whispered that "the manuscript had been so *cobbled* by Burke and Johnson, that Crabbe did not know it again when it was returned to him." If these kind persons survived to read "The Parish Register," their amiable conjectures must have received a sufficient rebuke.

"The Village" was published in May, 1783; and its success exceeded the author's utmost expectations. It was praised in the leading journals; the sale was rapid and extensive; and my father's reputation was, by universal consent, greatly raised, and permanently established by this poem. "The Library," and "The Village," are sufficient evidence of the care and zeal with which the young poet had studied Pope; and, without doubt, he had gradually, though in part perhaps unconsciously, formed his own style mainly on that polished model. But even those early works, and especially "The Village," fairly entitled Mr. Crabbe to a place far above the "mechanick echoes" of the British Virgil. Both poems are framed on a regular and classical plan—perhaps, in that respect, they may be considered more complete and faultless

[1] Croker's Boswell, vol. v, p. 55.

than any of his later pieces; and though it is only here and there that they exhibit that rare union of force and minuteness for which the author was afterwards so highly distinguished, yet such traces of that marked and extraordinary peculiarity appeared in detached places—above all, in the description of the Parish Workhouse in "The Village"—that it is no wonder the new poet should at once have been hailed as a genius of no slender pretensions.

The sudden popularity of "The Village" must have produced, after the numberless slights and disappointments already mentioned, and even after the tolerable success of "The Library," about as strong a revulsion in my father's mind as a ducal chaplaincy in his circumstances; but there was no change in his temper or manners. The successful author continued as modest as the rejected candidate for publication had been patient and long-suffering.

No sleeping apartment being vacant at the Duke of Rutland's residence in Arlington Street, Mr. Crabbe accidentally procured the very rooms shortly before occupied by the highly talented, but rash and miserable Hackman, the infatuated admirer and assassin of the beautiful mistress of the Earl of Sandwich. Here he again found himself in that distinguished society into which Mr. Burke had introduced him. He now very frequently passed his mornings at the easel of Sir Joshua Reynolds, conversing on a variety of subjects, while this distinguished artist was employed upon that celebrated painting the Infant Hercules,[2] then preparing for the Empress of Russia.

I heard him speak of no public character of that time (except Mr. Burke) with that warmth of feeling with which he regarded Sir Joshua. I have no doubt but that, in some respects, there was a similarity of character—an enlarged mind, and the

[2] Sir Joshua mentioned that this was his fourth painting on the same canvas.

love of ease and freedom, were common to both; but it is probable that those qualities also prepossessed my father greatly in his favour which he himself did *not* possess. Sir Joshua was never apparently discomposed by anything under the sun—under all circumstances, and at all times, he was ever the same cheerful, mild companion, the same perfect gentleman—happy, serene, and undisturbed. My father spoke with particular pleasure of one day passed at that house, when his Grace of Rutland and a select company dined there—Miss Palmer the great artist's niece, afterwards Marchioness of Thomond, presiding. The union of complete, and even homely, comfort and ease with perfect polish and the highest manners, had in it a charm which impressed the day especially on his memory.

It was now considered desirable that Mr. Crabbe, as the chaplain to a nobleman, should have a university degree; and the Bishop of Llandaff (Dr. Watson) very kindly entered his name on the boards of Trinity College, Cambridge, that he might have the privilege of a degree, after a certain number of terms, and without residence.

This arrangement, however, had hardly been made, when he received an invitation to dine with Lord Thurlow; and this is another of those incidents in his life, which I much regret that he himself has given no account of; for I should suppose many expressions characteristic of the rough old Chancellor might have been recorded. My father only said, that, before he left the house, his noble host, telling him, that, "by G——d, he was as like Parson Adams as twelve to a dozen," gave him the small livings of Frome St. Quintin, and Evershot, in Dorsetshire; and Mr. Crabbe, that he might be entitled to hold this preferment, immediately obtained the degree of LL.B. from the Archbishop of Canterbury (Dr. Moore), instead of waiting for it at Cambridge.

In the autumn of 1783, after a long absence, my father went to Suffolk; and Miss Elmy being then at Beccles with her mother, he bent his steps thither; and it was in one of their rides in that neighbourhood, that they had the good fortune to view the great and memorable meteor which appeared in the month of August in that year. At that moment my mother and he were returning, in the evening, over a wide open common near Beccles. It was late, dull, and cloudy: in an instant the dark mass opened just in front of them. The clouds were rolled back like a scroll; and the glorious phenomenon burst forth as large as the moon, but infinitely more brilliant; majestically sailed across the heavens, varying its form every instant, and, as it were, unfolding its substance in successive sheaths of fire, and scattering lesser meteors, as it moved along. My mother, who happened to be riding behind, said that, even at that awful moment (for she concluded that the end of all things was at hand), she was irresistibly struck with my father's attitude. He had raised himself from his horse, lifted his arm, and spread his hand towards the object of admiration and terror, and appeared transfixed with astonishment.

Mr. Crabbe returned from thence to Belvoir, and again went to London with the family at the latter end of the year. Being now in circumstances which enabled him to afford himself a view of those spectacles which he had hitherto abstained from, and with persons who invited him to accompany them, he went occasionally to the theatres, especially to see Mrs. Siddons. Of her talents he expressed, of course, the most unbounded admiration; but I have heard him also speak of Mrs. Abingdon and Mrs. Jordan (the latter especially, in the character of Sir Harry Wildair), in such terms as proved that he fully appreciated the exquisite grace, and then unrivalled excellency, of those comic actresses. Being one night introduced by Mr. Thoroton into the box of the Prince of

Wales's equerries, his royal highness inquired, with some displeasure, who he was that had so intruded there; but hearing it was the poetical chaplain of his friend the Duke of Rutland, he expressed himself satisfied, and a short time after, Mr. Crabbe was presented to his royal highness by his noble patron.

Before the end of the year 1783, it was fixed that his Grace of Rutland should soon be appointed Lord-Lieutenant of Ireland. Had the Chancellor's livings, which Mr. Crabbe held, been of any considerable value, he would no doubt have embraced this opportunity to retire and settle; but the income derived from them was very trifling, and, as it happened, no preferment on the Belvoir list was then vacant; and therefore, when it was decided that he should remain on this side the Channel and marry, the Duke very obligingly invited him to make the castle his home, till something permanent could be arranged. At parting, the Duke presented him with a portrait of Pope, by Sir Godfrey Kneller, and assured him it was his intention to place him in an eligible situation on the first opportunity. He little thought at that time (his Grace being by but a few months his senior) that he should never see his kind and noble patron again.

By some it has been thought remarkable that Mr. Crabbe, recommended to the Duke of Rutland by such a character as Mr. Burke, and afterwards by his own reputation and conduct, should not have accompanied his Grace to Dublin, and finally been installed in a dignitary's seat in some Irish cathedral. Whether he had the offer of proceeding to Ireland I do not know, but it would have been extremely inconsistent with his strong attachment to Miss Elmy, and his domestic disposition and habits, to have accepted it; and his irregular education was an effectual bar to any very high preferment in the church. That he should not desire to retain his chaplaincy, was not only to be attributed to his wish to settle, but his consciousness that he was by no means calculated to hold such an office. In fact, neither nature nor circumstances had qualified him for it. The aristocracy of genius approaches too near the aristocracy of station: superiority of talent is apt, without intention, to betray occasional presumption. It is true, subserviency would be always despised; but a cool, collected mind—never thrown off its guard—pleased with what passes—entering into the interests of the day, but never betrayed into enthusiasm—is an indispensable qualification for that station. Mr. Crabbe could never conceal his feelings, and he felt strongly. He was not a stoic, and freedom of living was prevalent in almost all large establishments of that period; and, when the conversation was interesting, he might not always retire as early as prudence might suggest; nor, perhaps, did he at all times put a bridle to his tongue, for he might feel the riches of his intellect more than the poverty of his station. It is also probable that, brought up in the warehouse of Slaughden, and among the uneducated, though nature had given him the disposition of a gentleman—the politeness of a mild and Christian spirit—he may at that early period have retained some repulsive marks of the degree from whence he had so lately risen; he could hardly have acquired all at once the ease and self-possession for which he was afterwards distinguished. I must also add, that although he owed his introduction to Burke, his adherence, however mild, to the Whig tenets of Burke's party may not have much gratified the circles of Belvoir.

These circumstances will easily account for his not accompanying the family into Ireland, without supposing the least neglect or unkindness in his patrons, or any insensibility on their part to his sterling merits: on the contrary, he never ceased to receive from every individual of that noble house the strongest testimonies of their regard; and he was not only most amply satisfied with the favours they had conferred, but felt a strong personal attachment to the members of the family of both generations.

A few weeks before the Duke embarked for Ireland, my father once more repaired to Suffolk, and hastened to Beccles with the grateful intelligence that he was at length entitled, without imprudence, to claim the long-pledged hand of Miss Elmy.

CHAPTER VI

1784—1792

Mr. Crabbe marries—He resides successively at Belvoir Castle, at his Curacy of Stathern, and at his Rectory of Muston—Increase of his Family—Publication of "The Newspaper"—Visits and Journeys—His mode of Life, Occupations, and Amusements.

IN THE MONTH of December, 1783, my father and mother were married in the church of Beccles, by the Rev. Peter Routh, father to the learned and venerable president of Magdalen College, Oxford. Shortly after, they took up their residence in the apartments destined for their use, at Belvoir Castle; but, although there were many obvious advantages to a couple of narrow income in this position, and although the noble owner of the seat had given the most strict orders that their convenience should be consulted in every possible manner by his servants, it was soon found to be a disagreeable thing to inhabit the house, and be attended by the domestics, of an absent family; and Mr. Crabbe, before a year and a half had elapsed, took the neighbouring curacy of Stathern, and transferred himself to the humble parsonage attached to that office, in the village of the same name. A child born to my parents, while still at Belvoir, survived but a few hours; their next, the writer of these pages, saw the light at Stathern, in November, 1785. They continued to reside in this obscure parsonage for four years; during which two more children were added to their household—John Crabbe, so long the affectionate and unwearied assistant of his father in his latter days (born in 1787), and a daughter (born in 1789), who died in infancy.

Of these four years, my father often said they were, on the whole, the very happiest in his life. My mother and he could now ramble together at their ease, amidst the rich woods of Belvoir, without any of the painful feelings which had before chequered his enjoyment of the place: at home, a garden afforded him healthful exercise and unfailing amusement; and his situation as a curate prevented him from being drawn into any sort of unpleasant disputes with the villagers about him. His great resource and employment was, I believe, from the first, the study of natural history: he cultivated botany, especially that of the grasses, with insatiable ardour. Entomology was another especial favourite; and he gradually made himself expert in some branches of geological science also. He copied with his own hand several expensive works on such subjects, of which his situation could only permit him to obtain a temporary loan; and, though manual dexterity was never his forte, he even drew and coloured after the prints in some of these books with tolerable success; but this sort of labour, he, after a little while, discontinued, as an unprofitable waste of time. I may also add, that in accordance with the usual habits of the clergy then resident in the vale of Belvoir, he made some efforts to become a sportsman; but he wanted precision of eye and hand to use the gun with success. As to coursing, the cry of the first hare he saw killed, struck him as so like the wail of an infant, that he turned heart-sick from the spot:

and, in a word, although Mr. Crabbe did, for a season, make his appearance now and then in a garb which none that knew him in his latter days could ever have suspected him of assuming, the velveteen jacket and all its appurtenances were soon laid aside for ever.

He had another employment, which, indeed, he never laid aside until, many years after this time, he became the rector of a populous *town*. At Stathern, and at all his successive country residences, my father continued to practise his original profession among such poor people as chose to solicit his aid. The contents of his medicine chest, and, among the rest, cordials, were ever at their service: he grudged no personal fatigue to attend the sick-bed of the peasant, in the double capacity of physician and priest; and had often great difficulty in circumscribing his practice strictly within the limits of the poor, for the farmers would willingly have been attended gratis also. On some occasions, he was obliged to act even as accoucheur. I cannot quit this matter without observing, that I have heard it said, by persons who had met my father in humble abodes of distress, that, however nature might have disqualified him for the art of a surgeon, he exhibited a sagacity which, under better circumstances, might have conducted him to no mean rank as a physician.

In the course of 1784, my father contributed a brief memoir of Lord Robert Manners to the Annual Register, published by his friend, Mr. Dodsley; and in 1785 he appeared again as a poet. "The Newspaper," then published, was considered as in all respects of the same class and merits with "The Library"; and the author was anew encouraged by the critics, and by the opinions of Mr. Burke and others of his eminent friends in London. Yet, successful as his poetical career had been, and highly flattering as was the reception which his works had procured him in the polished circles of life, if we except a

I

valueless sermon put forth on the death of his patron, the Duke of Rutland, in 1787, and a chapter on the Natural History of the Vale of Belvoir, which he contributed to Mr. Nichols's account of Leicestershire, shortly afterwards, he, from this time, withdrew entirely from the public view. His "Parish Register" was published at the interval of *twenty-two years* after "The Newspaper"; and, from his thirty-first year to his fifty-second, he buried himself completely in the obscurity of domestic and village life, hardly catching, from time to time, a single glimpse of the brilliant society in which he had for a season been welcomed, and gradually forgotten as a *living* author by the public, who only, generally speaking, continued to be acquainted with the name of Crabbe from the extended circulation of certain striking passages in his early poems, through their admission into "The Elegant Extracts." It might, under such circumstances, excite little surprise, if I should skip hastily over the whole interval from 1785 to 1807—or even down to my father's sixtieth year (1813), when he at last reappeared in the metropolis, and figured as a member of various literary institutions there, and among the *lions*, as they are called, of fashionable life; but I feel that, in doing so, I should be guilty of a grave omission; and I hope the son of such a father will be pardoned for desiring to dwell a little on him as he appeared in those relations which are the especial test of moral worth—which, if well sustained, can impart a brightness to the highest intellectual reputation, and which dwell on my memory as affording the most estimable traits of his character.

Not long after his marriage, in passing through London, on his way to visit his livings in Dorsetshire, he had the satisfaction of presenting his wife to Mr. and Mrs. Burke, when he and she experienced the kindest reception; but this was only a casual glimpse of his illustrious friend. I believe my father

offered him the dedication of "The Newspaper," as well as of
some of his earlier publications; but that great man, probably
from modesty, declined anything of this kind; and as for Dr.
Johnson, who, no doubt, must have been the next in his
view, that giant of literature was by this time lost to the
world. In Dorsetshire, they were hospitably received by Mr.
Baker, once a candidate for that county; and they returned
charmed with their excursion, yet resumed with undiminished zest the enjoyment of their own quiet little parsonage.

Never, indeed, was any man more fitted for domestic life
than my father; and, but for circumstances not under his con-
trol—especially the delicate state of health into which my
mother ere long declined—I am sure no man would have
enjoyed a larger share of every sort of domestic happiness. His
attachment to his family was boundless; but his contentment
under a long temporary oblivion may also, in great part, be
accounted for, by the unwearied activity of his mind. As the
chief characteristic of his heart was benevolence, so that of his
mind was a buoyant exuberance of thought and perpetual
exercise of intellect. Thus he had an inexhaustible resource
within himself, and never for a moment, I may say, suffered
under that *ennui* which drives so many from solitude to the
busy search for notoriety. I can safely assert, that, from the
earliest time I recollect him, down to the fifth or sixth year before his death, I never saw him (unless in company) seated in a
chair, enjoying what is called a lounge—that is to say, doing
nothing. Out of doors he had always some object in view—
a flower, or a pebble, or his note-book, in his hand; and in the
house, if he was not writing, he was reading. He read aloud
very often, even when walking, or seated by the side of his
wife, in the huge old-fashioned one-horse chaise, heavier than
a modern chariot, in which they usually were conveyed in
their little excursions, and the conduct of which he, from

awkwardness and absence of mind, prudently relinquished to my mother on all occasions. Some may be surprised to hear me speak of his writing so much; but the fact is, that although he for so many years made no fresh appeal to the public voice, he was all that time busily engaged in composition. Numberless were the manuscripts which he completed; and not a few of them were never destined to see the light. I can well remember more than one grand incremation—not in the chimney, for the bulk of paper to be consumed would have endangered the house—but in the open air—and with what glee his children vied in assisting him, stirring up the fire, and bringing him fresh loads of the fuel as fast as their little legs would enable them. What the various works thus destroyed treated of, I cannot tell; but among them was an Essay on Botany in English; which, after he had made great progress in it, my father laid aside, in consequence merely, I believe, of the remonstrances of the late Mr. Davies, vice-master of Trinity College, Cambridge, with whom he had become casually acquainted, and who, though little tinged with academical peculiarities, could not stomach the notion of degrading such a science by treating of it in a modern language.

My father used to say that, had this treatise come out at the time when his friend arrested its progress, he might perhaps have had the honour of being considered as the first discoverer of more than one addition to the British Flora, since those days introduced to notice, classed and named, by other naturalists. I remember his mentioning, as one instance, the humble trefoil, now known as the *Trifolium suffocatum*. But, even if Mr. Crabbe had sent no "Parish Register" before him, when he, after his long retirement, reappeared in the upper walks of life, there would have been no possibility of suspecting that his village existence had been one of intellectual torpor. He mixed, on that occasion, with a much wider circle than that to which Burke introduced him; and it was obvious to the few who could compare what he then was with what he had been on his first *début*, that all his social feelings had been quickened, all his mental powers expanded and strengthened, in the interval that had passed. Why, such being the case, he for so great a period of his life remained unmoved by the stimuli of reputation or money, or the pleasure of select society, is a question which will never, I suppose, be quite satisfactorily answered.

It was, I think, in the summer of 1787, that my father was seized, one fine summer's day, with so intense a longing to see the sea, from which he had never before been so long absent, that he mounted his horse, rode alone to the coast of Lincolnshire, sixty miles from his house, dipped in the waves that washed the beach of Aldborough, and returned to Stathern.

During my father's residence here, and also at his other country places, he very rarely either paid or received visits, except in his clerical capacity; but there was one friend whose expanding versatility of mind and rare colloquial talents made him a most welcome visiter at Stathern—and he was a very frequent one. I allude to Dr. Edmund Cartwright, a poet and a mechanist of no small eminence, who at this period was the incumbent of Goadby, and occasionally lived there, though his principal residence was at Doncaster, where vast machines were worked under his direction. Few persons could tell a good story so well; no man could make more of a trite one. I can just remember him—the portly, dignified, old gentleman of the last generation—grave and polite, but full of humour and spirit. In the summer of 1787, my father and mother paid Dr. Cartwright a visit at Doncaster; but when she entered the vast building, full of engines thundering with resistless power, yet under the apparent management of children, the bare idea of the inevitable hazard attendant on such stupendous undertakings, quite overcame her feelings, and she burst into tears. On their return, Mrs. Elmy paid them a visit, and remained for some months with them. My mother's mother was a calm, composed, cheerful old lady, such as all admire, and as grandchildren adore. She had suffered many heavy afflictions, and had long made it her aim to suppress all violent emotions; and she succeeded, if perfect serenity of appearance, and the ultimate age of ninety-two, be fair indications of the peace within.

In October of the same year occurred a most unexpected event, to which I have already alluded—the untimely death of the Duke of Rutland, at the vice-regal palace, in Ireland. My father had a strong personal regard for his Grace, and grieved sincerely for the loss of a kind and condescending friend. Had he cherished ambitious views, he might have grieved for himself too. I have stated, that the Duke's disposition was generous and social: these traits meeting the spirit of the Irish, whom it was his wish to attach, and the customs of that period unhappily tempting him to prolonged festivity, he became a prey to an attack of fever; and the medical attendants were said to have overlooked that nice point, in inflammatory cases, where reduction should cease. He was only in the thirty-fifth year of his age; leaving a young and lovely widow, with six children, the eldest in his ninth year. His remains were brought to Belvoir Castle, to be interred in the family vault at Bottesford, and my father, of course, was present at the melancholy solemnity.

The widowed Duchess did not forget the *protégé* of her lamented husband: kindly desirous of retaining him in the neighbourhood, she gave him a letter to the Lord Chancellor, earnestly requesting him to exchange the two small livings Mr. Crabbe held in Dorsetshire for two of superior value in the vale of Belvoir. My father proceeded to London but was not, on this occasion, very courteously received by Lord Thurlow. "No," he growled; "by G——d, I will not do this for any man in England." But he did it, nevertheless, for a woman in England. The good Duchess, on arriving in town, waited on him personally, to renew her request; and he yielded. My father, having passed the necessary examination at Lambeth, received a dispensation from the Archbishop, and became rector of Muston, in Leicestershire, and the neighbourhood parish of Allington, in Lincolnshire.

It was on the 25th of February, 1789, that Mr. Crabbe left Stathern, and brought his family to the parsonage of Muston. Soon after this his father died. My grandfather, soon after my grandmother's death, had married again; and his new wife bringing home with her several children by a former husband, the house became still more uncomfortable than it had for many years before been to the members of his own family. It was on the appearance of these strangers that my uncle William, the hero of the "Parting Hour," went to sea, never to return. For many years, the old man's habits had been undermining his health; but his end was sudden.

I am now arrived at that period of my father's life when I became conscious of existence; when, if the happiness I experienced was not quite perfect, there was only alloy enough to make it felt the more. The reader himself will judge what must have been the lot of a child of such parents—how indulgence and fondness were mingled with care and solicitude.

What a pity it seems that the poignant feelings of early youth should ever be blunted, and, as it were, absorbed in the interests of manhood; that they cannot remain, together with the stronger stimuli of mature passions—passions so liable to make the heart ultimately selfish and cold. It is true, no one could endure the thoughts of remaining a child for ever; but with all that we gain, as we advance, some of the finer and better spirit of the mind appears to evaporate; seldom do we again feel those acute and innocent impressions, which recalling for a moment, one could almost cry to retain. Now and then, under peculiar circumstances, this youthful tenderness of feeling does return, when the spirits are depressed either by fatigue or illness, or some other softening circumstance; and then, especially if we should happen to hear some pleasing melody, even chimes or distant bells, a flood of early remembrances and warm affections flows into the mind, and we dwell on the past with the fondest regret; for such scenes are never to return: yet, though painful, these impressions are ever mingled with delight; we are tenacious of their duration, and feel the better for the transient susceptibility—indeed transient: for soon the music ceases, the fatigue yields to rest, the mind recovers its strength, and straightway all is (to such salutary sensations) cold and insensible as marble. Surely the most delightful ideas one could connect with this sublunary state would be a union of these vivid impressions of infancy with the warmth and purity of passion in early youth, and the judgment of maturity: perhaps such a union might faintly shadow the blessedness that may be hereafter.

How delightful is it to recall the innocent feelings of unbounded love, confidence, and respect, associated with my earliest visions of my parents. They appeared to their children not only good, but free from any taint of the corruption common to our nature; and such was the strength of the impressions then received, that hardly could subsequent experience ever enable our judgments to modify them. Many a happy and indulged child has, no doubt, partaken in the same fond exaggeration; but ours surely had every thing to excuse it.

Always visibly happy in the happiness of others, especially of children, our father entered into all our pleasures, and soothed and cheered us in all our little griefs with such over-flowing tenderness, that it was no wonder we almost worshipped him. My first recollection of him is of his carrying me up to his private room to prayers, in the summer evenings, about sunset, and rewarding my silence and attention afterwards with a view of the flower-garden through his prism. Then I recall the delight it was to me to be permitted to sleep with him during a confinement of my mother's; how I longed for the morning, because then he would be sure to tell me some fairy tale, of his own invention, all sparkling with gold and diamonds, magic fountains and enchanted princesses. In the eye of memory I can still see him as he was at that period of his life, his fatherly countenance, unmixed with any of the less loveable expressions that, in too many faces, obscure that character—but pre-eminently *fatherly;* conveying the ideas of kindness, intellect, and purity; his manner grave, manly, and cheerful, in unison with his high and open forehead: his very attitudes, whether as he sat absorbed in the arrangement of his minerals, shells, and insects—or as he laboured in his garden until his naturally pale complexion acquired a tinge of fresh healthy red; or as, coming lightly towards us with some unexpected present, his smile of indescribable benevolence spoke exultation in the foretaste of our raptures.

But I think, even earlier than these are my first recollections of my mother. I think the very earliest is of her as combing my hair one evening, by the light of the fire, which hardly broke the long shadows of the room, and singing the plaintive air of "Kitty Fell," till, though I could not have been more than three years old, the melody found its way into my heart, and the tears dropped down so profusely that I was glad the darkness concealed them. How mysterious is shame without guilt!

There are few situations on earth more enviable than that of a child on his first journey with indulgent parents; there is perpetual excitement and novelty—"*omne ignotum pro magnifico*"—and at the same time a perfect freedom from care. This blessed ignorance of limits and boundaries, and absence of all forecast, form the very charm of the enchantment; each town appears indefinitely vast, each day as if it were never to have a close: no decline of any kind being dreamt of, the present is enjoyed in a way wholly impossible with those who have a long past to remember, and a dark future to anticipate. Never can I forget my first excursion into Suffolk, in company with my parents. It was in the month of September, 1790—(shortly after my mother had recovered from her confinement with her fourth son, Edmund Crabbe, who died in his sixth year)—that, dressed in my first suit of boy's clothes (and that scarlet), in the height of a delicious season, I was mounted beside them in their huge old gig, and visited the scenes and the persons familiar to me, from my earliest nursery days, in their conversation and anecdotes. Sometimes, as we proceeded, my father read aloud; sometimes he left us for a while to botanise among the hedgerows, and returned with some unsightly weed or bunch of moss, to him precious. Then, in the evening, when we had reached our inn, the happy child, instead of being sent early as usual to bed, was permitted to stretch himself on the carpet, while the reading was resumed, blending with sounds which, from novelty, appeared delightful—the buzzing of the bar, the rattling of wheels, the horn of the mail-coach, the gay glamour of the streets—everything to excite and astonish, in the midst of safety and repose. My father's countenance at such moments is still before me; with what gentle sympathy did he seem to enjoy the happiness of childhood!

On the third day we reached Parham, and I was introduced to a set of manners and customs, of which there remains, perhaps, no counterpart in the present day. My great-uncle's establishment was that of the first-rate yeoman of that period —the Yeoman that already began to be styled by courtesy an Esquire. Mr. Tovell might possess an estate of some eight hundred pounds per annum, a portion of which he himself cultivated. Educated at a mercantile school, he often said of himself, "Jack will never make a gentleman"; yet he had a native dignity of mind and of manners, which might have enabled him to pass muster in that character with any but very fastidious critics. His house was large, and the surrounding moat, the rookery, the ancient dovecot, and the well-stored fishponds, were such as might have suited a gentleman's seat of some consequence; but one side of the house immediately overlooked a farm-yard, full of all sorts of domestic animals, and the scene of constant bustle and noise. On entering the house, there was nothing at first sight to remind one of the farm: a spacious hall, paved with black and white marble—at one extremity a very handsome drawing-room, and at the other a fine old staircase of black oak, polished till it was as slippery as ice, and having a chime-clock and a barrel-organ on its landing-places. But this drawing-room, a corresponding dining parlour, and a handsome sleeping apartment up stairs, were all *tabooed* ground, and made use of on great and solemn occasions only—such as rent days, and an occasional visit with which Mr. Tovell was honoured by a neighbouring peer. At all other times the family and their visiters lived entirely in the old-fashioned kitchen along with the servants. My great-uncle occupied an arm-chair, or, in attacks of gout, a couch on one side of a large open chimney. Mrs. Tovell sat at a small table, on which, in the evening, stood one small candle, in an iron candlestick, plying her needle by the feeble glimmer, surrounded by her maids, all busy at the same employment; but in winter a noble block of wood, sometimes the whole circumference of a pollard, threw its comfortable warmth and cheerful blaze over the apartment.

At a very early hour in the morning, the alarum called the maids, and their mistress also; and if the former were tardy, a louder alarum, and more formidable, was heard chiding the delay—not that scolding was peculiar to any occasion, it regularly ran on through all the day, like bells on harness, in spiriting the work, whether it were done ill or well. After the important business of the dairy, and a hasty breakfast, their respective employments were again resumed; that which the mistress took for her especial privilege being the scrubbing of the floors of the state apartments. A new servant, ignorant of her presumption, was found one morning on her knees, hard at work on the floor of one of these preserves, and was thus addressed by her mistress: "*You* wash such floors as these? Give me the brush this instant, and troop to the scullery and wash that, madam! . . . As true as G——d's in heaven, here comes Lord Rochford, to call on Mr. Tovell.— Here, take my mantle (a blue woollen apron), and I'll go to the door!"

If the sacred apartments had not been opened, the family dined on this wise: the heads seated in the kitchen at an old table; the farm-men standing in the adjoining scullery, door open—the female servants at a side table, called a *bouter*; with the principals, at the table, perchance some travelling rat-catcher, or tinker, or farrier, or an occasional gardener in his shirt-sleeves, his face probably streaming with perspiration. My father well describes, in "The Widow's Tale," my mother's situation, when living in her younger days at Parham:

"But when the men beside their station took,
The maidens with them, and with these the cook;
When one huge wooden bowl before them stood,
Fill'd with huge balls of farinaceous food;
With bacon, mass saline! where never lean
Beneath the brown and bristly rind was seen.
When from a single horn the party drew
Their copious draughts of heavy ale and new;
When the coarse cloth she saw, with many a stain,
Soil'd by rude hinds who cut and came again;
She could not breathe, but, with a heavy sigh,
Rein'd the fair neck, and shut the offended eye;
She minced the sanguine flesh in frustums fine,
And wondered much to see the *creatures* dine."

On ordinary days, when the dinner was over, the fire re-
plenished, the kitchen sanded and lightly swept over in waves,
mistress and maids, taking off their shoes, retired to their
chambers for a nap of one hour to the minute. The dogs
and cats commenced their siesta by the fire. Mr. Tovell dozed
in his chair, and no noise was heard, except the melancholy
and monotonous cooing of a turtle-dove, varied, however,
by the shrill treble of a canary. After the hour had expired, the
active part of the family were on the alert, the bottles (Mr.
Tovell's tea equipage) placed on the table; and as if by in-
stinct, some old acquaintance would glide in for the evening's
carousal, and then another, and another. If four or five arrived, the punchbowl was taken down, and emptied and filled
again. But, whoever came, it was comparatively a dull evening, unless two especial Knights Companions were of the
party—one was a jolly old farmer, with much of the person
and humour of Falstaff, a face as rosy as brandy could make it,
and an eye teeming with subdued merriment; for he had

that prime quality of a joker, superficial gravity—the other was a relative of the family, a wealthy yeoman, middle-aged, thin, and muscular. He was a bachelor, and famed for his indiscriminate attachment to all who bore the name of woman —young or aged, clean or dirty, a lady or a gipsy, it mattered not to him; all were equally admired. He had peopled the village green; and it was remarked that, whoever was the mother, the children might be recognised in an instant to belong to him. Such was the strength of his constitution, that, though he seldom went to bed sober, he retained a clear eye and stentorian voice to his eightieth year, and coursed when he was ninety. He sometimes rendered the colloquies over the bowl peculiarly piquant; and so soon as his voice began to be elevated, one or two of the inmates, my father and mother for example, withdrew with Mrs. Tovell into her own *sanctum sanctorum*; but I, not being supposed capable of understanding much of what might be said, was allowed to linger on the skirts of the festive circle; and the servants, being considered much in the same point of view as the animals dozing on the hearth, remained, to have the full benefit of their wit, neither producing the slightest restraint, nor feeling it themselves.

After we had spent some weeks amidst this primitive set, we proceeded to Aldborough, where we were received with the most cordial welcome by my father's sister and her worthy husband, Mr. Sparkes. How well do I remember that morning!—my father watching the effect of the first view of the sea on my countenance, the tempered joyfulness of his manner when he carried me in his arms to the verge of the rippling waves, and the nameless delight with which I first inhaled the odours of the beach. What variety of emotions had he not experienced on that spot!—how unmingled would have been his happiness then, had his mother survived to see him as a husband and a father!

We visited also on this occasion my grandmother, Mrs. Elmy, and her two daughters, at the delightful town of Beccles; and never can I forget the admiration with which I even then viewed this gem of the Waveney, and the fine old church (Beata Ecclesia), which gives name to the place; though, as there were no other children in the house, there were abundant attractions of another kind more suited to my years. In fact, Beccles seemed a paradise, as we visited from house to house with our kind relations. From this town we proceeded to a sweet little villa called Normanston, another of the early resorts of my mother and her lover, in the days of their anxious affection. Here four or five spinsters of independent fortune had formed a sort of Protestant nunnery, the abbess being Miss Blacknell, who afterwards deserted it to become the wife of the late Admiral Sir Thomas Graves, a lady of distinguished elegance in her tastes and manners. Another of the sisterhood was Miss Waldron, late of Tamworth—dear, good-humoured, hearty, masculine Miss Waldron, who could sing a jovial song like a fox-hunter, and like him, I had almost said, toss a glass; and yet was there such an air of high *ton*, and such intellect mingled with these manners, that the perfect lady was not veiled for a moment— no, not when, with a face rosy red, and an eye beaming with mirth, she would seize a cup and sing "Toby Fillpot," glorying as it were in her own jollity. When we took our morning rides, she generally drove my father in her phaeton, and interested him exceedingly by her strong understanding and conversational powers.

After morning prayers read by their clerical guest in the elegant boudoir, the carriages came to the door, and we went to some neighbouring town, or to the sea-side, or to a camp then formed at Hopton, a few miles distant; more frequently to Lowestoft; where, one evening, all adjourned to a dissenting chapel, to hear the venerable John Wesley on one of the last of his peregrinations. He was exceedingly old and infirm, and was attended, almost supported in the pulpit, by a young minister on each side. The chapel was crowded to suffocation. In the course of the sermon, he repeated, though with an application of his own, the lines from Anacreon—

> "Oft am I by women told,
> Poor Anacreon! thou grow'st old;
> See, thine hairs are falling all,
> Poor Anacreon! how they fall!
> Whether I grow old or no,
> By these signs I do not know;
> But this I need not to be told.
> 'Tis time to *live* if I grow old."

My father was much struck by his reverend appearance and his cheerful air, and the beautiful cadence he gave to these lines; and, after the service, introduced himself to the patriarch, who received him with benevolent politeness.

Shortly after our return from Suffolk, the parsonage at Muston was visited by the late Mr. John Nichols, his son (the present "Mr. Urban"), and an artist engaged in making drawings for the History of Leicestershire. Mr. Crabbe on this occasion rendered what service he could to a work for which he had previously, as I have stated, undertaken to write a chapter of natural history; and was gratified, after his friend's return to London, by a present of some very fine Dutch engravings of plants, splendidly coloured.

In the spring of the next year (1792) my father preached a sermon at the visitation at Grantham, which so much struck the late Mr. Turner, rector of Denton and Wing, who had been commissioned to select a tutor for the sons of the Earl of Bute, that he came up after the service and solicited the preacher to receive these young noblemen into his family. But this he at once declined; and he never acted more wisely than in so doing. Like the late Archbishop Moore, when tutor to the sons of the Duke of Marlborough, he might easily have "read ahead" of his pupils, and thus concealed or remedied the defects of his own education; but the restraint of strange inmates would have been intolerable in my father's humble parsonage, and nothing could have repaid him for submitting to such an interruption of all his domestic habits and favourite pursuits.

About this time he became intimately acquainted with the late Dr. Gordon, precentor of Lincoln, father to the present dean, and my mother and he passed some time with him at his residence near the cathedral. This was another of those manly, enlarged minds, for which he ever felt a strong partiality; and on the same grounds he felt the same regard, many years afterwards, for his son.

In October of this year, Mr. Crabbe was enclosing a new garden for botanic specimens, and had just completed the walls, when he was suddenly summoned into Suffolk to act as executor to Mr. Tovell, who had been carried off before there was time to announce his illness; and on his return, after much deliberation (many motives contending against very intelligible scruples), my father determined to place a curate at Muston, and to go and reside at Parham, taking the charge of some church in that neighbourhood.

Though tastes and affections, as well as worldly interests, prompted this return to native scenes and early acquaintances, it was a step reluctantly taken, and, I believe, sincerely repented of. The beginning was ominous. As we were slowly quitting the place, preceded by our furniture, a stranger, though one who knew my father's circumstances, called out in

K

an impressive tone, "You are wrong, you are wrong." The sound, he said, found an echo in his own conscience, and during the whole journey seemed to ring in his ears like a supernatural voice.

CHAPTER VII

1792—1804

Mr. Crabbe's Residence in Suffolk—at Parham—at Glemham—and at Rendham.

IN NOVEMBER, 1792, we arrived once more at Parham: but how changed was every thing since I had first visited that house, then the scene of constant mirth and hospitality! As I got out of the chaise, I remember jumping for very joy, and exclaiming, "Here we are—here we are, little Willy[1] and all!" but my spirits sunk into dismay when, on entering the well-known kitchen, all there seemed desolate, dreary, and silent. Mrs. Tovell and her sister-in-law, sitting by the fireside weeping, did not even rise up to welcome my parents, but uttered a few chilling words, and wept again. All this appeared to me as inexplicable as forbidding. How little do children dream of the alterations that elder people's feelings towards each other undergo, when death has caused a transfer of property! Our arrival in Suffolk was by no means palatable to all my mother's relations.

Mrs. Elmy and her sister, Miss Tovell, were their brother's co-heiresses; the latter was an ancient maiden, living in a cottage hard by, and persuaded that every thing ought to have been left to her own management. I think I see her now, with her ivory-tipped walking-cane, a foot, at least, above her head, scolding about some change that would, as she said, have

[1] My father's seventh and youngest child.

made "Jacky" (her late brother), if he had seen it, shake in his grave—the said change being, perhaps, the removal of a print from one room to another, and my father having purchased every atom of the furniture when he came into the house.

My father being at least as accessible to the slightest mark of kindness as to any species of offence, the cool old dame used to boast, not without reason, that she could "screw Crabbe up and down like a fiddle." Every now and then she screwed her violin too tightly; but still there was never any real malice on either side. When, some time after, the hand of death was on Miss Tovell, she sent for Mr. Crabbe, and was attended by him with the greatest tenderness; nor did she at last execute her oft-repeated threat of making a *cadicy*—Anglicè, a codicil —to her will.

In many circumstances, besides, my father found the disadvantage of succeeding such a man as Mr. Tovell. He invited none of the old compotators, and if they came received them but coolly; and it was soon said that "Parham had passed away, and the glory thereof." When the paper of parish rates came round, he perceived that he was placed on a much higher scale of payment than his wealthy predecessor had ever been for the very same occupation; and when he complained of this, he was told very plainly: "Why, sir, Mr. Tovell was a good neighbour: we all miss him sadly; and so, I suppose, do you, sir; and—and——" "I understand you," said my father, "perfectly; now, sir, I refuse this rate: take your remedy." He resisted this charge; and the consequences may be guessed.

Having detected the bailiff in some connection with smugglers, he charged him with the fact. The man flew into a violent passion, grasped a knife, and exclaimed with an inflamed countenance, "No man shall call me a rogue!" My father smiled at his rage, and said, in a quiet tone,—"Now, Robert, you are too much for me: put down your knife, and

then we can talk on equal terms." The man hesitated:
my father added, lifting his voice, "Get out of the house,
you scoundrel!" and he was obeyed. On all occasions,
indeed, he appeared to have a perfect insensibility to physical
danger.

I have said that Mr. and Mrs. Crabbe were not in the habit
of visiting. In fact, his father's station and straitened circumstances, and the customs of his native place, had prevented his
forming any early habit of such intercourse. His own domestic
and literary pursuits indisposed him still further; and my
mother's ill health combined to prevent any regular sociality
with the families in their neighbourhood; but both at Muston
and Parham they had some valued friends occasionally residing
with them for many weeks, especially an old lady of Aldborough, who had been intimate with my father's family,
and was fallen into poverty, and who was ever received with
cordiality and respect. But, at one house in the vicinity of
Parham, my father was a frequent visitor. To Mr. Dudley
North he felt himself attached by the ties of gratitude, and
strongly attracted both by the mutual knowledge of Mr.
Burke, Mr. Fox, and other public characters, and by his own
superior mind and manners; for though, according to Mr.
Boswell's account of a conversation, Dr. Johnson mentions
him somewhat lightly to Mrs. Thrale, yet it is to be remembered that that lady provoked him to it by her reiterated
eulogium, and, moreover, that Mr. North was a Whig. But
he was distinguished, even among the eminent characters of
the day, for the high polish of his manners and the brilliancy
of his wit. Though a silent member of the house (for he had a
strong impediment in his utterance), "yet," said Mr. Fox,
"we owe to Dudley's suggestions some of the best hits we
have made."

From this friend, whose seat (Little Glemham Hall) was

within two miles of Parham, my father received every kindness and attention. I remember a well-stored medicine-chest arriving one morning—for Mr. Crabbe still continued to administer to the poor, gratis—and game, fruit, and other produce of his domain were sent in profusion. It was in the autumn of 1794, or 1795, that he had the honour of meeting at Mr. North's, a large party of some of the most eminent men in the kingdom—the Honourable Charles (now Earl) Grey, the Earl of Lauderdale, Mr. Fox, Mr. Roger Wilbraham, Dr. Parr, Mr. St. John, and several other public characters. Mr. Fox, cordially recognising my father, expressed his disappointment that his pen had been so long unemployed; and it was then that he promised to revise any future poem which Mr. Crabbe might prepare for publication. One day—for it was a shooting party, and they stayed about a fortnight—in passing from the saloon to the dining-room, while there was a momentary pause, Mr. Fox playfully pushed my father first, saying, "If he had had his deserts,[2] he would have walked before us all." If this was an unmerited compliment, it was assuredly a very good-humoured one.

Annoyances out of doors and within probably induced him, shortly after his arrival in Suffolk, to pay a visit of several months to his sister at Aldborough; and when there, he had the great satisfaction of placing my brother John and myself under the tuition of one of the good old dames who had taught himself his letters. On returning to Parham, he undertook the charge of Sweffling, for the respected incumbent of that parish, the Reverend Richard Turner, of Great Yarmouth. Another curacy (Great Glemham) was shortly added to this; and henceforth, his occupations and habits were very much what they used to be at Muston.

---

[2] Alluding to his station at Belvoir.

He had been about four years at Parham before another residence, quite suitable to his views, presented itself; and the opportunity of changing occurred at a moment when it was more than ever to be desired. In March, 1796, Mr. Crabbe lost his third son, a fine promising lad, then in his sixth year. His family had been seven, and they were now reduced to two. The loss of this child was so severely felt by my mother, that it caused a nervous disorder, from which she never entirely recovered; and it became my father's very earnest wish to quit Parham, where the thoughts of that loss were unavoidably cherished. Great Glemham Hall, a house belonging to Mr. North, becoming vacant at that time, he very obligingly invited my father to be his tenant, at a greatly reduced rent; and, on the 17th of October, the *lares* were removed from Parham, where they had been always unpropitious, to this beautiful residence, where my parents remained for four or five years, to their entire satisfaction. The situation was delightful in itself, and extremely convenient for the clerical duties my father had to perform. I was now placed at school at Ipswich, under the care of the late excellent Mr. King, in whom my father had the most perfect confidence; but I passed, of course, my vacations at home; and never can I cease to look back to my days at Glemham as the golden spot of my existence.

In June, 1798, on Mr. King's retiring from the school at Ipswcih, I returned home finally; for it was soon resolved that I should not be sent to any other master, but that my brother and myself should prepare for the University under our father's own care. If I except occasional visits of a month or two to Muston, the associations of our happiest years are all with Glemham and other scenes in his native county. Glemham itself is, and ever will be, the Alhambra of my imagination. That glorious palace yet exists; ours is levelled with the ground.[3] A small well-wooded park occupied the whole mouth of the glen, whence, doubtless, the name of the village was derived. In the lowest ground stood the commodious mansion; the approach wound down through a plantation on the eminence in front. The opposite hill rose at the back of it, rich and varied with trees and shrubs scattered irregularly; under this southern hill ran a brook, and on the banks above it were spots of great natural beauty, crowned by whitethorn and oak. Here the purple scented violet perfumed the air, and in one place coloured the ground. On the left of the front, in the narrower portion of the glen, was the village; on the right, a confined view of richly wooded fields. In fact, the whole parish and neighbourhood resemble a combination of groves, interspersed with fields cultivated like gardens, and intersected with those green dry lanes which tempt the walker in all weathers, especially in the evenings, when in the short grass of the dry sandy banks lies, every few yards, a glowworm, and the nightingales are pouring forth their melody in every direction.

My father was a skilful mathematician; and imperfectly as he had been grounded in the classics at school, he had, as I have stated, been induced, by various motives, to become a very respectable scholar; and not the least of these motives was his strong partiality for Latin poetry, which continued to the last, his library table, and even his bed-room, being seldom without some favourite work of this description. But there may be great defects in a domestic education, without any want of knowledge in the master. Seldom is such tuition carried on with strict regularity and perseverance, for family interruptions unavoidably occur daily; and such an indulgent mind as his, conscious, too, of its own hatred to restraint,

---

[3] A new and elegant mansion has been built on the hill, by Dr. Kilderbee, who bought the estate.

e necessary discipline. So that, to
his new academy had much more of
: contrasted with Ipswich, it seemed
little   ious holiday.

The   ngs especially, at this place, dwell on
my mem   elightful dream. When we had finished
our lesson: d not adjourn with my father to the garden to wo   own plats, we generally took a family
walk throu   green lanes around Glemham; where, at
every turn, s   as a cottage or a farm, and not collected into a
street, as in some parts of the kingdom, leaving the land naked
and forlorn. Along these we wandered sometimes till the
moon had risen, my mother leading a favourite little niece
who lived with us, my father reading some novel aloud, while
my brother and I caught moths or other insects to add to his
collection. Since I have mentioned novels, I may say that
even from the most trite of these fictions, he could sometimes
catch a train of ideas that was turned to an excellent use; so
that he seldom passed a day without reading part of some such
work, and was never very select in the choice of them. To us
they were all, in those days, interesting, for they suggested
some pleasing imaginings, the idea of some pretty little in-
nocent-looking village heroine, perhaps, whom we had seen
at church, or in a ramble; and while he read Mrs. Inchbald's
deeply pathetic story, called "Nature and Art," one evening,
I believe some such association almost broke our hearts.
When it was too dark to see, he would take a battledore and
join us in the pursuit of the moths, or carry his little favourite
if she were tired, and so we proceeded homeward while on
the right and left, before and behind, the nightingales (I
never heard so many as among those woods) were pouring
out their melody, sometimes three or four at once. And now
we fill the margin of our hats with glow-worms to place

upon the lawn before our windows, and reach the house only in time for supper.

In the winter evenings the reading was carried out more systematically, and we had generally books of a superior description; for a friend lent us every Christmas a large box of the most reputable works recently published, especially of travels; and never can I forget the deep interest with which we heard my father read Stedman's Surinam, Park's Africa, Macartney's China, and several similar publications of that period. He read in that natural and easy manner, that permits the whole attention to be given to the subject. Some (I think miscalled "good readers") are so wonderfully correct and emphatic, that we are obliged to think of the reading, instead of the story. In repeating anything of a pathetic nature, I never heard his equal; nay, there was a nameless something about his intonation which could sometimes make even a ludicrous stanza affecting. We had been staying a week at a friend's house (a very unusual circumstance), and among his large and fine family was one daughter so eminently beautiful and graceful as to excite general admiration; and the writer (now fifteen) very naturally fancied himself deeply in love with her. On returning home, my heart was too full to trust myself near the chaise, so I rode far behind, calling the setting sun and the golden tints of the west to witness my most solemn determination to raise myself to a rank worthy of this young enchantress. We stopped at an inn to rest the horses, and my father began to read aloud the well-known mock heroic from the "Anti-jacobin," —

> "Barbs! barbs! alas! how swift ye flew
>   Her neat post-wagon trotting in!
> Ye bore Matilda from my view.
>   Forlorn I languish'd at the U–

niversity of Gottingen,
niversity of Gottingen."

In itself the song is an exquisite burlesque; but the cadence
he gave it was entirely irresistible, and at the words, "Sweet,
sweet, Matilda Pottingen," I could suppress the accumulated
grief no longer. "O ho!" said he, "I see how the case is now!"
and he shut the book, and soothed me with inexpressible
kindness.

My father, now about his forty-sixth year, was much more
stout and healthy than when I first remember him. Soon after
that early period, he became subject to vertigoes, which he
thought indicative of a tendency to apoplexy; and was
occasionally bled rather profusely, which only increased the
symptoms. When he preached his first sermon at Muston, in
the year 1789, my mother foreboded, as she afterwards told
us, that he would preach very few more: but it was on one
of his early journeys into Suffolk, in passing through Ipswich,
that he had the most alarming attack. Having left my mother
at the inn, he walked into the town alone, and suddenly staggered in the street, and fell. He was lifted up by the passengers,
and overhead some one say, significantly, "Let the gentleman
alone, he will be better by and by"; for his fall was attributed
to the bottle. He was assisted to his room, and the late Dr.
Clubbe was sent for, who, after a little examination, saw
through the case with great judgment. "There is nothing the
matter with your head," he observed, "nor any apoplectic
tendency; let the digestive organs bear the whole blame: you
must take opiates." From that time his health began to amend
rapidly, and his constitution was renovated; a rare effect
of opium, for that drug almost always inflicts some partial
injury, even when it is necessary; but to him it was only
salutary, and to a constant but slightly increasing dose of it may

be attributed his long and generally healthy life. His personal appearance also was improved with his health and his years. This is by no means an uncommon case: many an ordinary youth has widened and rounded into a well-looking, dignified, middle-aged man. His countenance was never ordinary, but health of itself gives a new charm to any features; and his figure, which in his early years had been rather thin and weakly, was now muscular and almost athletic.

During the whole time my father officiated in Suffolk, he was a popular preacher, and had always large congregations; for, notwithstanding what I have observed on this subject, and that he adopted not what are called evangelical principles, yet was he deemed a gospel preacher: but this term, as it was applied then and there, fell short of the meaning it now conveys. It signified simply a minister who urges his flock to virtuous conduct, by placing a future award ever full in their view, instead of dwelling on the temporal motives rendered so prominent at that time by many of his brethren.

His style of reading in the desk was easy and natural— at any rate, natural to him, though a fastidious ear might find in it a species of affectation, something a little like assumed authority; but there was no tone, nothing of singsong. He read too rapidly, it is true: but surely this was an error on the right side. The extremely slow enunciation of matter so very familiar is enough to make piety itself impatient. In the pulpit he was entirely unaffected; read his sermon with earnestness, and in a voice and manner, on some occasions, peculiarly affecting; but he made no attempt at extempore preaching, and utterly disregarded all the mechanism of oratory. And he had at that time another trait, very desirable in a minister—the most complete exemption from fear or solicitude. "I must have some money, gentlemen," he would say, in stepping from the pulpit. This was his notice of tithe-day. Once or twice, finding it grow dark, he abruptly shut his sermon, saying, "Upon my word I cannot see; I must give you the rest when we meet again." Or, he would walk into a pew near a window, and stand on the seat and finish his sermon, with the most admirable indifference to the remarks of his congregation. He was always, like his own Author-Rector, in the Parish Register, "careless of hood and band," &c.

I have mentioned that my mother was attacked, on the death of her son Edmund, by a nervous disorder; and it proved of an increasing and very lamentable kind; for, during the hotter months of almost every year, she was oppressed by the deepest dejection of spirits I ever witnessed in any one, and this circumstance alone was sufficient to undermine the happiness of so feeling a mind as my father's. Fortunately for both, there were long intervals, in which, if her spirits were a little too high, the relief to herself and others was great indeed. Then she would sing over her old tunes again—and be the frank, cordial, charming woman of earlier days.

This severe domestic affliction, however, did not seriously interrupt my father's pursuits and studies, although I think it probable that it was one of the main causes of that long abstinence from society, which has already been alluded to as one of the most remarkable features in his personal history. He continued at Glemham, as he had done at Parham and Muston, the practice of literary composition. My brother says, in a memorandum now before me, "While searching for and examining plants or insects, he was moulding verses into measure and smoothness. No one who observed him at these times could doubt that he enjoyed exquisite pleasure in composing. He had a degree of action while thus walking and versifying, which I hardly ever observed when he was preaching or reading. The hand was moved up and down;

the pace quickened. He was, nevertheless, fond of considering poetical composition as a species of task and labour, and would say, "I have been hard at work, and have had a good morning."

My father taught himself both French and Italian, so as to read and enjoy the best authors in either language, though he knew nothing of their pronunciation. He also continued all through his residence in Suffolk the botanical and entomological studies to which he had been so early devoted. I rather think, indeed, that this was, of his whole life, the period during which he carried the greatest and most indefatigable zeal into his researches in Natural History. There was, perhaps, no one of its departments to which he did not, at some time or other, turn with peculiar ardour; but, generally speaking, I should be inclined to say, that those usually considered as the least inviting had the highest attractions for him. In botany, grasses, the most useful, but the least ornamental, were his favourites; in minerals, the earths and sands; in entomology, the minuter insects. His devotion to these pursuits appeared to proceed purely from the love of science and the increase of knowledge—at all events, he never seemed to be captivated with the mere beauty of natural objects, or even to catch any taste for the arrangement of his own specimens. Within the house was a kind of scientific confusion; in the garden, the usual showy foreigners gave place to the most scarce flowers, and especially to the rarer weeds, of Britain; and these were scattered here and there only for preservation. In fact, he neither loved order for its own sake, nor had any very high opinion of that passion in others; witness his words, in the tale of Stephen Jones, the "Learned Boy"—

"The *love of order*—I the thing receive
From reverend men—and I in part believe—

Shows a clear mind and clean, and whoso needs
This love, but seldom in the world succeeds.
Still has *the love of order* found a place
With all that's low, degrading, mean, and base;
With all that merits scorn, and all that meets disgrace.
In the cold miser of all change afraid,
In pompous men in public seats obeyed,
In humble placemen, heralds, solemn drones,
Fanciers of flowers, and lads like Stephen Jones;
Order to these is armour and defence,
And love of method serves for lack of sense."

Whatever truth there may be in these lines, it is certain
that this insensibility to the beauty of order was a defect in his
own mind; arising from what I must call his want of taste.
There are, no doubt, very beautiful detached passages in his
writings—passages apparently full of this very quality. It is
not, however, in detached parts of a poem that the
criterion of principle properly lies, but in the conduct of
the whole; in the selection of the subject and its amplifications;
in the relative disposition and comparative prominency of the
parts, and in the contrasts afforded by bearing lightly or
heavily on the pencil. In these things Mr. Crabbe is generally
admitted to be not a little deficient; and what can demonstrate
the high rank of his other qualifications better than the fact,
that he could acquire such a reputation in spite of so serious a
disadvantage? This view of his mind, I must add, is confirmed
by his remarkable indifference to almost all the proper objects of taste. He had no real love for painting, or music, or
architecture, or for what a painter's eye considers as the
beauties of landscape. But he had a passion for science—the
science of the human mind, first; then, that of nature in
general; and, lastly, that of abstract quantities. His powerful

intellect did not seem to require the ideas of sense to move it to enjoyment, but he could at all times find luxury in the most dry and forbidding calculations.

One of his chief labours at this period was the completion of the English Treatise on Botany, which I mentioned at an earlier page of this narrative, and the destruction of which I still think of with some regret. He had even gone so far as to propose its publication to Mr. Dodsley, before the scruples of another interfered, and made him put the manuscript into the fire. But among other prose writings of the same period some were of a class which, perhaps, few have ever suspected Mr. Crabbe of meddling with, though it be one in which so many of his poetical contemporaries have earned high distinction. During one or two of his winters in Suffolk, he gave most of his evening hours to the writing of Novels, and he brought not less than three such works to a conclusion. The first was entitled "The Widow Grey"; but I recollect nothing of it except that the principal character was a benevolent humourist, a Dr. Allison. The next was called "Reginald Glanshaw, or the Man who commanded Success"; a portrait of an assuming, overbearing, ambitious mind, rendered interesting by some generous virtues, and gradually wearing down into idiotism. I cannot help thinking that this Glanshaw was drawn with very extraordinary power; but the story was not well managed in the details. I forget the title of his third novel; but I clearly remember that it opened with a description of a wretched room, similar to some that are presented in his poetry, and that, on my mother's telling him frankly that she thought the effect very inferior to that of the corresponding pieces in verse, he paused in his reading, and, after some reflection, said, "Your remark is just." The result was a leisurely examination of all these manuscript novels, and another of those grand incremations which, at an earlier period, had been sport to his children. The prefaces and dedications to his poems have been commended for simple elegance of language; nor was it in point of diction, I believe, that his novels would have been found defective, but rather in that want of skill and taste for order and arrangement, which I have before noticed as displayed even in his physiological pursuits.

He had now accumulated so many poetical pieces of various descriptions, that he began to think of appearing once more in the capacity which had first made him known to fame. In the course of the year 1799, he opened a communication with Mr. Hatchard, the well-known bookseller, and was encouraged to prepare for publication a series of poems, sufficient to fill a volume—among others, one on the Scripture story of Naaman; another, strange contrast! entitled "Gipsy Will"; and a third founded on the legend of the Pedlar of Swaffham. But before fully committing his reputation to the hazards of a new appearance, he judiciously paused to consult the well-known taste of the Reverend Richard Turner, already mentioned as rector of Sweffling. This friendly critic advised further revision, and his own mature opinion coinciding with that thus modestly hinted, he finally rejected the tales I have named altogether; deferred for a further period of eight years his re-appearance as a poetical author; and meantime began "The Parish Register," and gradually finished it and the smaller pieces, which issued with it from the press in 1807.

Since I have been led to mention Mr. Turner in this manner, let me be pardoned for adding, that one of the chief sources of comfort all through my father's residence in Suffolk was his connection with this honoured man. He considered his judgment a sure safeguard and reliance in all cases practical and literary. The peculiar characteristic of his vigorous mind being an interest, not a seeming, but a real interest, in every object of nature and art, he had stored it with multifarious knowledge, and had the faculty of imparting some portion of the interest he felt on all subjects, by the zeal and relish with which he discussed them. With my father he would converse on natural history, as if this had been his whole study; with my mother, on mechanical contrivances and new inventions, for use or ornament, as if that were an exclusive taste; while he would amuse us young folks with well-told anecdotes, and to walk or ride with him was considered our happiest privilege. Mr. Turner is too extensively and honourably known to need any such eulogy as I can offer; but my father's most intimate friend and chosen critic will forgive the effusion of my regard and respect. While at Glemham, as at Parham, my father rarely visited any neighbours except Mr. North and his brother Mr. Long; nor did he often receive any visitors. But one week in every year was to him, and to all his household, a period of peculiar enjoyment—that during which he had Mr. Turner for his guest.

About this time the bishops began very properly to urge all non-resident incumbents to return to their livings; and Mr. Dudley North, willing to retain my father in his neighbourhood, took the trouble to call upon the Bishop of Lincoln, Dr. Prettyman, and to request that Mr. Crabbe might remain in Suffolk; adding, as an argument in favour of the solicited indulgence, his kindness and attention to his present parishioners. But his Lordship would not yield—observing that they of Muston and Allington had a prior claim. "Now," said Mr. North, when he reported his failure, "we must try and procure you an incumbency here"; and one in his own gift becoming vacant, he very obligingly offered it to my father. This living[4] was, however, too small to be held singly, and he

[4] The two Glemhams, both in the gift of Mrs. North, were lately presented to my brother John, who is now the incumbent.

prepared ultimately (having obtained an additional furlough of four years) to return to his own parishes. His strong partiality to Suffolk was not the only motive for desiring to remain in that county, and near to all our relatives on both sides; he would have sacrificed mere personal inclination without hesitation, but he was looking to the interests of his children.

In the autumn of 1801, Mr. North and his brother, having a joint property in the Glemham estate, agreed to divide by selling it; and in October we left this sweet place, and entered a house at Rendham, a neighbouring village, for the four years we were to remain in the East Angles.

In July, 1802, my father paid his last visit to Muston, previous to his final return. We passed through Cambridge in the week of the commencement; and he was introduced by the Vice-Master of Trinity to the present Duke of Rutland, whom he had not seen since he was a child, and to several other public characters. I then saw from the gallery of the Senate House the academical ceremonies in all their imposing effect, and viewed them with the more interest, because I was soon after to be admitted to Trinity. The area below was entirely filled. The late Duchess of Rutland attracted much admiration. There were the Bishops of Lincoln and Bath and Wells, and many others of high rank; but, conspicuous above all, the commanding height and noble bust, and intellectual and dignified countenance of Mr. Pitt. I fancied—perhaps it was only partiality—that there was, in that assembly, another high forehead very like his.

My father haunted the Botanic Garden whenever he was at Cambridge, and he had a strong partiality for the late worthy curator, Mr. James Donn. "Donn is—Donn is ——" said he one day, seeking an appropriate epithet; "a man," said my mother; and it was agreed that it was the very word. And, should any reader of these pages remember that independent, unassuming, but uncompromising character, he will assent to the distinction. He had no little-minded suspicions, or narrow self-interest. He read my father's character at once—felt assured of his honour, and when he rang at the gate for admission to pass the morning in selecting such duplicates of plants as could well be spared from the garden, Donn would receive us with a grave, benevolent smile, which said, "Dear Sir, you are freely welcome to wander where, and to select what, you will—I am sure you will do us no injury."

On our return through Cambridge, I was examined, and entered; and in October, 1803, went to reside. When I left college for the Christmas vacation, I found my father and mother stationed at Aldborough for the winter, and was told of a very singular circumstance which had occurred while I was absent. My father had received a letter from a stranger, signing his name "Aldersey" (dated from Ludlow), stating that, having read his publications, he felt a strong inclination to have the pleasure of his society—that he possessed property enough for both, and requested him to relinquish any engagements he might have of a professional nature, and reside with him. The most remarkable part of the matter was, the perfect coherency with which this strange offer was expressed.

One day about this time, casually stepping into a bookseller's at Ipswich, my father first saw the "Lay of the last Minstrel." A few words only riveted his attention, and he read it nearly through while standing at the counter, observing, "a new and great poet has appeared!" How often have I heard him repeat those striking lines near the commencement of that poem:

> "The lady's gone into her secret cell,
> Jesu Maria! shield us well!"

He was for several years, like many other readers, a cool
admirer of the earlier and shorter poems of what is called the
Lake School; but, even when he smiled at the exceeding
simplicity of the language, evidently found something in it
peculiarly attractive; for there were few modern works
which he opened so frequently—and he soon felt and acknowledged, with the public, that in that simplicity was veiled
genius of the greatest magnitude. Of Burns he was ever as
enthusiastic an admirer as the warmest of his own countrymen. On his high appreciation of the more recent works of
his distinguished contemporaries, it is needless to dwell.[5]

I have not much more to say with respect to my father's
second residence in Suffolk; but I must not dismiss this period
—a considerable one in the sum of his life—without making
some allusion to certain rumours which, long before it
terminated, had reached his own parish of Muston, and dis-
inclined the hearts of many of the country people there to receive him, when he again returned among them, with all the
warmth of former days. When first it was reported among
those villagers by a casual traveller from Suffolk, that Mr.
Crabbe was a *Jacobin*, there were few to believe the story—
"it must be a *loy*, for the rector had always been a good, kind

[5] My brother says on this subject—"He heartily assented to the maxim, that
—allowing a fair time, longer in some cases than in others—a book would
find its proper level; and that a well-filled theatre would form a just opinion of
a play or an actor. Yet he would not timidly wait the decision of the public, but
give his opinion freely. Soon after Waverley appeared, he was in a company
where a gentleman of some literary weight was speaking of it in a disparaging
tone. A lady defended the new novel, but with a timid reserve. Mr. Crabbe
called out, 'Do not be frightened, Madam; you are right: speak your opinion
boldly.' Yet he did not altogether like Sir Walter's principal male characters.
He thought they wanted gentleness and urbanity; especially Quentin Durward,
Halbert Glendinning and Nigel. He said Colonel Mannering's age and peculiar
situation excused his haughtiness; but he disliked fierceness and glorying, and
the trait he especially admired in Prince Henry, was his greatness of mind in
yielding the credit of Hotspur's death to his old companion Falstaff. Henry, at
Agincourt, 'covetous of honour,' was ordinary, he said, to this."

gentleman, and much noticed by *the Duke*"; but by degrees the tale was more and more disseminated, and at length it gained a pretty general credence among a population, which being purely agricultural—and, therefore, connecting every notion of what was praiseworthy with the maintenance of the war that, undoubtedly, had raised agricultural prices to an unprecedented scale—was affected in a manner extremely disagreeable to my father's feelings, and even worldly interests, by such an impression as thus originated. The truth is, that my father never was a politician—that is to say, he never allowed political affairs to occupy much of his mind at any period of his life, or thought either better or worse of any individual for the bias he had received. But he did not, certainly, approve of the *origin* of the war that was raging while he lived at Parham, Glemham, and Rendham; nor did he ever conceal his opinion, that this war might have been avoided—and hence, in proportion to the weight of his local character, he gave offence to persons maintaining the diametrically opposite view of public matters at that peculiar crisis. As to the term *Jacobin*, I shall say only one word. None could have been less fitly applied to him at any period of his life. He was one of the innumerable good men who, indeed, hailed the beginning of the French Revolution, but who execrated its close. No syllable in approbation of Jacobins or Jacobinism ever came from his tongue or from his pen; and as to the "child and champion of Jacobinism," Napoleon had not long pursued his career of ambition, before my father was well convinced that to put *him* down was the first duty of every nation that wished to be happy and free.

With respect to the gradual change which his early sentiments on political subjects in general unquestionably underwent, I may as well, perhaps, say a word or two here; for the topic is one I have no wish to recur to again.

Perhaps the natural tendency of every young man who is conscious of powers and capabilities above his station, is, to adopt what are called popular or liberal opinions. He peculiarly feels the disadvantages of his own class, and is tempted to look with jealousy on all those who, with less natural talent, enjoy superior privileges. But, if this young man should succeed in raising himself by his talents into a higher walk of society, it is perhaps equally natural that he should imbibe aristocratic sentiments: feeling the reward of his exertions to be valuable in proportion to the superiority of his acquired station, he becomes an advocate for the privileges of rank in general, reconciling his desertion of the exclusive interests of his former caste, by alleging the facility of his own rise. And if he should be assisted by patronage, and become acquainted with his patrons, the principle of gratitude, and the opportunity of witnessing the manners of the great, would contribute materially to this change in his feelings. Such is, probably, the natural tendency of such a rise in society; and, in truth, I do not think Mr. Crabbe's case was an exception. The popular opinions of his father were, I think, originally embraced by him rather from the unconscious influence I have alluded to, than from the deliberate conviction of his judgment. But his was no ordinary mind, and he did not desert them merely from the vulgar motive of interest. At Belvoir he had more than once to drink a glass of salt water, because he would not join in Tory toasts. He preserved his early partialities through all his trying time of Tory patronage; and of course he felt, on the whole, a greater political accord with the owner of Glemham and his distinguished guests. But when, in the later portion of his life, he became still more intimate with the highest ranks of society, and mingled with them, not as a young person whose fortune was not made, and who had therefore to assert his independence, but as one whom talent had placed above the suspicion of subserviency; when he felt the full advantages of his rise, and became the rector of a large town, and a magistrate, I think again, the aristocratic and Tory leanings he then showed were rather the effect of these circumstances than of any alteration of judgment founded upon deliberate inquiry and reflection. But of this I am sure, that his own passions were never violently enlisted in any political cause whatever; and that to purely *party* questions he was, first and last, almost indifferent. The dedication of his poems to persons of such opposite opinions arose entirely from motives of personal gratitude and attachment; and he carried his impartiality so far, that I have heard him declare, he thought it very immaterial who were our representatives in parliament, provided they were men of integrity, liberal education, and possessed an adequate stake in the country.

I shall not attempt to defend this apathy on a point of such consequence, but it accounts for circumstances which those who feel no such moderation might consider as aggravated instances of inconsistency. He not only felt an equal regard for persons of both parties, but would willingly have given his vote to either; and at one or two general elections, I believe he actually did so; for example, to Mr. ·Benett, the Whig candidate for Wiltshire, and to Lord Douro and Mr. Croker,[6] the Tory candidates at Aldborough.

[6] I take the liberty of quoting what follows, from a letter with which I have lately been honoured by the Right Honourable J. W. Croker: "I have heard, from those who knew Mr. Crabbe earlier than I had the pleasure of doing (and his communications with me led to the same conclusion), that he never was a violent nor even a zealous politician. He was, as a conscientious clergyman might be expected to be, a church-and-king man; but he seemed to me to think and care less about party politics than any man of his condition in life that I ever met. At one of my elections for Aldeburgh, he happened to be in the neighbourhood, and he did me the honour of attending in the Town Hall, and proposing me. This was, I suppose, the last act of his life which had any reference to politics—at least, to local politics; for it was, I believe, his last visit to the place of his nativity. My opinion of his admirable works, I took the

He says, in a letter on this subject, "With respect to the parties themselves, Whig and Tory, I can but think, two dispassionate, sensible men, who have seen, read, and observed, will approximate in their sentiments more and more; and if they confer together, and argue—not to convince each other, but for pure information, and with a simple desire for the truth—the ultimate difference will be small indeed. The Tory, for instance, would allow that, but for the Revolution in this country, and the noble stand against the arbitrary steps of the house of Stuart, the kingdom would have been in danger of becoming what France once was; and the Whig must also grant, that there is at least an equal danger in an unsettled, undefined democracy; the ever-changing laws of a popular government. Every state is at times on the inclination to change: either the monarchical or the popular interest will predominate; and in the former case, I conceive, the well-meaning Tory will incline to Whiggism—in the latter, the honest Whig will take the part of declining monarchy." I quote this as a proof of the political moderation I have ascribed to him; and I may appeal with safety, on the

liberty of recording in a note on Boswell's Johnson. To that opinion, on reconsideration, and frequent reperusals of his poems, I adhere with increased confidence; and I hope you will not think me presumptuous for adding, that I was scarcely more struck by his genius, than by the amiable simplicity of his manners, and the dignified modesty of his mind. With talents of a much higher order, he realised all that we read of the personal amiability of Gay."

The note on Boswell, to which Mr. Croker here refers, is in these terms:— "The writings of this amiable gentleman have placed him high on the roll of British poets; though his having taken a view of life too minute, too humiliating, too painful, and too just, may have deprived his works of so extensive, or, at least, so brilliant, a popularity as some of his contemporaries have attained; but I venture to believe that there is no poet of his times who will stand higher in the opinion of posterity. He generally deals with 'the short and simple annals of the poor'; but he exhibits them with such a deep knowledge of human nature, with such general ease and simplicity, and such accurate force of expression—whether gay or pathetical,—as, in my humble judgment, no poet except Shakspeare, has excelled."

same head, to the whole tenour, not only of his published works, but of his private conversations and pastoral discourse.

We happened to be on a visit at Aldborough, when the dread of a French invasion was at its height. The old artillery of the fort had been replaced by cannon of a large calibre; and one, the most weighty I remember to have seen, was constantly primed, as an alarm gun. About one o'clock one dark morning, I heard a distant gun at sea; in about ten minutes another, and at an equal interval a third; and then at last, the tremendous roar of the great gun on the fort, which shook every house in the town. After inquiring into the state of affairs, I went to my father's room, and, knocking at the door, with difficulty waked the inmates, and said, "Do not be alarmed, but the French are landing." I then mentioned that the alarm gun had been fired, that horsemen had been despatched for the troops at Ipswich, and that the drum on the quay was then beating to arms. He replied, "Well, my old fellow, you and I can do no good, or we would be among them; we must wait the event." I returned to his door in about three quarters of an hour, to tell him that the agitation was subsiding, and found him fast asleep. Whether the affair was a mere blunder, or there had been a concerted manoeuvre to try the fencibles, we never could learn with certainty; but I remember that my father's coolness on the occasion, when we mentioned it next day, caused some suspicious shakings of the head among the ultra-loyalists of Aldborough.

But the time was now at hand that we were all to return finally to Leicestershire; and when, in the year 1805, we at length bade adieu to Suffolk, and travelled once more to Muston, my father had the full expectation that his changes of residence were at an end, and that he would finish his days in his own old parsonage. I must indulge myself, in closing this chapter, with part of the letter which he received, when on the eve of starting for Leicestershire, from the honoured rector of Sweffling:—

"It would be very little to my credit, if I could close, without much concern, a connection which has lasted nearly twelve years—no inconsiderable part of human life—and never was attended with a cross word or a cross thought. My parish has been attended to with exemplary care; I have experienced the greatest friendship and hospitality from you and Mrs. Crabbe; and I have never visited or left you without bringing away with me the means of improvement. And all this must return no more! Such are the awful conditions upon which the comforts of this life must be held. Accept, my dear sir, my best thanks for your whole conduct towards me, during the whole time of our connection, and my best wishes for a great increase of happiness to you and Mrs. Crabbe, in your removal to the performance of more immediate duties. Your own parishioners will, I am persuaded, be as much gratified by your residence amongst them as mine have been by your residence in Suffolk. Our personal intercourse must be somewhat diminished; yet, I hope, opportunities of seeing each other will arise, and if subjects of correspondence be less frequent, the knowledge of each other's and our families' welfare will always be acceptable information. Adieu, my dear sir, for the present. Your much obliged and faithful friend, R. TURNER."

CHAPTER VIII

1805—1814

WHEN, IN October, 1805, Mr. Crabbe resumed the charge of his own parish of Muston, he found some changes to vex him, and not the less, because he had too much reason to suspect that his long absence from his incumbency had been, partly at least, the cause of them. His cure had been served by respectable and diligent clergymen, but they had been often changed, and some of them had never resided within the parish; and he felt that the binding influence of a settled and permanent minister had not been withdrawn for twelve years with impunity. A Wesleyan missionary had formed a thriving establishment in Muston, and the congregations at the parish church were no longer such as they had been of old. This much annoyed my father; and the warmth with which he began to preach against dissent only irritated himself and others, without bringing back disciples to the fold.

But the progress of the Wesleyans, of all sects the least unfriendly in feeling, as well as the least dissimilar in tenets, to the established church, was, after all, a slight vexation compared to what he underwent from witnessing the much more limited success of a disciple of Huntington in spreading in the same neighbourhood the pernicious fanaticism of his half-crazy master. The *social* and *moral* effects of that new mission were well calculated to excite not only regret, but indignation; and, among other distressing incidents, was the departure from his own household of two servants, a woman and a man, one of whom had been employed by him for twenty years. The man, a conceited ploughman, set up for a Huntingtonian preacher himself; and the woman, whose moral character had been sadly deteriorated since her adoption of the new lights, was at last obliged to be dismissed, in consequence of intolerable insolence. I mention these things, because they may throw light on some passages in my father's later poetry.

By the latter part of the year 1806, Mr. Crabbe had nearly completed his "Parish Register," and the shorter poems that accompanied it, and had prepared to add them to a new edition of his early works; and his desire to give his second son also the benefits of an academical education was, I ought to add, a principal motive for no longer delaying his re-appearance as a poet. He had been, as we have seen, promised, years before, in Suffolk, the high advantage of Mr. Fox's criticism; but now, when the manuscript was ready, he was in office, and in declining health; so that my father felt great reluctance to remind him of his promise. He wrote to the great statesman to say that he could not hope, under such circumstances, to occupy any portion of his valuable time, but that it would afford much gratification if he might be permitted to dedicate the forthcoming volume to Mr. Fox. That warm and energetic spirit, however, was not subdued by all the pressure of his high functions added to that of an incurable disease; and "he repeated an offer," says my father, in his preface, "which though I had not presumed to expect, I was happy to receive." The manuscript was immediately sent to him at St. Anne's Hill; "and," continues Mr. Crabbe, "as I have the information from Lord Holland, and his Lordship's permission to inform my readers, the poem which I have named 'The Parish Register,' was heard by Mr. Fox and it excited interest enough, by some of its parts, to gain for me the benefit of his judgment upon the whole. Whatever he approved the reader will readily believe that I carefully retained; the parts he disliked are totally expunged, and others are substituted, which, I hope, resemble those more conformable to the taste of so admirable a judge. Nor can I deny myself the melancholy satisfaction of adding, that this poem (and more especially the story of Phoebe Dawson, with some parts of the second book), were the last compositions of their kind that engaged and amused the capacious, the candid, the benevolent mind of this great man." In the same preface my father acknowledges his obligations to Mr. Turner. "He, indeed," says Mr. Crabbe, "is the kind of critic for whom every poet should devoutly wish, and the friend whom every man would be happy to acquire. To this gentleman I am indebted more than I am able to express, or than he is willing to allow, for the time he has bestowed upon the attempts I have made."

This preface is dated Muston, September, 1807; and in the same month the volume was published by Mr. Hatchard. It contained, with the earlier series, "The Parish Register," "Sir Eustace Grey," "The Birth of Flattery," and other minor pieces; and its success was not only decided, but nearly unprecedented. By "The Parish Register," indeed, my father must be considered as having first assumed that station among British poets which the world has now settled to be peculiarly his own. The same character was afterwards still more strikingly exemplified and illustrated—but it was henceforth the same; whereas there was but little in the earlier series that could have led to the expectation of such a performance as "The Register." In the former works, a few minute descriptions had been introduced—but here there was nothing but a succession of such descriptions; in them there had been no tale—this was a chain of stories; they were didactic—here no moral inference is directly inculcated: finally, they were regularly constructed poems—this boldly defies any but the very slightest and most transparently artificial connections. Thus differing from his former self, his utter dissimilarity to any other author then enjoying public favour was still more striking; the manner of expression was as entirely his own as the singular minuteness of his delineation, and the strictness of his adherence to the literal truth of nature; and it was now universally admitted, that, with lesser peculiarities, he mingled the conscious strength, and, occasionally, the profound pathos, of a great original poet.

Nor was "Sir Eustace Grey" less admired on other grounds, than "The Parish Register" was for the singular combination of excellences which I have been fairly alluding to, and which called forth the warmest eulogy of the most powerful critical authority of the time, which was moreover considered as the severest. The other periodical critics of the day agreed substantially with the "Edinburgh Review"; and I believe that within two days after the appearance of Mr. Jeffrey's admirable and generous article, Mr. Hatchard sold off the whole of the first edition of these poems.

Abundantly satisfied with the decision of professional critics, he was further encouraged by the approbation of some old friends and many distinguished individuals to whom he had sent copies of his work; and I must gratify myself by inserting a few of their letters to him on this occasion.

From Mr. Bonnycastle.

"Woolwich Common, Oct. 24, 1807.

"DEAR SIR,—Being from home when your kind letter, with a copy of your Poems, arrived, I had no opportunity of answering it sooner, as I should certainly otherwise have done. The pleasure of hearing from you, after a silence of more than twenty-eight years, made me little solicitous to inquire how it has happened that two persons, who have always mutually esteemed each other, should have no intercourse whatever for so long a period. It is sufficient that you are well and happy, and that you have not forgot your old friend; who, you may be assured, has never ceased to cherish the same friendly remembrance of you.—You are as well known in my family as you are pleased to say I am in yours; and whenever you may find it convenient to come to this part of the world, both you and yours may depend upon the most sincere and cordial reception. I have a daughter nearly twenty, a son upon the point of becoming an officer in the engineers and two younger boys, who at this moment are deeply engaged in your poems, and highly desirous of seeing the author, of whom they have so often heard me speak. They are, of course, no great critics; but all beg me to say, that they are much pleased with your beautiful verses, which I promised to read to them again when they have done; having conceded to their eagerness the *prémices* of the treat. It affords me the greatest gratification to find that, in this world of chances, you are so comfortably and honourably established in your profession, and I sincerely hope your sons may be as well provided for. I spent a few days at Cambridge a short time since, and had I known they had been there, I should not have failed making myself known to them, as an old friend of their father's. For myself, I have little to complain of, except the anxiety and fatigue attending the duties of my calling; but as I have lately succeeded to the place of Dr. Hutton, who has resigned the attendance at the academy, this has made it more easy, and my situation as respectable and pleasant as I could have any reason to expect. Life, as my friend Fuseli constantly repeats, is very short, therefore do not delay coming to see us any longer than you can possibly help. Be assured we shall all rejoice at the event.

In the meantime, believe me, my dear Sir, your truly sincere friend,

"J. BONNYCASTLE."

From Mrs. Burke.[1]

"Beaconsfield, Nov. 30, 1807.

"SIR,—I am much ashamed to find that your very kind letter and very valuable present have remained so long unacknowledged. But the truth is, when I received them, I was far from well; and procrastination being one of my natural vices, I have deferred returning you my most sincere thanks for your gratifying my feelings, by your beautiful preface and poems. I have a full sense of their value and your attention. *Your friend* never lost sight of worth and abilities. He found them in you, and was most happy in having it in his power to bring them forward. I beg you, Sir, to believe, and to be assured, that your situation in life was not indifferent to me, and that it rejoices me to know that you are happy. I beg my compliments to Mrs. Crabbe, and my thanks for her remembering that I have had the pleasure of seeing her. I am, Sir, with great respect and esteem, &c.,

"JANE BURKE."

From Dr. Mansel.[2]

"Trinity Lodge, Cambridge, Oct. 29, 1807.

"DEAR SIR,—I could not resist the pleasure of going completely through your delightful poems, before I returned you,

[1] Of this lady, who died in 1812, Mr. Prior says:—"Added to affectionate admiration of Mr. Burke's talents, she possessed accomplishments, good sense, goodness of heart, and a sweetness of manners and disposition, which served to allay many of the anxieties of his career. He repeatedly declared, that 'every care vanished the moment he entered under his own roof.'"—*Life of Burke.*

[2] Afterwards Bishop of Bristol. His Lordship died in 1820.

as I now do, my best thanks for so truly valuable a proof of your remembrance. The testimony of my opinion is but of small importance, when set by the side of those which have already been given of this accession to our standard national poetry; but I must be allowed to say, that so much have I been delighted with the perusal of the incomparable descriptions which you have laid before me; with the easiness and purity of the diction, the knowledge of life and manners, and the vividness of that imagination which could produce, and so well sustain and keep up such charming scenes—that I have found it to be almost the only book of late times which I could read through without making it a sort of duty to do so. Once more, dear Sir, accept of my best thanks for this very flattering remembrance of me; and be assured of my being, with much regard, your faithful, &c.,

"W. L. Mansell."

From Earl Grey.

"Hertford Street, Feb. 28, 1808.

"Sir,—I have many excuses to offer for not having sooner returned my thanks for your letter of the 10th of October, and the valuable present which accompanied it. I did not receive it till I arrived in London, about the middle of the last month, and I waited till I should have had time—for which the first business of an opening session of parliament was not favourable—to read a work from which I anticipated much pleasure. I am now able, at the same time, to offer you my best thanks in sending me the poems you have lately published, and to say that my admiration of the author of the 'Library,' has not been diminished by the perusal of the 'Parish Register,' and the other additional poems. But all other praise must appear insipid after that of Mr. Fox; and I will only add, that I think that highest praise, for such I esteem it, was justly due to you.

M

I well remember the pleasure which I had in meeting you at Mr. Dudley North's, and wish I could look to a revival of it. I have the honour to be, with great regard, Sir, &c.,

"GREY."

From Roger Wilbraham, Esq.

"Stratton Street, May 23, 1808.

"DEAR SIR,—Unless I had heard from our friend, Mr. North, that you had received complimentary letters from most of your friends on your late publication, I should not have thought of adding my name to the number. The only reason for my silence was the fear of assuming much more of a literary character than belongs to me; though, on the score of friendship for the author, and admiration of his works, I will not yield to the most intelligent and sagacious critic. Perhaps, indeed, an earlier letter from me might have been authorised by the various conversations we have had together at Glemham, in which I so frequently took the liberty to urge you not to rest contented with that sprig of bays which your former publications had justly acquired, but to aim at a large branch of thicker foliage. This I can truly say, my dear Sir, you have obtained by universal consent; and I feel considerable pride in having the honour to be known to a person who has afforded so much real delight to a discerning public.—No, no, Sir, when we thought you idle, you were by no means so; you were observing man, and studying his character among the inferior orders of the community; and the varieties that belong to his character you have now described with the most perfect truth, and in the most captivating language. When I took up your book, the novelties of it first attracted my notice, and afterwards I visited my old acquaintances with as much pleasure as ever. The only regret I felt at the end was, that the book was not marked Vol. I; but that may be amended. In which hope I take my leave, assuring you of the very sincere regard, and real admiration of, your most truly and sincerely,

.   "ROGER WILBRAHAM."

From Mr. Canning.

"Stanhope Street, Nov. 13, 1807.

"SIR,—I have deferred acknowledging the civility of your letter, until I should at the same time acknowledge the pleasure which I had derived from the perusal of the volume which accompanied it. I have lately made that volume the companion of a journey into the country. I am now therefore able to appreciate the value of your present, as well as to thank you for your obliging attention in sending it to me. With some of the poems—the 'Village,' particularly—I had been long acquainted; but I was glad to have them brought back to my recollection; and I have read with no less pleasure and admiration those which I now saw for the first time. I have the honour to be, Sir, &c., &c.,

"GEORGE CANNING."

From Lord Holland.

"SIR,—Having been upon a tour in Scotland, I did not receive your book till my arrival at York, and was unwilling to answer your very obliging letter till I read the 'Parish Register' in print. I can assure you that its appearance in this dress has increased my opinion of its beauty: and, as you have done me, very undeservedly, the honour of calling me a judge of such matters, I will venture to say that it seems to me calculated to advance the reputation of the author of the 'Library' and the 'Village,' which, to any one acquainted with those two excellent poems, is saying a great deal. With regard to the very flattering things you are pleased to say of me, I am conscious that your willingness to oblige had blinded your judg-

ment; but cannot conclude my letter without returning you thanks for such expressions of your partiality. I am, Sir, &c.,
"HOLLAND."

To these I may add a letter from Mr. Walter Scott, dated "Ashestiel, October 21st, 1809"—acknowledging the receipt of a subsequent edition of the same volume.

"DEAR SIR,—I am just honoured with your letter, which gives me the more sensible pleasure, since it has gratified a wish of more than twenty years' standing. It is, I think, fully that time since I was, for great part of a very snowy winter, the inhabitant of an old house in the country, in a course of poetical study, so very like that of your admirably painted 'Young Lad,' that I could hardly help saying, 'That's me!' when I was reading the tale to my family. Among the very few books which fell under my hands was a volume or two of Dodsley's Annual Register, one of which contained copious extracts from 'The Village,' and 'The Library,' particularly the conclusion of book first of the former, and an extract from the latter, beginning with the description of the old Romancers. I committed them most faithfully to my memory, where your verses must have felt themselves very strangely lodged, in company with ghost stories, border riding-ballads, scraps of old plays, and all the miscellaneous stuff which a strong appetite for reading, with neither means nor discrimination for selection, had assembled in the head of a lad of eighteen. New publications, at that time, were very rare in Edinburgh, and my means of procuring them very limited; so that, after a long search for the poems which contained these beautiful specimens, and which had afforded me so much delight, I was fain to rest contented with the extracts from the Register, which I could repeat at this moment. You may, therefore, guess my sincere delight when I saw your poems at a later period assume the rank in the public consideration which they so well deserve. It was a triumph to my own immature taste to find I had anticipated the applause of the learned and of the critical, and I became very desirous to offer my *gratulor*, among the more important plaudits which you have had from every quarter. I should certainly have availed myself of the freemasonry of authorship (for our trade may claim to be a mystery as well as Abhorson's) to address to you a copy of a new poetical attempt, which I have now upon the anvil, and I esteem myself particularly obliged to Mr. Hatchard, and to your goodness acting upon his information, for giving me the opportunity of paving the way for such a freedom. I am too proud of the compliments you honour me with, to affect to decline them; and with respect to the comparative view I have of my own labours and yours, I can only assure you, that none of my little folks, about the formation of whose taste and principles I may be supposed naturally solicitous, have ever read any of my own poems; while yours have been our regular evening's amusement. My eldest girl begins to read well, and enters as well into the humour as into the sentiment of your admirable descriptions of human life. As for rivalry, I think it has seldom existed among those who know, by experience, that there are much better things in the world than literary reputation, and that one of the best of these good things is the regard and friendship of those deservedly and generally esteemed for their worth or their talents. I believe many dilettanti authors do cocker themselves up into a great jealousy of anything that interferes with what they are pleased to call their fame; but I should as soon think of nursing one of my own fingers into a whitlow for my private amusement, as encouraging such a feeling. I am truly sorry to observe you mention bad health: those who contribute so much to the improvement as well as the delight of society should escape this evil. I hope, however, that one day your state of health may permit you to view this country. I have very few calls to London, but it will greatly add to the interest of those which may occur, that you will permit me the honour of waiting upon you in my journey, and assuring you, in person, of the early admiration and sincere respect with which I have the honour to be, dear Sir, yours, &c.,

"WALTER SCOTT."

In the manly and sensible views of literature and literary fame expressed in the last of these letters, Mr. Crabbe fully concurred. He enjoyed the sweetness of well-earned credit; but at his mature years, and with his strong religious bias, he was little likely to be intoxicated with the applause of critics. His feelings on this occasion were either not perceptible, or only seen in those simple, open demonstrations of satisfaction which show that no proud exulting spirit lurks within. Of some men it is said, that they are too proud to be vain; but of him it might be said, that the candid manner in which he testified his satisfaction at success, was a proof that, while he felt the pleasure, he felt also its limited value—limited by the consciousness of defects; limited by the consciousness that there were higher, nearer, and dearer interests in life than those of poetical ambition. How gratifying is the contemplation of such success, when it is only accessory to the more substantial pleasures of existence, namely, the consciousness of having fulfilled the duties for which that existence was especially given, and the bright hope that higher and better things than this world can afford await those who have borne the trials of adversity and prosperity with a humble and pious spirit! How poor is such success when it is made "the pearl of great price!"

My brother now residing at Caius College, Cambridge, Mr. Crabbe more than once went thither, and remained a considerable time, dining in that college or Trinity every day, and passing his mornings chiefly in the botanic garden. The new poems, and the remarks of the Reviews, had brought him again under the public eye; so that he was now received, in that seat of learning, not only as a man who had formerly deserved the encouragements of literature, but as one of the popular writers of the day—became an object of attention and curiosity, and added many distinguished names to the number of his acquaintance.

On one occasion, happening to be at Cambridge during the Newmarket season, my father was driven by his son John in a tandem to the course; and though he booked no bets, I have reason to think he enjoyed his ride quite as much as many of of the lads by whom he was surrounded. Ever tenacious of important points of morality, no one looked with a more enlarged and benignant eye upon such juvenilities; it always seemed to me as if his mind was incapable of seeing and apprehending the little in anything.

Our respected friend, Donn, being one of the congregation of the celebrated Mr. Simeon, and having a sincere regard for my father, persuaded him to occupy his pew in Little St. Mary's; hoping, probably, that he might become a convert to his own views of religion. Accordingly, he took his seat there, and paid great attention to the sermon, and on his return from church wrote the substance of it, and preached it at Muston the following Sunday; telling his congregation where he had heard it, in what points he entirely assented to the opinions it contained, and where he felt compelled to differ from the pious author.

He also accompanied the worthy curator to the Book Society, consisting chiefly of inhabitants of the town; and they had the kindness to enrol his name as an honorary member. But few of his friends at Cambridge survive him; Dr. Mansel, Mr. Davis, Mr. Lambert, Mr. Tovell, and Mr. Donn, all died before him. Nowhere do we perceive the effects of times so evidently as in a visit to the universities.

In the beginning of 1809, Dr. Cartwright expressed a wish that my father would prepare some verses, to be repeated at the ensuing meeting of that admirable institution for the benefit of distressed authors, "The Literary Fund"; and it happened that a portion of a work then on the stocks, "The Borough," was judged suitable for the occasion: with some additions, accordingly, it was sent, and spoken at the anniversary, with all the advantage that Mr. Fitzgerald gave to whatever he recited.

Mr. Crabbe was now diligently occupied in finishing this poem, which had been begun while he lived at Rendham; and as our kind friends at Aldborough had invited us to taste the sea air after four years' residence in the centre of the kingdom, my father carried his manuscript for completion, and for the inspection of that judicious friend at Great Yarmouth, without whose council he decided on nothing. Can it be questioned that he trod that beach again, to which he had so often returned after some pleasing event, with somewhat more of honest satisfaction, on account of the distinguished success of his late poems! The term exultation, however, could no longer be applicable; he was now an elderly clergyman, and much too deeply did he feel the responsibilities of life to be "carried off his feet," as the Duchess of Gordon playfully expressed it, by any worldly fascinations. Mr. Turner's opinion of "The Borough" was, upon the whole, highly favourable; but he intimated, that there were portions of the new work which might be liable to rough treatment from the critics, and his decision, in both its parts, was confirmed by the public voice. As soon as we returned to Muston, Mr. Hatchard put it to the press: it was published in 1810, and in 1816 it had attained its sixth edition.

The opinion of the leading Reviews was again nearly unanimous; agreeing that "The Borough" had greater beauties and greater defects than its predecessor, "The Parish Register." With such a decision an author may always be well pleased; for he is sure to take his rank with posterity by his beauties; defects, where there are great and real excellences, serve but to fill critical dissertations. In fact, though the character was still the same, and the blemishes sufficiently obvious, "The Borough" was a great spring upwards. The incidents and characters in "The Parish Register" are but excellent sketches —there is hardly enough matter even in the most interesting description, not even in the story of Phoebe Dawson, to gain a firm hold of the reader's mind—but, in the new publication, there was a sufficient evolution of event and character, not only to please the fancy; but grapple with the heart. I think the "Highwayman's Tale", in the twenty-third letter (Prisons), is an instance in point. We see the virtuous young man, the happy lover, and the despairing felon in succession, and enough of each state to give full force to its contrasts. I know that my father was himself much affected when he drew that picture, as he had been, by his own confession, twice before; once at a very early period (see the "Journal to Mira"), and again when he was describing the terrors of a poor distracted mind, in his Sir Eustace Grey. The tale of the Condemned Felon arose from the following circumstances: while he was struggling with poverty in London, he had some reason to fear that the brother of a very intimate friend, a wild and desperate character, was in Newgate under condemnation for a robbery. Having obtained permission to see the man who bore the same name, a glance at once relieved his mind from the dread of beholding his friend's brother; but still he never forgot the being he then saw before him. He was pacing the cell, or small yard, with a quick and hurried step; his eye was as glazed and abstracted as that of a corpse:—

"Since his dread sentence, nothing seem'd to be
As once it was; seeing he could not see,
Not hearing hear aright . . .
Each sense was palsied!"

In the common-place book of the author the following observations were found relative to "The Borough"; and they apply perhaps with still more propriety to his succeeding poems:—"I have chiefly, if not exclusively, taken my subjects and characters from that order of society where the least display of vanity is generally to be found, which is placed between the humble and the great. It is in this class of mankind that more originality of character, more variety of fortune, will be met with; because, on the one hand, they do not live in the eye of the world, and, therefore, are not kept in awe by the dread of observation and indecorum; neither, on the other, are they debarred by their want of means from the cultivation of mind and the pursuits of wealth and ambition, which are necessary to the development of character displayed in the variety of situations to which this class is liable."

The preface to "The Borough" shows how much his mind was engrossed and irritated, at this period, by the prevalence of Mr. Huntington's injurious doctrines in his neighbourhood, and even in his household. And his "Letter on Sects" not only produced a ridiculous threat from a Swedenborgian (dated from Peterborough) of personal chastisement; but occasioned a controversy between the writer and the editor of the "Christian Observer," which appeared likely to become public. It ended, however, in mutual expressions of entire respect; and I am happy to think that the difference in their views was only such as different circumstances of education, &c., might cause between two sincere Christians.

"The Borough" was dedicated, in very grateful terms, to the present Duke of Rutland; from whom, and all the members of that noble family, more especially the Duchess Dowager, my father continued to receive polite attention during the whole period of his residence at Muston. At Belvoir he enjoyed from time to time the opportunity of mixing with many public characters, who, if their pursuits and turn of mind differed widely from his own, were marked by the stamp and polish of perfect gentlemen; and no one could appreciate the charm of high manners more fully than he whose muse chose to depict, with rare exceptions, those of the humbler classes of society. He was particularly pleased and amused with the conversation of the celebrated "Beau Brummell."

My brother and I (now both clergymen), having curacies in the neighbourhood, still lived at Muston, and all the domestic habits which I have described at Glemham were continued, with little exception. My father having a larger and better garden than in Suffolk, passed much of his time amongst his choice weeds, and though (my mother growing infirm) we did not take a family walk as heretofore, yet in no other respect was that perfect domestication invaded. When the evening closed, winter or summer, my father read aloud from the store which Mr. Colburn, out of his circulating library, sent and renewed, and nineteen in every twenty books of these were, as of old, novels; while, as regularly, my brother took up his pencil, and amused our unoccupied eyes by some design strikingly full of character; for he had an untaught talent in this way, which wanted only the mechanical portion of the art to give him a high name among the masters of the time. One winter he copied and coloured some hundreds of insects for his father, from expensive plates sent for his inspection by the Vice-Master of Trinity; and this requiring no genius but pains only, I joined in the employment. "Now, old fellows," said my father, "it is my duty to read to you."

The landscape around Muston was open and uninteresting. Here were no groves nor dry green lanes, nor gravel roads to tempt the pedestrian in all weather; but still the parsonage and its premises formed a pretty little oasis in the clayey desert. Our front windows looked full on the churchyard, by no means like the common forbidding receptacles of the dead, but truly ornamental ground; for some fine elms partially concealed the small beautiful church and its spire, while the eye, travelling through their stems, rested on the banks of a stream and a picturesque old bridge.[3] The garden enclosed the other two sides of this churchyard; but the crown of the whole was a Gothic archway, cut through a thick hedge and many boughs, for through this opening, as in the deep frame of a picture, appeared, in the centre of the aerial canvas, the unrivalled Belvoir.

Though we lived just in the same domestic manner when alone, yet my father visited much more frequently than in Suffolk; besides the Castle, he occasionally dined at Sir Robert Heron's, Sir William Welby's, with Dr. Gordon, Dean of Lincoln, the Rector of the next village, and with others of the neighbouring clergy. And we had now and then a party at our house; but where the mistress is always in ill-health and the master a poet, there will seldom be found the nice tact

---

[3] See the lines on Muston in "The Borough," Letter 1:—

"Seek then thy garden's shrubby bound, and look
As it steals by, upon the bordering brook;
That winding streamlet, limpid, lingering, slow,
Where the reeds whisper when the zephyrs blow," &c.

to conduct these things just as they ought to be. My father was conscious of this; and it gave him an appearance of inhospitality quite foreign to his nature. If he neither shot nor danced, he appeared well pleased that we brought him a very respectable supply of game, and that we sometimes passed an evening at the assembly-room of our metropolis, Grantham. My mother's declining state becoming more evident, he was, if possible, more attentive to her comforts than ever. He would take up her meals when in her own room, and sometimes cook her some little nicety for supper, when he thought it would otherwise be spoiled. "What a father you have!" was a grateful exclamation often on her lips.

In the early part of the year 1812, Mr. Crabbe published—(with a dedication to the Duchess Dowager of Rutland)—his "Tales in Verse"; a work as striking as, and far less objectionable than, its predecessor, "The Borough"; for here no flimsy connection is attempted between subjects naturally separate; nor consequently, was there such temptation to compel into verse matters essentially prosaic. The new tales had also the advantage of ampler scope and development than his preceding ones. The public voice was again highly favourable, and some of these relations were spoken of with the utmost warmth of commendation; as, the "Parting Hour," "The Patron," "Edward Shore," and "The Confidant."

My father wrote a letter at the time to Mr. Scott, and sent him a copy of all his works. His brother poet honoured him with the following beautiful reply:—

"Abbotsford, June 1, 1812.
"MY DEAR SIR,—I have too long delayed to thank you for the most kind and acceptable present of your three volumes. Now am I doubly armed, since I have a set for my cabin at Abbotsford as well as in town; and, to say truth, the auxiliary

copy arrived in good time, for my original one suffers as much by its general popularity among my young people as a popular candidate from the hugs and embraces of his democratical admirers. The clearness and accuracy of your painting, whether natural or moral, renders, I have often remarked, your works generally delightful to those whose youth might render them insensible to the other beauties with which they abound. There are a sort of pictures—surely the most valuable, were it but for that reason—which strike the uninitiated as much as they do the connoisseur, though the last alone can render reason for his admiration. Indeed, our old friend Horace knew what he was saying, when he chose to address his ode, "*Virginibus puerisque*"; and so did Pope when he told somebody he had the mob on the side of his version of Homer, and did not mind the high-flying critics at Button's. After all, if a faultless poem could be produced, I am satisfied it would tire the critics themselves, and annoy the whole reading world with the spleen.

"You must be delightfully situated in the Vale of Belvoir— a part of England for which I entertain a special kindness, for the sake of the gallant hero, Robin Hood, who, as probably you will readily guess, is no small favourite of mine; his indistinct ideas concerning the doctrine of *meum* and *tuum* being no great objection to an outriding borderer. I am happy to think that your station is under the protection of the Rutland family, of whom fame speaks highly. Our lord of the 'cairn and the scaur' waste wilderness and hundred hills, for many a league round, is the Duke of Buccleugh, the head of my clan; a kind and benevolent landlord, a warm and zealous friend, and the husband of a lady, 'comme il y en a peu.' They are both great admirers of Mr. Crabbe's poetry, and would be happy to know him, should he ever come to Scotland, and venture into the Gothic halls of a border chief. The early and uniform kindness of this family, with the friendship of the late and present Lord Melville, enabled me, some years ago, to exchange my toils as a barrister for the lucrative and respectable situation of one of the clerks of our supreme court, which only requires a certain routine of official duty, neither laborious nor calling for any exertion of the mind. So that my time is entirely at my own command, except when I am attending the court, which seldom occupies more than two hours of the morning during sitting. I besides hold *in commendam* the sheriffdom of Ettrick Forest,—which is now no forest;—so that I am a sort of pluralist as to law appointments, and have, as Dogberry says, two gowns, and every thing handsome about me. I have often thought it is the most fortunate thing for bards like you and me, to have an established profession and professional character, to render us independent of those worthy gentlemen, the retailers, or, as some have called them, the midwives of literature, who are so much taken up with the abortions they bring into the world, that they are scarcely able to bestow the proper care upon young and flourishing babes like ours. That, however, is only a mercantile way of looking at the matter; but did any of my sons show poetical talent, of which, to my great satisfaction, there are no appearances, the first thing I should do, would be to inculcate upon him the duty of cultivating some honourable profession, and qualify himself to play a more respectable part in society than the mere poet. And as the best corollary of my doctrine, I would make him get your tale of 'The Patron,' by heart from beginning to end. It is curious enough that you should have republished 'The Village' for the purpose of sending your young men to college, and I should have written the 'Lay of the Last Minstrel' for the purpose of buying a new horse for the Volunteer Cavalry. I must now send this scrawl into town to get a frank, for God knows it is not worthy of postage. With the warmest wishes for your health, prosperity, and increase of fame—though it needs not—I remain most sincerely and affectionately yours,

"WALTER SCOTT."

My father's answer to this kind communication has been placed in my hands; and I feel convinced that no offence will be taken by any one at an extract which I am about to give from it. The reader will presently discover, that my father had no real cause to doubt the regard of the noble person to whom he alludes, and who subsequently proved a most efficient patron and friend. Mr. Crabbe says to Sir Walter:

"Accept my very sincere congratulations on your clerkship, and all things beside which you have had the goodness to inform me of. It is indeed very pleasant to me to find that the author of works that give me and thousands delight, is so totally independent of the midwives you speak of. Moreover, I give you joy of an honourable intercourse with the noble family of Buccleugh, whom you happily describe to me, and by whose notice or rather notice of my book, I am much favoured. With respect to my delightful situation in the Vale of Belvoir, and under the very shade of the castle, I will not say that your imagination has created its beauties, but I must confess it has enlarged and adorned them. The Vale of Belvoir is flat and unwooded, and save that an artificial straight-lined piece of water, and one or two small streams, intersect it, there is no other variety than is made by the different crops, wheat, barley, beans. The castle, however, is a noble place, and stands on one entire hill, taking up its whole surface, and has a fine appearance from the window of my parsonage, at which I now sit, at about a mile and a half distance. The duke also is a duke-like man, and the duchess a very excellent lady. They have great possessions, and great patronage, *but*—you see this unlucky particle, in one or other of Horne Tooke's senses, will occur—*but* I am now of the *old race*. And what then?—Well, I will explain. Thirty years since I was taken to Belvoir by its late possessor, as a domestic chaplain. I read the service on a Sunday, and fared sumptuously every day. At that time, the Chancellor, Lord Thurlow, gave me a rectory in Dorsetshire, small, but a living; this the duke taught me to disregard as a provision, and promised better things. While I lived with him on this pleasant footing I observed many persons in the neighbourhood who came occasionally to dine, and were civilly received: 'How do you do, Dr. Smith? How is Mrs. Smith?'—'I thank your Grace, well': and so they took their venison and claret. 'Who are these?' said I to a young friend of the duke's. 'Men of the *old race*, Sir; people whom the *old duke* was in the habit of seeing—for some of them he had done something, and had he yet lived all had their chance. They now make way for us, but keep up a sort of connection.' The son of the *old duke* of that day and I were of an age to a week; and with the wisdom of a young man I looked distantly on his death and my own. I went into Suffolk and married, with decent views, and prospects of views more enlarging. His Grace went into Ireland—and died. Mrs. Crabbe and I philosophised as well as we could; and after some three or four years, Lord Thurlow, once more at the request of the Duchess Dowager, gave me the crown livings I now hold, on my resignation of that in Dorsetshire. They were at that time worth about 70*l*. or 80*l*. a-year more than that, and now bring me about 400*l*.; but a long minority ensued,—new connections were formed; and when, some few years since, I came back into this country, and expressed a desire of inscribing my verses to the duke, I obtained leave, indeed, but I almost repented the attempt, from the coldness

N

of the reply. Yet, recollecting that great men are beset with applicants of all kinds, I acquitted the duke of injustice, and determined to withdraw myself, as one of the *old race,* and give way to stronger candidates for notice. To this resolution I kept strictly, and left it entirely to the family whether or no I should consider myself as a stranger, who, having been disappointed in his expectation, by unforeseen events, must take his chance, and ought to take it patiently. For reasons I have no inclination to canvass, his Grace has obligingly invited me, and I occasionally meet his friends at the castle, without knowing whether I am to consider that notice as the promise of favour, or as favour in itself,—I have two sons, both in orders, partly from a promise given to Mrs. Crabbe's family that I would bring them up precisely alike, and partly because I did not know what else to do with them. They will share a family property that will keep them from pining upon a curacy. And what more?—I must not perplex myself with conjecturing. You find, Sir, that you are much the greater man; for except what Mr. Hatchard puts into my privy purse, I doubt whether 600*l.* be not my total receipts; but he at present helps us, and my boys being no longer at college, I can take my wine without absolutely repining at the enormity of the cost. I fully agree with you respecting the necessity of a profession for a youth of moderate fortune. Woe to the lad of genius without it! and I am flattered by what you mention of my *Patron.* Your praise is current coin."

In the summer of 1813, my mother, though in a very declining state of health, having a strong inclination to see London once more, a friend in town procured us those very eligible rooms for sight-seers, in Osborne's Hotel, Adelphi, which were afterwards occupied by their sable majesties of Otaheite. We entered London in the beginning of July, and returned at the end of September. My mother being too infirm to accompany us in our pedestrian expeditions, they were sometimes protracted to a late hour, and then we dropped in and dined at any coffee-house that was near. My father's favourite resorts were the botanic gardens, where he passed many hours; and in the evenings he sometimes accompanied us to one of the minor theatres, the larger being closed. He did not seem so much interested by theatrical talent as I had expected; but he was one evening infinitely diverted at the Lyceum by Liston's Solomon Wiseacre, in "Sharp and Flat," especially where he reads the letter of his dear Dorothy Dimple, and applies his handkerchief to his eyes, saying, "It is very foolish, but I cannot help it." He pronounced Liston "a true genius in his way."

Mr. Dudley North called upon my father, and he had again the pleasure of renewing his intercourse with that early friend and patron, dining with him several times during our stay.

One morning, to our great satisfaction, the servant announced Mr. Bonnycastle. A fine, tall, elderly man cordially shook hands with my father; and we had, for the first time, the satisfaction of seeing one whose name had been from childhood familiar to us. He and my father had, from some accidental impediment, not seen one another since their days of poverty, and trial, and drudgery; and now, after thirty-three years, when they met again, both were in comparative affluence, both had acquired a name and reputation, and both were in health. Such meetings rarely occur. He entertained us with a succession of anecdotes, admirably told, and my father went as frequently to Woolwich as other engagements would permit.

I have already mentioned, that, ever mindful when in town of his early struggle and providential deliverance, he sedulously sought out some objects of real distress. He now went to

the King's Bench, and heard the circumstances that incarcer-
ated several of the inmates, and rejoiced in administering the
little relief he could afford. We were not with him on these
occasions; but I knew incidentally that he was several mornings engaged in this way.

Soon after our return to Muston, my father was requested
by the Rev. Dr. Brunton, of Edinburgh, the husband of the
celebrated novelist, to contribute to a new collection of
psalmody, then contemplated by some leading clergymen
of the Church of Scotland. He consulted Sir Walter Scott,
and received the following interesting letter:

"MY DEAR SIR,—I was favoured with your kind letter some
time ago. Of all people in the world, I am least entitled to demand regularity of correspondence; for being, one way and
another, doomed to a great deal more writing than suits my
indolence, I am sometimes tempted to envy the reverend
hermit of Prague, confessor to the niece of Queen Gorboduc,
who never saw either pen or ink. Mr. Brunton is a very
respectable clergyman of Edinburgh, and I believe the work in
which he has solicited your assistance is one adopted by the
General Assembly, or Convocation, of the Kirk. I have no
notion that he has any individual interest in it; he is a well-
educated and liberal-minded man, and generally esteemed, I
have no particular acquaintance with him myself, though we
speak together. He is at this very moment sitting on the
outside of the bar of our supreme court, within which I am
fagging as a clerk; but as he is hearing the opinion of the
judges upon an action for augmention of stipend to him and
to his brethren, it would not, I conceive, be a very favourable
time to canvass a literary topic. But you are quite safe with
him; and having so much command of scriptural language,
which appears to me essential to the devotional poetry of

Christians, I am sure you can assist his purpose much more than any man alive.

"I think those hymns which do not immediately recall the warm and exalted language of the Bible are apt to be, however elegant, rather cold and flat for the purposes of devotion. You will readily believe that I do not approve of the vague and indiscriminate scripture language which the fanatics of old and the modern Methodists have adopted; but merely that solemnity and peculiarity of diction, which at once puts the reader and hearer upon his guard as to the purpose of the poetry. To my Gothic ear, indeed, the *Stabat Mater,* the *Dies Irae,* and some of the other hymns of the Catholic church, are more solemn and affecting than the fine classical poetry of Buchanan: the one has the gloomy dignity of a Gothic church, and reminds us instantly of the worship to which it is dedicated; the other is more like a Pagan temple, recalling to our memory the classical and fabulous deities. This is, probably, all referable to the association of ideas—that is, if 'the association of ideas' continues to be the universal pick-lock of all metaphysical difficulties, as it was when I studied moral philosophy —or to any other more fashionable universal solvent which may have succeeded to it in reputation. Adieu, my dear Sir. I hope you and your family will long enjoy all happiness and prosperity. Never be discouraged from the constant use of your charming talent. The opinions of reviewers are really too contradictory to found anything upon them, whether they are favourable or otherwise; for it is usually their principal object to display the abilities of the writers of the critical lucubrations themselves. Your Tales are universally admired here. I go but little out, but the few judges whose opinions I have been accustomed to look up to are unanimous. Ever yours, most truly,

"WALTER SCOTT."

I know not whether my father ever ventured to engage in the work patronised by Dr. Brunton. That same autumn, an event occurred which broke up the family, and spoiled, if it did not entirely terminate, the domestic habits of years. My mother died October 21st, in her sixty-third year, and was buried in the chancel of Muston. During a long period before her departure, her mind had been somewhat impaired by bodily infirmities; and at last it sank under the severity of the disease. She possessed naturally a great share of penetration and acuteness; a firm unflinching spirit, and very warm and feeling heart. She knew the worth of her husband; and was grateful for his kindness; for she had only to express her wishes and his own inclinations, if at variance, were cheerfully sacrificed. "Never," said her own sister, "was there a better husband, except that he was too indulgent." But so large a portion of her married life was clouded by her lamentable disorder, that I find written by my father on the outside of a beautiful letter of her own, dated long before this calamity: "Nothing can be more sincere than this, nothing more reasonable and affectionate; and yet happiness was denied."

Perhaps it was a fortunate circumstance for my father, that anxiety and sorrow brought on an alarming illness two days after her decease; for any other calamity occurring at the same time with this heaviest of human ills, divides and diverts its sting. And yet, I am not sure that his own danger had this absorbing effect; for he appeared regardless of life, and desired, with the utmost coolness, that my mother's grave might not be closed till it was seen whether he should recover. The disease bore a considerable resemblance to acute cholera without sickness, and was evidently, at last, carrying him off rapidly. At length emetics were fortunately tried, although he had always a great aversion to this species of medicine, and the effect was palpably beneficial, though his recovery was very gradual. His demeanour, while the danger lasted, was that of perfect humility, but of calm hope, and unshaken firmness.

A very short time after he resumed his duties, a letter arrived from the Duke of Rutland, offering him the living of Trowbridge, in Wiltshire, of which his Grace had the alternate presentation. To this offer, of which the Duke had at first rather mistaken the value, as compared with Muston, &c., and which my father had, though with much gratitude, hesitated to accept, his noble patron afterwards added that of the incumbency of Croxton, near Belvoir; and, the proposition being then accepted, we prepared to vacate Muston. And my father looked to a new residence without that feeling of regret which generally accompanies even an advantageous removal in later life; for, with a strong attachment to some very friendly and estimable individuals in the vicinity, he felt the change produced by the late event in every part of the house and premises. His garden had become indifferent to him, nor was that occupation ever resumed again: besides, that diversity of religious sentiment, which I mentioned before, had produced a coolness in some of his parishioners, which he felt the more painfully, because whatever might be their difference of opinion, he was ever ready to help and oblige them all by medical and other aid to the utmost extent of his power. They carried this unkind feeling so far as to ring the bells for his successor, before he himself had left the residence.

Before he quitted Leicestershire he witnessed a scene of hospitality at the castle which has not often been exceeded in magnificence. In January, 1814, the infant heir of the House of Rutland was publicly baptised in the chapel of Belvoir, by the Archbishop of Canterbury, Dr. Manners Sutton, himself a near branch of the ducal family, and of whom my father was accustomed to say, that he carried as much personal grace and dignity about with him as any individual he ever met with. On this high occasion the Prince Regent and Duke of York were present as sponsors. A variety of magnificent entertainments ensued; and my father, who was one of the company, had the honour of being presented, for the second time, to his late Majesty, and to the Duke of York, by both of whom he was received in a very flattering manner.

Before finally quitting Leicestershire, my father paid a short visit to his sister at Aldborough, from whom he was about to be still more widely divided; and one day was given to a solitary ramble among the scenery of bygone years—Parham and the woods of Glemham, then in the first blossom of May. He did not return until night and in his note-book I find the following brief record of this mournful visit:

"Yes, I behold again the place,
    The seat of joy, the source of pain;
It brings in view the form and face
    That I must never see again.

The night-bird's song that sweetly floats
    On this soft gloom—this balmy air,
Brings to the mind her sweeter notes
    That I again must never hear.

Lo! yonder shines that window's light,
    My guide, my token, heretofore;
And now again it shines as bright,
    When those dear eyes can shine no more.

Then hurry from this place away!
  It gives not now the bliss it gave:
For Death has made its charm his prey,
  And joy is buried in her grave."

I may introduce, in connection with the above, some lines
which were long afterwards found written on a paper in which
my dear mother's wedding-ring, nearly worn through before
she died, was wrapped:

"The ring so worn, as you behold,
  So thin, so pale, is yet of gold:
The passion such it was to prove;
  Worn with life's cares, love yet was love."

On the 3rd of June, 1814, he was inducted to Trowbridge church by the Rev. Mr. Fletcher. His diary has,
among others, the following very brief entries:—"5th June,—
first sermon at Trowbridge. 8th, Evening,—solitary walk—
night—change of opinion—easier, better, happier." To what
these last words refer, I shall not guess; but I well remember
that, even after he had mingled with the lively society of
Trowbridge, he was subject to very distressing fits of melancholy. My brother and I did not for some little time follow
him to that place. The evening of our arrival, seeing us conversing cheerfully as we walked together in the garden before
his window, it seemed to have brought back to his memory
the times when he was not alone: for happening to look up,
I saw him regarding us very earnestly, and he appeared deeply
affected. That connection had been broken, which no other
relationship can supply. These visitations of depression were,
however, gradually softened;—he became contented and
cheerful, and I hope I may add, positively happy.

CHAPTER IX

1814—1819

WHEN MY brother and myself arrived, on the occasion already alluded to, within a mile of Trowbridge, my father appeared on the road, having walked out to meet us; and, as he returned with us in the chaise, the manner in which he pointed out various houses to our notice satisfied us that he had met with a very gratifying reception among the principal inhabitants of his new parish. On the very night of his coming to Trowbridge, he had been most cordially received by the family of the late Mr. Waldron; and there, but not there only, we found the foundations already laid of intimacy, that soon ripened into friendship which death alone could break; for such casual variations of humour as he was subject to, serve only to prove the strength of the sentiment that survived them.

We were soon satisfied that Mr. Crabbe had made a wise and happy choice in this change of residence. While my mother lived, her infirm health forbade her mingling much in society, nor, with her to care for, did he often miss it; but he was naturally disposed for, and calculated to find pleasure in, social intercourse; and after his great loss, the loneliness of Muston began to depress him seriously. In answering the Duke of Rutland's kind letter, offering him the rectory of Trowbridge, he said, "It is too true that Muston is no longer what is has been to me: here I am now a solitary with a social disposition,—a hermit without a hermit's resignation." What wonder that he was healthfully excited by the warm reception he was now experiencing among the most cultivated families of Trowbridge and its vicinity: by the attractive attentions of the young and gay among them, in particular, who, finding the old satirist in many things very different from what they had looked for, hastened to show a manifest partiality for his manners, as well as admiration of his talents? We were surprised, certainly, as well as delighted, to observe the tempered exuberance to which, ere many weeks had passed, his spirits, lately so sombre and desponding, were raised,—how lively and cheerful he appeared in every company, pleased with all about him, and evidently imparting pleasure wherever he went.

But a physical change that occurred in his constitution, at the time of the severe illness that followed close on my mother's death, had, I believe, a great share in all these happy symptoms. It always seemed to be his own opinion that at that crisis his system had, by a violent effort, thrown off some weight or obstruction which had been, for many years previously, giving his bodily condition the appearances of a gradual decline,—afflicting him with occasional fits of low fever, and vexatiously disordering his digestive organs. In those days, "life is as tedious as a twice-told tale," was an expression not seldom in his mouth; and he once told me, he felt that he could not possibly live more than six or seven years. But now it seemed that he had recovered not only the enjoyment of sound health, but much of the vigour and spirit of youthful feelings. Such a renovation of health and strength at sixty is rare enough; and never, I believe, occurs unless there has been much temperance in the early period of life. Perhaps, he had never looked so well, in many respects, as he did about this time; his temples getting more bare, the height of his well-developed forehead appeared as increased, and more than ever like one of those heads by which Wilkie makes so many converts to the beauty of human decay. He became stouter in person than he had been, though without fatness; and, although he began to stoop, his limbs and motions were strong and active.

Notwithstanding his flattering reception among the principal people of the place, he was far from being much liked, for some years, by his new parishioners in general: nor, in truth, is it at all difficult to account for this. His immediate predecessor, the curate of the previous rector, had been endeared to the more serious inhabitants by warm zeal and a powerful talent for preaching extempore, and had moreover, been so universally respected, that the town petitioned the Duke of Rutland to give him the living. His Grace's refusal had irritated many even of those who took little interest in the qualifications of their pastor, and engendered a feeling bordering on ill-will, towards Mr. Crabbe himself, which was heightened by the prevalence of some reports so ridiculous, that I am almost ashamed to notice them; such as, that he was a dissipated man—a dandy—even a gambler. And then, when he appeared among them, the perfect openness of his nature,— that, perhaps, impolitic frankness which made him at all times scorn the assumption of a scruple which he did not really feel, led him to violate occasionally, what were considered, among many classes in that neighbourhood, the settled laws of clerical decorum. For example, though little delighting in such scenes, except as they were partaken by kind and partial friends, he might be seen occasionally at a concert, a ball, or even a play. Then, even in the exercise of his unwearied and extensive charity, he often so conducted himself as to neutralise, in coarse and bad minds, all the natural movements of gratitude; mixing the clergyman too much with the almsgiver, and reading a lecture, the severity of which, however just, was more thought of than the benefaction it accompanied. He, moreover, soon after his arrival, espoused the cause of a candidate for the county representation, to whom the manufacturing interest, the prevalent one in his parish, was extremely hostile. Lastly, to conclude this long list, Mr. Crabbe, in a town remarkable for diversity of sects and warmth of discussion, adhered for a season unchanged to the same view of scriptural doctrines which had latterly found little favour even at Muston. As he has told us of his own Rector, in the Tales of the Hall:—

> " 'A moral teacher!' some contemptuous cried;
> He smiled, but nothing of the fact denied;
> Nor, save by his fair life, to charge so strong replied.
> Still, though he bade them not on aught rely
> That was their own, but all their worth deny,
> They call'd his pure advice his cold morality,
> 'Heathens,' they said, 'can tell us right from wrong,
> But to a Christian higher points belong.' "

But, while these things were against him, there were two or three traits in his character which wrought slowly, but steadily, in his favour. One was his boldness and uncompromising perseverance in the midst of opposition and reproach. During the violence of that contested election, while the few friends of Mr. Benett were almost in danger of their lives, he was twice assailed by a mob of his parishioners, with hisses and the most virulent abuse. He replied to their formidable menaces by "rating them roundly"; and though he was induced to retire by the advice of some friends, who hastened to his succour, yet this made no change in his vote, habits, or conduct. He continued to support Mr. Benett; he walked in the streets always alone, and just as frequently as before; and spoke as fearlessly. Mr. Canon Bowles says, in a letter to the present writer:

"A riotous, tumultuous, and most appalling mob, at the time of election, besieged his house, when a chaise was at the door, to prevent his going to the poll and giving his vote in favour of my most worthy friend, John Benett of Pyt House, the present member for the county. The mob threatened to destroy the chaise and tear him to pieces, if he attempted to set out. In the face of the furious assemblage, he came out calmly, told them they might kill him if they chose, but, whilst alive, nothing should prevent his giving a vote at the election, according to his promise and principles, and set off, undisturbed and unhurt, to vote for Mr. Benett."

He manifested the same decision respecting his religious opinions; for one or two reproachful letters made no impression, nor altered his language in the least. Such firmness, where it is the effect of principle, is sure to gain respect from all Englishmen. But mildness was as natural to him as his fortitude; and this, of course, had a tendency to appease enmity even at its height. A benevolent gentle heart was seen in his manner and countenance, and no occasional hastiness of temper could conceal it;—and then it soon became known that no one left his house unrelieved.

But, above all, the liberality of his conduct with respect to dissenters brought a counter-current in his favour. Though he was warmly attached to the established church, he held that

"A man's opinion was his own, his due
And just possession, whether false or true";[1]

[1] He wrote thus to a friend on the subject:—"Thousands and tens of thousands of sincere and earnest believers in the Gospel of our Lord, and in the general contents of Scripture, seeking its meaning with veneration and prayer, agree, I cannot doubt, in essentials, but differ in many points, and in some which unwise and uncharitable persons deem of much importance; nay, think that there is no salvation without them. Look at the good—good, comparatively speaking—just, pure, pious; the patient and suffering amongst recorded characters—and were they not of different opinions in many articles of their faith? and can we suppose their heavenly Father will select from this number a few, a very few, and that for their assent to certain tenets, which causes, independent of any merit of their own, in all probability, led them to embrace?"

and in all his intercourse with his much-divided parishioners he acted upon this principle, visiting and dealing indiscriminately, and joining the ministers of the various denominations in every good work. In the course of a few years, therefore, not only all opposition died away, but he became generally and cordially esteemed. They who differed from him admitted that he had a right also to his own religious and political opinions. His integrity and benevolence were justly appreciated; his talents acknowledged, and his disposition loved.

In the spring of 1815, my brother and I, thinking it probable that we might soon settle, for life, each in some village parsonage, and that this was the only opportunity of seeing something of our native country—leaving my father in sound health and among attached friends, absorbed by his duties, his new connections and amusements—quitted Trowbridge about the same time, and continued absent from it, sometimes in London together, sometimes apart in distant places in the kingdom, for nearly two years. In that interval, though we constantly corresponded, I saw my father only twice.

Calling, one day, at Mr. Hatchard's, in Piccadilly, he said, "Look round," and pointed to his inner room; and there stood my father, reading intently, as his manner was—with his knees somewhat bent, insensible to all around him. How homelike was the sight of that venerable white head among a world of strangers! He was engaged, and I was leaving town; and, after appointing a day to meet at Beccles, and a short cheerful half hour, we parted.

When the time arrived, he joined my brother and me at Beccles, at the house of his kind sister-in-law, Miss Elmy; where, after staying about a week, and being introduced to Lady Byron, who attracted his just admiration, he left us *via*

Aldborough, and returned into Wiltshire. This was about the end of October, 1816.

I cannot pass this date—October, 1816—without offering a remark or two, suggested by my father's diary and note-book of that period. He was peculiarly fond of the society and correspondence of females: all his most intimate friends, I think, were ladies; and I believe no better proof could be given of the delicacy and purity of his mind and character. He loved the very failings of the female mind: men in general appeared to him too stern, reserved, unyielding and worldly; and he ever found relief in the gentleness, the tenderness, and the unselfishness of woman. Many of his chosen female friends were married, but this was not uniformly the case; and will it seem wonderful, when we consider how he was situated at this time, that with a most affectionate heart, a peculiar attachment to female society, and with unwasted passions, Mr. Crabbe, though in his sixty-second year, should have again thought of marriage? He could say with Shakespeare's good old Adam—I quote lines which, for their surpassing beauty, he himself never could read steadily—

> "Though I look old, yet am I strong and lusty;
> For in my youth I never did apply
> Hot and rebellious liquors to my blood;
> Nor did not with unbashful forehead woo
> The means of weakness and debility:
> Therefore, my age is as a lusty winter,
> Frosty but kindly."

Moreover, a poet's mind is proverbially always young. If, therefore, youth and beauty could more than once warm his imagination to outrun his prudence—for, surely, the union of youth and beauty with a man of such age can never be *wise*—I feel satisfied that no one will be seriously shocked with such an evidence of the freshness of his feelings. The critics of his last publication bestowed some good-natured raillery on the warmth with which he there expressed himself on certain subjects—the increased tenderness of his love-scenes especially—and there occurred various incidents in his own later history that might afford his friends fair matter for a little innocent jesting: but none that knew him ever regarded him with less respect on account of this pardonable sort of weakness; and though *love* might be out of the question, I believe he inspired feelings of no ordinary regard in more than one of the fair objects of his vain devotion. These things were so well known among the circle of which at this period he formed the delight and ornament, that I thought it absurd not to allude to them. I have, however, no great wish to dwell on the subject; though, I must add, it was one that never for a moment disturbed the tranquillity of his family; nay, that, on one occasion at least, my brother and myself looked with sincere pleasure to the prospect of seeing our father's happiness increased by a new alliance.

Whether the two following sets of stanzas refer to the same period, I have not been curious to inquire. It is even possible that I may be wrong in suspecting any allusion to his personal feelings.

I

"Unhappy is the wretch who feels
  The trembling lover's ardent flame,
And yet the treacherous hope conceals
  By using Friendship's colder name.

He must the lover's pangs endure,
  And still the outward sign suppress;
Nor may expect the smiles that cure
  The wounded heart's concealed distress.

When her soft looks on others bend,
  By him discern'd, to him denied,
He must be then the silent friend,
  And all his jealous torments hide.

When she shall one blest youth select,
  His bleeding heart must still approve;
Must every angry thought correct,
  And strive to like, where she can love.

Heaven from my heart such pangs remove,
  And let these feverish sufferings cease—
These pains without the hope of love,
  These cares of friendship, not its peace."

II

"And wilt thou never smile again;
  Thy cruel purpose never shaken?
Hast thou no feeling for my pain,
  Refused, disdain'd, despised, forsaken?

Thy uncle, crafty, careful, cold,
  His wealth upon my mind imprinted;
His fields described, and praised his fold,
  And jested, boasted, promised, hinted.

Thy aunt—I scorn'd the omen—spoke
  Of lovers by thy scorn rejected;
But I the warning never took
  When chosen, cheer'd, received, respected.

Thy brother, too—but all was plann'd
  To murder peace—all freely granted;
And then I lived in fairy land,
  Transported, bless'd, enrapt, enchanted.

> Oh, what a dream of happy love!
>   From which the wise in time awaken;
> While I must all its anguish prove,
>   Deceived, despised, abused, forsaken!"

I am persuaded that but few men have, even in early life, tasted either of the happiness or the pain which attend the most exquisite of passions, in such extremes as my father experienced at this period of his life. In his young "true love," indeed, he was so soon assured of a full return, that one side of the picture could scarcely have been then revealed to his view, and I cannot but consider it as a very interesting trait in the history of his mind, that he was capable at so late a stage, of feeling, with regard to the other side of it, so exactly as a man of five-and-twenty would have done under the same circumstances.

But my brother, in December, 1816, married, with his entire approbation, the daughter of the late William Crowfoot, Esq., and sister to the present Dr. Crowfoot, of Beccles, and immediately came to reside as his curate at Trowbridge, thus relieving him from much of the fatigue of his professional duties, as well as from domestic cares and the weariness of a solitary house. Soon after this I again joined the family; and early in 1817, my father had the satisfaction of marrying me to the daughter of the late Thomas Timbrell, Esq., of Trowbridge, and of seeing my wife and myself established, within twenty miles of him, in the curacy of Pucklechurch; where, during the rest of his life, he had always at his command a second, and, what was often refreshing to him, a rural home.

In relating my own impressions of my father, I have often been apprehensive that I have described him in terms which those who did not know him may deem exaggeration;

yet am I supported by the testimony, not only of many who were well acquainted with his worth, but of one who knew him not, except by his publications and his letters. The talented individual who began the following correspondence, which was continued till her death in 1826, read and appreciated his character nearly as well as the most intimate of his friends. The daughter of Richard Shackleton, the intimate friend of Burke, had met my father at Mr. Burke's table in the year 1784, when, just after his marriage, he had the pleasure of introducing his bride to his patron. This distinguished lady possessed that superiority of intellect which marked her family, and was evidently honoured by Mr. Burke, not merely as the daughter of his old friend, but as one worthy to enjoy that high title herself. Her correspondence with Mr. Burke forms an interesting feature in Mr. Prior's able work. She was a poet, though not of the highest class, and sent to her eminent friend some pleasing verses on his residence at Beaconsfield, which drew forth a long and warm reply. How would he have been gratified had he lived to read the very superior publications in prose, "Cottage Dialogues," "Cottage Biography," &c., which she gave to the world after she had changed her name to Leadbeater! This excellent woman had not forgotten that early meeting with Mr. Crabbe; and in November, 1816, he had the unexpected pleasure of receiving from her the first of a long series of letters; his replies to which are rendered particularly interesting by the playful ingenuousness with which he describes himself. They are, in fact, most valuable additions to his autobiographical sketch.

From Mrs. Leadbeater.

"Ballitore, 7th of 11th month, 1816.
"I believe it will surprise George Crabbe to receive a letter

from an entire stranger, whom, most probably, he does not remember to have ever seen or heard of, but who cannot forget having met him at the house of Edmund Burke, Charles Street, James's Square, in the year 1784. I was brought thither by my father, Richard Shackleton, the friend, from their childhood, of Edmund Burke. My dear father told thee, that 'Goldsmith's would now be the *deserted village*.' Perhaps thou dost not remember this compliment; but I remember the ingenuous modesty which disclaimed it. He admired the 'Village,' the 'Library,' and the 'Newspaper' exceedingly; and the delight with which he read them to his family could not but be acceptable to the author, had he known the sound judgment and the exquisite taste which that excellent man possessed. But he saw no more of the productions of the Muse he admired, whose originality was not the least charm. He is dead— the friend whom he loved and honoured, and to whose character thou dost so much justice in the Preface to the 'Parish Register,' is also gone to the house appointed for all living. A splendid constellation of poets arose in the literary horizon. I looked around for Crabbe. 'Why does not he, who shines as brightly as any of these, add his lustre?' I had not long thought thus, when, in an Edinburgh Review, I met with reflections similar to my own, which introduced the 'Parish Register.' Oh! it was like the voice of a long-lost friend: and glad was I to hear that voice again in 'The Borough!'—still more in the 'Tales,' which appear to me excelling all that preceded them. Every work is so much in unison with our own feelings, that a wish for information concerning them and their author, received into our hearts, is strongly excited. One of our friends, Dykes Alexander, who was in Ballitore, in 1810 I think, said, he was personally acquainted with thee, and spoke highly of thy character. I regretted I had not an opportunity of conversing with him on this subject, as perhaps he would have been able to decide arguments which have arisen; namely, whether we owe to truth or to fiction that 'ever new delight' which thy poetry affords us? Thy characters, however singular some of them may be, are never unnatural; and thy sentiments, so true to domestic and social feelings, as well as to those of a higher nature, have the convincing power of reality over the mind; and *I* maintain that all thy pictures *are drawn from life*. To inquire whether this be the case, is the excuse which I make to myself for writing this letter. I wish the excuse may be accepted by thee; for I greatly fear I have taken an unwarrantable liberty in making the inquiry. Though advanced in life, yet, from an education of peculiar simplicity, and from never having been long absent from my retired native village, I am too little acquainted with decorum. If I have now transgressed the rules it prescribes, I appeal to the candour and liberality of thy mind to forgive a fault caused by strong enthusiasm.

"I am thy sincere friend,

"MARY LEADBEATER."

"P.S. Ballitore is the village in which Edmund Burke was educated by Abraham Shackleton, whose pupil he became in 1741, and from whose school he entered the college of Dublin in 1744. The school is still flourishing."

To Mrs. Leadbeater.

"Trowbridge, 1st of 12th month, 1816.

"MARY LEADBEATER!—Yes, indeed, I do well remember you! Not Leadbeater then, but a pretty demure lass, standing a timid auditor while her own verses were read by a kind friend, but a keen judge. And I have in my memory your father's person and countenance, and you may be sure that my vanity retained the compliment which he paid me in the moment when he permitted his judgment to slip behind his good humour and desire of giving pleasure—Yes, I remember all who were present; and, of all, are not you and I the only survivors? It was the day—was it not?—when I introduced my wife to my friend. And now both are gone! and your father, and Richard Burke, who was present (yet again I must ask—was he not?)—and Mrs. Burke! All departed—and so, by and by, they will speak of us. But, in the mean time, it was good of you to write. Oh very—very good.

"But, are you not your father's own daughter? Do you not flatter after his manner? How do you know the mischief that you may do in the mind of a vain man, who is but too susceptible of praise, even while he is conscious of so much to be placed against it? I am glad that you like my verses: it would have mortified me much if you had not, for you can judge as well as write . . . Yours are really very admirable things; and the morality is as pure as the literary merit is conspicuous. I am not sure that I have read all that you have given us; but what I have read has really that rare and almost undefinable quality—genius: that is to say, it seizes on the mind, and commands attention; and on the heart, and compels its feelings.

"How could you imagine that I could be otherwise than pleased—delighted rather—with your letter? And let me not omit the fact, that I reply the instant I am at liberty, for I was enrobing myself for church. You are a child of simplicity, I know, and do not love robing; but you are a pupil of liberality, and look upon such things with a large mind, smiling in charity. Well! I was putting on the great black gown, when my servant—(you see I can be pompous, to write of gowns and servants with such familiarity)—when he brought me a letter first directed, the words yet legible, to 'George Crabbe, at Belvoir Castle,' and then by Lord Mendip to 'the Reverend' at Trowbridge; and at Trowbridge I hope again to receive these welcome evidences of your remembrance, directed in all their simplicity, and written, I trust, in all sincerity. The delay was occasioned by a change in my place of residence. I now dwell in the parsonage of a busy, populous, clothing town, sent thither by ambition, and the Duke of Rutland. It is situated in Wiltshire, not far from Bath.

"There was a Suffolk family of Alexanders, one of whom you probably mean; and as he knew very little of me, I see no reason why he should not give me a good character. Whether it was merited is another point, and that will depend upon our ideas of a good character. If it means, as it generally does, that I paid my debts, and was guilty of no glaring world-defying immorality—why yes! I was so far a good character. But before the Searcher of Hearts what are our good characters?

"But your motive for writing to me was your desire of knowing whether my men and women were really existing creatures, or beings of my own imagination? Nay, Mary Leadbeater, yours was a better motive: you thought that you should give pleasure by writing, and—yet you will think me very vain—you felt some pleasure yourself in renewing the acquaintance that commenced under such auspices! Am I not right? My heart tells me that I am, and hopes that you will confirm it. Be assured that I feel a very cordial esteem for the friend of my friend—the virtuous, the worthy character whom I am addressing. Yes, I will tell you readily about my creatures, whom I endeavoured to paint as nearly as I could and dared; for, in some cases, I dared not. This you will readily admit: besides, charity bade me be cautious. Thus far you are correct: there is not one of whom I had not in my mind the original; but I was obliged, in some cases, to take them from their real situations, in one or two instances to change even the sex, and, in many, the circumstances. The nearest to real life was the proud, ostentatious man in the 'Borough,' who disguises an ordinary mind by doing great things; but the others approach to reality at greater or less distances. Indeed, I do not know that I could paint merely from my own fancy; and there is no cause why we should. Is there not diversity sufficient in society? and who can go, even but a little, into the assemblies of our fellow-wanderers from the way of perfect rectitude, and not find characters so varied and so pointed, that he need not call upon his imagination?

"Will *you* not write again? 'Write *to* thee, or *for* the public?' wilt thou not ask? *To* me and *for* as many as love and can discern the union of strength and simplicity, purity and good sense. *Our* feeling and *our* hearts is the language you can adopt. Alas, *I* cannot with propriety use it—*our* I too could once say; but I am alone now and since my removing into a busy town among the multitude, the loneliness is but more apparent and more melancholy. But this is only at certain times; and then I have, though at considerable distances, six female friends unknown to each other, but all dear, very dear, to me. With men I do not much associate, not as deserting, and much less disliking, the male part of society, but as being unfit for it; not hardy nor grave, not knowing enough, nor sufficiently acquainted with the every-day concerns of men. But my beloved creatures have minds with which I can better assimilate. Think of you I must; and of me, I must entreat that you would not be unmindful. Thine, dear lady, very truly,

"GEORGE CRABBE."

I dare say no one will put an unfavourable interpretation on my father's condescension to Mrs. Leadbeater's feelings, if, indeed, it was anything but a playful one, in dating the above letter after the Quaker fashion, "1st of 12th month." I need not transcribe the whole of this excellent lady's next letter: but the first and last paragraphs are as follow:

"Ballitore, 29th of 12th month, 1816.

"RESPECTED FRIEND,—I cannot describe the sensations with which I began to read thy letter. They overpowered me. I burst into tears, and, even after I had recovered composure, found it necessary frequently to wipe my spectacles before I reached the conclusion. I felt astonishment mingled with delight, to find that I, in my lonely valley, was looked upon with such benevolence by him who sits upon the top of the hill. That benevolence encourages me again to take up the pen. That day on which I had the pleasure of seeing thee and thy wife was the tenth day of the sixth month (June), 1784. It was the day thou introduced thy bride to thy friends. She sat on a sofa with Jane Burke; thou stood with Edmund near the window. May I ask how long it is since thou wast visited by the affliction of losing her, and how many children are left to comfort thee? But this is a delicate chord, and perhaps I should not touch it. The report of my having received a letter from thee, quickly spread through Ballitore, and I was congratulated by my family, friends, and neighbours, with unfeigned cordiality, on this distinction; for we partake in each other's joys and sorrows, being closely united in friendship and good neighbourhood. We are mostly a colony of Quakers; and those who are not of our profession, in their social intercourse with us conform to our sober habits. None of us are wealthy, all depending on industry for our humble competence, yet we find time to recreate ourselves with books, and generally see every publication which is proper for our perusal. Some profess not to relish poetry; yet *thou* hast contrived to charm us all, and sorry shall we be if thy next visit be to take leave. Therefore do not mar the pleasure we anticipate by a threat so alarming. In thy partiality for female society, I discern a resemblance to dear Cowper, our other moral poet, but enlivened by that flow of cheerfulness, which he so sadly wanted.

*   *   *

"I cannot define my motives for writing to thee. I perfectly recollect that one of them *was* the wish to be assured of the reality of thy characters. I suppose, also, I wished to know thy own; but I did not imagine I could give pleasure to thee by such an address: indeed, I feared offending, though that fear was dissipated when I opened one of thy volumes. How condescending art thou to gratify my curiosity, and how glad am I to find myself right in my conjecture! But I felt confident that what impressed our hearts so deeply must be truth. I could say much more, but I curb myself, considering who I am, and whom I address; and am, with sentiments of gratitude and respect, sincerely thy friend,

"MARY LEADBEATER."

I am approaching the period of my father's return to the high society of London; and, perhaps, a few remarks on his qualifications for mixing in such circles may, with propriety, precede some extracts from the Journal which he kept during his first season in the metropolis. When he re-entered such society, his position was very different from what it had been when he sat at the tables of Mr. Burke, Sir Joshua Reynolds, and the Duke of Rutland. *Then* he was under the avowed patronage of persons, whose station must have ensured him easy admittance among their equals, whatever might have been his own talents for society: but when he returned to high life, though his poetical reputation would no doubt have procured him an extensive introduction, nothing but his personal qualifications, agreeable or shining, could have enabled him to retain his place—nay, continually to enlarge the circle of his acquaintance, and see the cordiality of his distinguished admirers growing into the warmth and attachment of friendship.

Now, certainly, all this was not to be attributed to any very shining qualities in his conversation. He had no talent for speaking—never, except at one or two public meetings, uttered a sentence in the form or tone of a speech in his life, but said (as was admirably remarked by Mr. Murray) "uncommon things in so natural and easy a way, that he often lost the credit of them." Nor were such conversational powers as as he did possess always at his command—they required to be drawn forth and fostered. Perhaps, no man with an appearance so prepossessing was ever more distrustful of his powers to please. Coldness and reserve would benumb them; and he would be abstracted and even distressed. But where he was once received warmly, he generally felt that strong partiality which ever unlocked his heart and drew forth his powers; and under particular circumstances, when his spirits were raised, he could be the most delightful of companions.

Argument he sustained with great impatience: he neither kept close to his point, nor preserved his temper. This dislike of controversial discourse arose, in part, probably, from a consciousness that he had not cultivated the faculty of close logical reasoning; but partly, also, from an opinion, or rather feeling, that he had, against all pretence of colloquial equality. He had seen the submission paid to the opinions of Johnson and Burke, and he always readily followed the lead of any one he thought skilled on the topic in question; but when he ventured an assertion himself, he expected similar deference. And, to be candid, though what he said was pretty sure to be just, yet there was an unfair and aristocratic principle in this expectation, which I never could think quite in harmony with the general modesty of his nature.

But he had a recommendation for the best society infinitely more availing than even the brilliancy of wit. In appearance, manners, and disposition, he was entirely the gentleman. Mr. Burke had discovered this stamp when he had recently left the warehouse at Slaughden, and since that time his walk had been at Belvoir, Glemham, and Cambridge; and his profession, his studies, his age, and his literary success had fully ripened the character. Perhaps it may be said, that no one so humbly born and bred, ever retained so few traces of his origin. His person and his countenance peculiarly led the mind from the suspicion of any, but a highly cultivated and polished education; venerable, clerical, intellectual—it seemed a strange inconsistency to imagine him, even in early youth, occupied as a warehouseman; and, in fact, there was no company in which his appearance would not have proclaimed him an equal. But, above all, he had the disposition of a gentleman, the genuine politeness of a virtuous mind, and a warm and benevolent heart, ready to enter into the interests of others, grateful for their attentions, and happy in their happiness.

The vicinity of Trowbridge to Bath, Bowood, &c., drew Mr. Crabbe by degrees into the distinguished society of London. He was first introduced to the noble family of Lansdowne by his brother poet, and, in latter days, attached friend, the Reverend W. L. Bowles; and it was, I believe, under that roof that he began an acquaintance, which also soon ripened into a strong friendship, with the author of the "Pleasures of Memory." Mr. Rogers urged him to pay a visit in the summer season to the metropolis: he did so, and, taking lodgings near his new friend's residence in St. James's Place, was welcomed in the most cordial manner by the whole of that wide circle—including almost every name distinguished in

politics, fashion, science, literature, and art—of which Mr.
Rogers has so long been considered as the brightest ornament.
His reception at Holland House was peculiarly warm, in consequence of his early acquaintance with the late Mr. Fox;
but, indeed, every mansion of that class was now open to receive him with pride and pleasure: nor were the attentions of
royalty withheld. In this brilliant society, to which after this
time he returned during some weeks for several successive
seasons, he became personally acquainted with Mr. Moore,
who soon afterwards came to reside at no great distance from
Trowbridge, and maintained an affectionate intercourse with
him to the last. He was also introduced, on one of these London visits, by Mr. Murray, of Albemarle Street, to his correspondent Sir Walter Scott; and the admiration and respect
they had long felt for each other were but heightened and confirmed by mutual observation. I am happy to say, that
among my father's papers have been found several note-books,
containing short memoranda of these exciting scenes, and
from them I shall extract various specimens. They will,
however artless, convey, perhaps, no inadequate impression of
the brilliant reception he met with. A friend who saw much of
him under these new circumstances, says, "It is not easy to
conjecture the effect which the modern world produced on
one who had associated with Burke, Reynolds, and Johnson.
As for himself, there can be no doubt that he produced a very
pleasing impression on those who now, for the first time, beheld and heard him. There was much of the old school in his
manners, and even in the disposition of his beautiful white
hair; but this sat gracefully on his time of life and professional
character, and an apparent simplicity, arising from his strange-
ness to some of the recent modes of high life, was mingled
with so much shrewdness of remark, that most people found
his conversation irresistibly amusing. When in society which

he particularly liked, he would manifest his writings, in keen pointed sarcastic humour, and pithy observations: and to this he joined, in the company of ladies, such a spice of the old-fashioned gallantry and politeness, as never fails to please when it is unaffected and genuine."

I proceed to make some extracts from his London Journal of 1817. He reached town in company with his friend, Mr. W. Waldron, on the 19th of June:

"*June 24th*.—Mr. Rogers; his brother, and family. Mr. and Mrs. Moore, very agreeable and pleasant people. Foscolo, the Italian gentleman. Dante, &c. Play, Kemble in Coriolanus.

"*26th*.—Mr. Rogers and the usual company at breakfast. Lady Holland comes and takes me to Holland House. The old building. Addison's room. Bacon. Mr. Fox. The busts and statue. Gardens very pleasant and walks extensive. Meet at Holland House Mr. Allen. He appears equally intelligent and affable. Must have a difficult part, and executes it well. A young Grecian under Lady Holland's protection. Meet Mr. Campbell. Mr. Moore with us. Mr. Rogers joins us in the course of the day. Met Mr. Douglas,[2] in my way, at the Horse Guards, and promised to dine with him on Saturday. He says I cannot leave Holland House; that it is *experimentum crucis*. Dinner. Mr. Brougham, who in some degree reminds me of Mr. Burke. Ready at all subjects, and willing; very friendly. Duchess of Bedford, daughter of the Duchess of Gordon. The confidence of high fashion. In the evening, Countess Besborough, a frank and affectionate character, mother of Lady Caroline Lamb, invites me to her house the next evening.— Miss Fox.[3] I remember meeting her thirty years since; but did not tell her so, and yet could not help appearing to know her; and she questions me much on the subject. Parry it pretty

[2] The late Hon. Sylvester Douglas.

[3] Sister to the late Mr. Fox.

well.—Mrs. Fox.[4] All the remains of a fine person; affectionate manners and informed mind. Diffident and retiring. Appeared to be much affected at meeting a friend of her husband. Invites me to her house; and I am told she was much in earnest. Retire very late.

"27th.—Breakfast with Mr. Brougham and Lady Holland. Lord Holland to speak at Kemble's retiring, at the meeting at Freemasons' Tavern to-morrow. Difficulty of procuring me an admission ticket, as all are distributed. Trial made by somebody, I knew not who, failed. This represented to Lady Holland, who makes no reply. Morning interview with Mr. Brougham. Mr. Campbell's letter.[5] He invites us to Syden-

[4] Widow of the Right. Hon. Charles James Fox.

[5] I take the liberty of inserting Mr. Campbell's letter;—a letter full of what only a high mind in such eminent station would express. My father had found Mr. Campbell a much younger man than he had expected.

"Sydenham, June 25, 1817.

"MY DEAR SIR,—I sent an apology to Lady Holland for not being able to dine at Holland House to-day; and at that very moment of writing, I felt that I owed also an apology to you for not testifying, by my acceptance of the invitation, the high value which I attached to an opportunity of meeting you. It was, indeed, an indispensable engagement that kept me, otherwise it would have been an humiliating self-reflection to have neglected such an occasion of being in the company of Crabbe. You thought me an old man; but, in addressing you, my dear Sir, I feel myself younger than even the difference of our years might seem to justify. I have a very youthful feeling of respect— nay, if you will pardon me for the liberty of saying so—something of a filial upward-looking affection for your matured genius and patriarchal reputation. This reverence for your classic name would have been equally strong in my mind if I had not been so fortunate as to form an acquaintance with you; which your kind manners have made a proud era in the little history of my life. That time, and that spot, in the library of Holland House, I shall never forget, when you shook me a second time by the hand. It must be one of the most enviable privileges of your senior, and superior merit to confer pleasure on such men as myself, by recognising them as younger brothers of your vocation. One token of your kindness was a promise to give me a day of your society. I would not be importunate on this head; but I cannot help reminding you of it, and assuring you that Mrs. Campbell has a very proper sympathy with me in the enthusiasm which I feel to have the honour of your presence under my roof. Our excellent friend, Mr. Rogers, I trust, will accompany you, and you will have the goodness to fix the day. Believe me, most estimable Sir, yours truly,

"T. CAMPBELL."

ham. I refer it to Mr. Rogers and Mr. Moore. Return to
town. The porter delivers to me a paper containing the admission ticket, procured by Lady Holland's means: whether
request or command I know not. Call on Mr. Rogers. We
go to the Freemasons' Tavern. The room filled. We find a
place about half-way down the common seats, but not where
the managers dine, above the steps. By us Mr. Smith, one of
the authors of the Rejected Addresses. Known, but no introduction. Mr. Perry, editor of the Morning Chronicle, and
Mr. Campbell, find us, and we are invited into the Com-
mittee-room. Kemble, Perry, Lord Erskine, Mr. Moore, Lord
Holland, Lord Ossory, whom I saw at Holland House. Dinner
announced. Music. Lord Erskine sits between me and a young
man, whom I found to be a son of Boswell. Lord Holland's
speech after dinner. The Ode recited.[6] Cambell's speech.
Kemble's—Talma's. We leave the company, and go to
Vauxhall to meet Miss Rogers and her party. Stay late.

"28th.—Go to St. James's Place. Lord Byron's new works,
Manfred, and Tasso's Lament. The tragedy very fine—but
very obscure in places. The Lament more perspicuous, and
more feeble. Seek lodgings, 37 Bury Street. Females only
visible. Dine as agreed with Mr. Douglas. Chiefly strangers.
My new lodgings a little mysterious.

"29th.—Breakfast at the Coffee-house in Pall Mall, and go
to Mr. Rogers and family. Agree to dine, and then join their
party after dinner. Mr. Stothard. Foscolo. Drive to Kensington Gardens in their carriage. Grosvenor Gate. Effect new
and striking. Kensington Gardens have a very peculiar effect;
not exhilarating, I think, yet alive and pleasant. Return to
my new lodgings. Inquire for the master. There is one, I understand, in the country. Am at a loss whether my damsel is
extremely simple, or too knowing.

[6] This beautiful Ode is now included in Mr. Campbell's collective works.

"*30th.*—Letter from Mrs. Norris.[7] Like herself. First hour at Mr. Murray's. A much younger and more lively man than I had imagined.—A handsome drawing-room, where he receives his friends, usually from two to five o'clock. Pictures by Phillips, of Lord Byron, Mr. Scott, Mr. Southey, Mr. Campbell, Rogers (yet unfinished), Moore, by Lawrence" (his last picture). "Mr. Murray wishes me to sit. Advise with Mr. Rogers. He recommends.[8] Dine with Lord Ossory. Meet Marquis and Marchioness of Lansdowne.[9] Engage to dine on Friday. Lord Gower.[10]

"*July 1st.*—I foresee a long train of engagements. Dine with Mr. Rogers. Company: Kemble, Lord Erskine, Lord Ossory, Sir George Beaumont, Mr. Campbell, and Mr. Moore. Miss R. retires early, and is not seen any more at home. Meet her, at the Gallery in Pall Mall, with Mr. Westall.

"*2nd.*—Duke of Rutland. List of pictures burned at Belvoir Castle. Dine at Sydenham, with Mr. and Mrs. Campbell, Mr. Moore, and Mr. Rogers. Poets' Club."

*   *   *

I here interrupt my father's Journal, in order to give part of a letter with which I have lately been honoured by Mr. Campbell.

"The first time I met Crabbe was at Holland House, where he and Tom Moore and myself lounged the better part of a

[7] Mr. Crabbe was on terms of intimate friendship with Mr. and Mrs. Norris, of Hughenden Hall, near Wycombe, Bucks.

[8] Mr. Crabbe did sit to Mr. Phillips.

[9] I take the liberty of inserting the following passage from a letter with which I have recently been honoured by the noble marquess:—"Any testimony to your father's amiable and unaffected manners, and to that simplicity of character which he united to the uncommon powers of minute observation, would indeed be uncalled for; as it could only express the common feeling of all who had access to his society."

[10] Now Duke of Sutherland.

morning about the park and library; and I can answer for one of the party at least being very much pleased with it. Our conversation, I remember, was about novelists. Your father was a strong Fieldingite, and I as sturdy a Smollettite. His mildness in literary argument struck me with surprise in so stern a poet of nature, and I could not but contrast the unassumingness of his manners with the originality of his powers. In what may be called the ready-money small-talk of conversation, his facility might not perhaps seem equal to the known calibre of his talents; but in the progress of conversation I recollect remarking that there was a vigilant shrewdness that almost eluded you by keeping its watch so quietly. Though an oldish man when I saw him, he was not a '*laudator temporis acti*,' but a decided lover of later times.

"The part of the morning which I spent at Holland House with him and Tom Moore, was one, to me at least, of memorable agreeableness. He was very frank, and even confidential, in speaking of his own feelings. Though in a serene tone of spirits, he confessed to me that since the death of his wife he had scarcely known positive happiness. I told him that in that respect, viz. the calculation of our own happiness, we are apt to deceive ourselves. The man whose manners are mild and tranquil, and whose conversation is amusing, cannot be positively unhappy.

"When Moore left us we were joined by Foscolo; and I remember as distinctly as if it had been yesterday, the contrasted light in which Crabbe and Foscolo struck me. It is not an invidious contrast—at least my feelings towards Ugo's memory intend it not to be so—yet, it was to me morally instructive, and, I need hardly say, greatly in favour of your father. They were both men of genius, and both simple. But what a different sort of simplicity! I felt myself between them as if I had been standing between a roaring cataract and a placid stream. Ugo raged and foamed in argument, to my amusement, but not at all to your father's liking. He could not abide him. What we talked about I do not recollect; but only that Ugo's impetuosity was a foil to the amenity of the elder bard.

"One day—and how can it fail to be memorable to me when Moore has commemorated it?—your father, and Rogers, and Moore, came down to Sydenham pretty early in the forenoon, and stopped to dine with me. We talked of founding a Poets' Club, and even set about electing the members, not by ballot, but *viva voce*. The scheme failed, I scarcely know how; but this I know, that a week or so afterwards, I met with Perry, of the Morning Chronicle, who asked me how our Poets' Club was going on. I said, 'I don't know—we have some difficulty of giving it a name,—we thought of calling ourselves *the Bees*.' 'Ah,' said Perry, 'that's a little different from the common report, for they say you are to be called *the Wasps*.' I was so stung with this waspish report, that I thought no more of the Poets' Club.

"The last time I saw Crabbe was, when I dined with him at Mr. Hoare's at Hampstead. He very kindly came with me to the coach to see me off, and I never pass that spot on the top of Hampstead Heath without thinking of him. As to the force and faith of his genius, it would be superfluous in me to offer any opinion. Pray, pardon me for speaking of his memory in this very imperfect manner, and believe me, dear sir, yours very truly,

"T. CAMPBELL."

*   *   *

I return to Mr. Crabbe's Journal:

"*July 3rd.*—Letter from Trowbridge. I pity you, my dear John, but I must plague you. Robert Bloomfield. He had better rested as a shoemaker, or even a farmer's boy; for he would have been a farmer perhaps in time, and now he is an unfortunate poet. By the way, indiscretion did much. It might be virtuous and affectionate in him to help his thoughtless relations; but his more liberal friends do not love to have their favours so disposed of. He is, however, to be pitied and assisted. Note from Mr. Murray respecting the picture. Go, with Mr. Rogers, in his carriage, to Wimbledon. Earl and Countess Spencer. The grounds more beautiful than any I have yet seen; more extensive, various, rich. The profusion of roses extraordinary. Dinner. Mr. Heber, to whom Mr. Scott addresses one canto of Marmion. Mr. Stanhope. A pleasant day. Sleep at Wimbledon.

"4th.—Morning view, and walk with Mr. Heber and Mr. Stanhope. Afterwards Mr. Rogers, Lady S., Lady H. A good picture, if I dare draw it accurately: to place in lower life, would lose the peculiarities which depend upon their station; yet, in any station. Return with Mr. Rogers. Dine at Lansdowne House. Sir James Mackintosh, Mr. Grenville, elder brother to Lord Grenville. My visit to Lord Lansdowne's father in this house, thirty-seven years since! Porter's lodge. Mr. Wynn. Lord Ossory.

"5th.—My thirty lines done; but not well I fear; thirty daily is the self-engagement. Dine at George's Coffee-house. Return. Stay late at Holborn. The kind of shops open at so late an hour. Purchase in one of them. Do not think they deceive any person in particular.

"6th.—Call at Mr. Rogers's and go to Lady Spencer. Go with Mr. Rogers to dine at Highbury with his brother and family. Miss Rogers the same at Highbury as in town. Visit to Mr. John Nichols. He relates the story of our meeting at Muston, and inquires for John, &c. His daughters agreeable women. Mr. Urban wealthy. Arrive at home in early time.

Go to Pall Mall Coffee-house and dine. Feel hurt about Hampstead. Mr. Rogers says I must dine with him to-morrow and that I consented when at Sydenham; and now certainly they expect me at Hampstead, though I have made no promise.

"7th.—Abide by the promise, and take all possible care to send my letter; so that Mr. Hoare[11] may receive it before dinner. Set out for Holborn Bridge to obtain assistance. In the way find the Hampstead stage, and obtain a promise of delivery in time. Prepare to meet our friends at Mr. Rogers's. Agree to go to Mr. Phillips, and sit two hours and a half. Mrs. Phillips a very agreeable and beautiful woman. Promise to breakfast next morning. Go to Holborn. Letter from Mr. Frere. Invited to meet Mr. Canning, &c. Letter from Mr. Wilbraham. Dinner at Mr. Rogers's with Mr. Moore and Mr. Campbell, Lord Strangford, and Mr. Spencer. Leave them, and go by engagement to see Miss O'Neil, in Lady Spencer's box. Meet there Lady Besborough, with whom I became acquainted at Holland House, and her married daughter. Lady B. the same frank character: Mr. Grenville the same gentle and polite one: Miss O'Neil natural, and I think excellent; and even her 'Catherine,' especially in the act of yielding the superiority to the husband, well done and touching. Lady Besborough obligingly offers to set me down at twelve o'clock. Agreed to visit the Hon. W. Spencer[12] at his house at Petersham, and there to dine next day with Mr. Wilbraham.

"8th.—Mr. Phillips. Sit again. Begin to think something may be made. Mrs. Phillips. Find a stray child. Mrs. Phillips takes him home. Mr. Murray's. Mr. Frere. To dine on Monday next. Dine this day with Mr. North. Meet Lord Dundas.

[11] The late Samuel Hoare, Esq., of Hampstead.

[12] Mr. Spencer, the well-known translator of "Leonora," &c. &c. &c.

Mrs. Wedall. Story of the poor weaver, who begged his master to allow him a loom, for the work of which he would charge nothing: an instance of distress. Thirty lines to-day; but not yesterday: must work up.—I even still doubt whether it be pure simplicity, a little romantic, or—a great deal simplified. Yet I may, and it is likely do, mistake.

"9th.—Agree to dine with Mr. Phillips. A day of indisposition unlike the former. Dine at George's Coffee-house, and in a stupid humour. Go to a play not very enlivening; yet the 'Magpie and Maid' was, in some parts, affecting, till you reflected.

"10th.—Apology for last night. Maiden at a ball; I hope not mistress too. Rise early for the coach to Twickenham, as I prefer going first to Mr. Wilbraham, who first invited me. Ask what is the name of every place except one, and that one is Twickenham, and so go a mile at least beyond. Walk back to Twickenham. Meet a man carrying a child. He passed me, but with hesitation; and there was, as I believed, both distress and honesty. As he watched my manner, he stopped, and I was unwilling to disappoint him. The most accomplished actor could not counterfeit the joy and surprise at first, and then the joy without the surprise afterwards. The man was simple, and had no roguish shrewdness. Pope's house.[13] Civil man, and something more. Mr. Wilbraham. A drive round the country three hours. Richmond Hill. Recollect Sir Joshua's house. Hampton Court. Petersham. In Mr. Wilbraham's carriage to Brentford. Take a chaise to Knightsbridge. Make up my thirty lines for yesterday and to-day. Take a story from the Dutch imposition, but with great variation.

"11th.—Breakfast with Mr. Rogers: talk of Mr. Frere. Mr. Douglas. Called for by Mr. Spencer. This gentleman is

---

[13] Pope's villa, now inhabited by Sir Wathen Waller, Bart., and his lady the Baroness Howe.

grandson to the Duke of Marlborough. He married, at nineteen, a very beautiful and most accomplished woman, in the court of the Duke of Weimar. She was sixteen. His manner is fascinating, and his temper all complacency and kindness. His poetry far beyond that implied in the character of *Vers de Société*. I am informed Mrs. S. has very extraordinary talents. Go in the carriage with his daughter to Petersham by Ham House. Introduced to Mrs. Spencer, Sir Harry Englefield, and Mr. Standish, a Bond-street man, but of a superior kind; and so is Sir Harry. A very delightful morning. Gardens. Miss Spencer drives me to Richmond in her pony-chaise. The Duke and Duchess of Cumberland and Madame W——— came in the evening. The duchess very engaging. Daughter of the Duke of Weimar, and sister to the Queen of Prussia. Mr. Spencer with them at the court. All this period pleasant, easy, gay, with a tincture of melancholy that makes it delicious. A drawback on mirth, but not on happiness, when our affection has a mixture of regret and pity.

"14th.—Some more intimate conversation this morning with Mr. and Mrs. Moore. They mean to go to Trowbridge. He is going to Paris, but will not stay long. Mrs. Spencer's album. Agree to dine at Curzon Street. A welcome letter from ———. This makes the day more cheerful. Suppose it were so. Well! 'tis not! Go to Mr. Rogers, and take a farewell visit to Highbury. Miss Rogers. Promise to go when——— Return early. Dine there, and purpose to see Mr. Moore and Mr. Rogers in the morning when they set out for Calais.

"15th.—Was too late this morning. Messrs. Rogers and Moore were gone. Go to church at St. James's. The sermon good; but the preacher thought proper to apologise for a severity which he had not used. Write some lines in the solitude of Somerset House, not fifty years from the Thames on one side, and the Strand on the other; but as quiet as the sands of Arabia. I am not quite in good humour with this day; but, happily, I cannot say why.

"16th.—Mr. Boswell the younger. Malone's papers. He is an advocate, like most of his countrymen, for Mary. Mr. Frere's poem.[14] Meet, at Mr. Murray's, Mr. Heber. Mr. Douglas takes me to Mr. Frere at Brompton. Meet Mr. Canning and Lord Binning. Conversation on church affairs. A little on the poem of the Stowmarket men. Go home with Mr. Douglas, and call for the ladies at St. James's Place. Write about eighty verses. Agree to stay over Sunday.

"16th.—Picture finished, which allows me more time. Lady Errol[15] and Lady Holland. Invitation from Lord Binning.[16] Write, in consequence of my second delay, to Mrs. Norris and Anna. Resolve not to stay beyond Tuesday. Farewell dinner with Mr. Canning. Dine to-day with my friends in Curzon Street. Pleasant, as all is there. Mrs. Spencer the same agreeable young woman. Besides the family, Sir Harry Englefield, a Catholic. His character opens upon me very much. He appeared to be in earnest, and I hope he was. It would be hard if we were judged by our youthful sins, or even if sins necessarily implied unbelief. Meet in my way Lady Besborough, with a gentleman and a young lady. She does not introduce me, and I pass on; but, describing the lady, I understand it was Lady Caroline Lamb. Lady Besborough comes at night to Mr. Spencer's, and confirms it. She invites me to Roehampton. Pleasant evening.

"17th.—Omitted a visit to the Duchess of Rutland at an earlier time. She invites me to dine; but our days did not

---

[14] "The Monks and the Giants," published under the name of Whistlecraft, of Stowmarket, Suffolk.

[15] The Countess Dowager of Errol, wife of the Right Honourable John Hookham Frere.

[16] Now Earl of Haddington.

accord. Notes from Mr. Frere and Mr. Canning. Dine with Mr.
Douglas. Mr. Boswell the younger: I met the elder in the
morning. Many gentlemen with us. Mr. Douglas sends us
home in his carriage. Good day, at least as far as relates to Mr.
Douglas, who is ever the same. I wrote to Trowbridge. They
are not correct in their opinion; yet I love London; and who
does not, if not confined to it? A visit from Sir Harry Englefield. There is an affectionate manner, which almost hides
his talents; and they are not trifling. Wrote my lines today,
but no more.

"18th.—Read the pamphlet Mr. Boswell recommended:
natural, certainly, and the man had too much provocation for
his act. There is the wish of the heart to acquit itself, but that
is very common. Dine with Mr. Murray. Very fine day. Sir
Harry in good spirits, except during his vehemence.
Mr. Phillips. Mr. Chantry. His 'Mother and Infants' in the
exhibition. Mr. and Mrs. Graham. The Mrs. Graham[17] who
wrote the lively India Journal, a delightful woman! Mr.
Phillips argued, and preserved his temper. Sir Harry was silent,
for fear of being tumultuous. The dinner in every respect as in
a nobleman's house. Join the ladies, Mrs. Graham still lively.
Sir Harry's account of the Isle of Wight; a folio, with prints.
At eleven o'clock enters Lady Caroline Lamb. She offers to
take me on a visit to her company at twelve o'clock. I
hesitated, for I had curiosity; but finally declined. Mr.
Wilkie. His picture in the exhibition much admired.

"19th.—Agreed to sit half an hour, for Mr. Phillips to re-
touch the picture. Breakfast with them once more.—Leave
them, and return to Bury Street, and find a note! What an
unaccountable! It is so ridiculous!—Foscolo; who said he
would call, and I must go with him to his friends, Lady
Flint, and sister, and nieces. He came, and I assented. I was

[17] Maria Graham now Mrs. Calcott.

paid for compliance. They are very delightful women. Go and call on Mrs. Spencer; find Sir Harry Englefield. These are two favourite characters. Dine at Lord Binning's. Lady Binning with one visitor. She knows me, and we are at ease. Mr. Canning more lively as with his friends, and very pleasant. Mr. Frere could not dine. Lady Errol indisposed. Mr. Robinson.[18] Conceive J. B.'s size and good temper, with a look of more understanding, and better manner. Mr. Huskisson—countenance less open; grew more free, and became pleasant. The Speaker[19] polite, and rather cheerful; a peculiar cast of the countenance; pleasing, certainly. Mrs. Canning I thought reserved; but all appearance of this retired. I was too much a stranger among friends; but, before we parted, all became easy. Lord Binning a sensible, polite man.

"20th.—I wake ill this morning and nervous; and so little do we judge of the future, that I was half inclined to make apologies, and not join the pleasantest of all parties. I must go from this infatuating scene.—Walk in the Park, and in some degree recover. Write two hours. At seven go to Sir Harry Englefield. A large house that overlooks the Park and Serpentine River. Disappointed of Mr. Spencer; but Mrs. Spencer, and Miss Churchill and Miss Spencer dine with us. Mr. Murray and Mr. Standish. Nothing particularly worthy of remark at dinner; but after dinner, one of the best conversations since I came to town. Mr. Spencer and Miss Churchill chiefly; on the effect of high polish on minds; chiefly female; Sir Harry sometimes joining, and Miss Spencer. A very delightful evening. Sir Harry's present of Aristo's inkstand. Of a double value, as a gift, and from the giver. Mr. Standish and Mr. Murray leave us. Part painfully at one o'clock. Yes, there are at Trowbridge two or three; and

---

[18] The Right Honourable Frederick Robinson, now Earl of Ripon.

[19] The Right Honourable Charles Manners Sutton.

it is well there are. Promise (if I live) to return in the winter. Miss Churchill a very superior and interesting woman. Take leave of my friend Sir Harry. The impression rather nervous, and they will smile at ——, I am afraid; but I shall still feel. I shall think of this evening.

"*21st.*—I would not appear to myself superstitious. I returned late last night, and my reflections were as cheerful as such company could make them, and not, I am afraid, of the most humiliating kind; yet, for the first time these many nights, I was incommoded by dreams such as would cure vanity for a time in any mind where they could gain admission. Some of Baxter's mortifying spirits whispered very singular combinations. None, indeed, that actually did happen in the very worst of times, but still with a formidable resemblance. It is, doubtless, very proper to have the mind thus brought to a sense of its real and possible alliances, and the evils it has encountered, or might have had; but why these images should be given at a time when the thoughts, the waking thoughts, were of so opposite a nature, I cannot account. So it was. Awake, I had been with the high, the apparently happy: we were very pleasantly engaged, and my last thoughts were cheerful. Asleep, all was misery and degradation, not my own only, but of those who had been.—That horrible image of servility and baseness—that mercenary and commercial manner! It is the work of imagination, I suppose; but it is very strange. I must leave it.[20]—Walk to Holborn. Call and pay for yesterday's coffee, which, with a twenty-pound note and some gold, I could not discharge then. A letter from Mrs.

[20] Mr. Moore, on reading this journal in MS., writes thus:

"The Journal of your father is a most interesting document; and it is rather curious that some parts of it should so much resemble the journalising style of Byron, particularly that describing his frightful dream after a day of enjoyment." A very striking poem, entitled "Dreams," &c., is given in the posthumous volume of his works.

Norris; like herself and all hers. Now for business. Called at Holborn, and stayed an hour with P——, York Coffeehouse. Return and write. Go to Oxford Street to take a place for Wycombe, a mile and a half from Mr. Norris. After a short delay, I pay my visit to Mrs. Spencer. Her husband's note left with me. Find her and the young people. Return by Mr. Murray's, and send to Lady Errol's from his house. He obligingly sent his servant to Bury Street. Lady Errol much better. May hope to meet Mr. Frere this day at dinner. Prepare to go with Mr. Douglas to Mr. Canning's.—Mr. Canning's dinner. Gardens and house in very beautiful style: doubly secluded, and yet very near town.[21] Mr. Huskisson, two younger gentlemen, Mr. Frere, Mr. Canning, Mr. Douglas, and myself. Claret more particularly excellent. Ministerial claret. A lively day. Shakespeare. Eton and Westminster. Mr. Canning.—This is the last evening in town, notwithstanding the very kind invitation of Mr. Douglas. And here I may close my journal, of certainly the most active, and, with very little exception,—that is, the exception of one or two persons— the most agreeable of all excursions—except——"

"22nd.—Oxford Street politician, who assures me nothing can be more true, than that ministers send spies to Ireland with money to intoxicate the poor people; who are persuaded to enter into treason while drunk, are taken next morning to a magistrate, condemned on the evidence of the seducer, and executed before noon; and this man seemed ready to testify on oath, as a major somebody had testified to him.—Three o'clock for Wycombe. Arrive at eight, and walk to the great house, as my guide was proud to call it. Mrs. Norris: she looks as one recovering, but not quite well. Her spirits as usual.

"23rd.—A vile engagement to an oratorio at church, by I

[21] Mr. Canning, at this time, resided at Gloucester Lodge, near Brompton.

know not how many noisy people; women as well as men. Luckily, I sat where I could write unobserved, and wrote forty lines, only interrupted by a song of Mrs. Brand—a hymn, I believe. It was less doleful than the rest. Party at dinner. Music after dinner, much more cheerful and enlivening than at church. Solitary evening walk. Things soon become familiarised, when the persons are well known. Thought of Sunday next, and wrote about half a sermon upon confirmation.

"24*th*.—Read Miss Edgeworth's dramas. Company at breakfast. Finish my sermon.—Must determine to go to-morrow. Younger dear's birthday."

* * *

The following is an extract from a letter of the 25th:

"This visit to London has, indeed, been a rich one. I had new things to see, and was, perhaps, something of a novelty myself. Mr. Rogers introduced me to almost every man he is acquainted with; and in this number were comprehended all I was previously very desirous to obtain a knowledge of."

Shortly after his return to Trowbridge from this excursion of 1817, my father wrote as follows to his friend at Ballitore:

"A description of your village society would be very gratifying to me—how the manners differ from those in larger societies, or in those under different circumstances. I have observed an extraordinary difference in village manners in England, especially between those places otherwise nearly alike, when there was and when there was not a leading man, or a squire's family, or a manufactory near, or a populous, vitiated town, &c. All these, and many other circumstances, have great influence. *Your* quiet village, with such influencing minds, I am disposed to think highly of. No one, perhaps, very rich—none miserably poor. No girls, from six years to sixteen, sent to a factory, where men, women, and children of all ages are continually with them breathing contagion. Not all, however: we are not so evil—there is a resisting power, and it is strong; but the thing itself, the congregation of so many minds, and the intercourse it occasions, will have its powerful and visible effect. But these you have not; yet as you mention your schools of both kinds, you must be more populous and perhaps not so happy as I was giving myself to believe.

"I will write my name and look for two lines; but complying with you, my dear lady, is a kind of vanity.[22] I find, however, no particular elevation of spirit, and will do as you desire; indeed, your desire must be very unlike yours, if I were not glad to comply with it; for the world has not spoiled you, Mary, I do believe: now it has me. I have been absorbed in its mighty vortex, and gone into the midst of its greatness, and joined in its festivities and frivolities, and been intimate with its children. You may like me very well, my kind friend, while the purifying water, and your more effectual imagination, is between us; but come you to England, or let me be in Ireland, and place us where mind becomes acquainted with mind,—

[22] Mrs. Leadbeater had requested Mr. Crabbe to give an autograph for Mr. Wilkinson, the Quaker poet, the same worthy man to whom Wordsworth refers in the verses,

"Spade with which Wilkinson hath till'd his lands," &c.
and he sent the following scrap:

"Enclosed, at Mrs. Leadbeater's request, for Thomas Wilkinson's collection of handwritings:

'One calm, cold evening, when the moon was high,
And rode sublime within the cloudy sky,
She sat within her hut, nor seemed to feel
Or cold, or want, but turn'd her idle wheel;
And with sad song its melancholy tone
Mix'd—all unconscious that she dwelt alone.'

"The above six lines are from a discarded poem: they are good for little, and the epithet 'idle' may not seem proper for a spinning-wheel: but my poor heroine was discarded, and, therefore, it was idle, because profitless."

and then! ah, Mary Leadbeater! you would have done
with your friendship with me! Child of simplicity and virtue,
how can you let yourself be so deceived? Am I not a great fat
Rector, living upon a mighty income, while my poor curate
starves with six hungry children, upon the scraps that fall
from the luxurious table? Do I not visit that horrible London,
and enter into its abominable dissipations? Am I not this day
going to dine on venison and drink claret?[23] Have I not been
at election dinners, and joined the Babel-confusion of a town-
hall? Child of simplicity! am I fit to be a friend to you, and to
the peaceful, mild, pure, gentle people about you? One thing
only is true—I wish I had the qualification; but I am of the
world, Mary. Though I hope to procure a free cover for you,
yet I dare not be sure, and so must husband my room. I am
sorry for your account of the fever among your poor. Would
I could suggest anything! I shall dine with one of our representatives to-day; but such subjects pass off: all say, 'Poor

[23] Mrs. Leadbeater says, in her answer to this letter:

"Have I given too partial an account of our little community? Ask those who
visit Ballitore; who quit it with regret, and return to it with delight; some of
whom call it the Classic Vale, some the Vale of Tempè, some the Happy
Valley, some Simplicity's Vale; while others take a higher flight, and dignify
it by the name of Athens: all agreeing, that we live like one large family. Thus,
from infancy to age preserved in this safe enclosure, surrounded by excellent
examples, have I not much to be accountable for? And yet how little am I
cleansed from secret faults, I shall not say, for I fear one of these is a desire to
appear better than I am to him whose good opinion I do indeed highly value,
and who, I believe, is disposed to be more severe upon himself than upon another; but if the graceful figure which I saw in London—designated by my
father 'the youth with the *sour* name and the *sweet* countenance'—has become
somewhat corpulent, that is a consequence of good humour as well as good
living; and why not partake of venison and claret with the moderation which
such a mind will dictate? The sentiment expressed in an old song has occurred
to me, when too little allowance has been made for those in exalted situations:

'Deceit may dress in linen gown,
And truth in diamonds shine.'

From my own contracted sphere I have had some opportunities of per-
ceiving the virtues which, beaming from the zenith of wealth and rank, diffuse
their influence to a wide extent."

people, I am sorry,' and there it ends. My new Tales are not
yet entirely ready, but do not want much that I can give them.
I return all your good wishes, think of you, and with much
regard, more than, indeed, belongs to *a man of the world!* Still
let me be permitted to address thee.—O! my dear Mrs. L., this
is so humble that I am afraid it is vain. Well! write soon, then,
and believe me to be most sincerely, and affectionately yours,

"GEORGE CRABBE."

I have introduced the above extract in this place, on account
of the allusions it contains to my father's reception in the gay
world of London,—a reception of the nature of which his own
family, until his journals came to light after his death, had
never had an exact notion. When he returned home after one
of these intoxicating visits to the metropolis, no one could
trace the slightest difference in his manners or habits. He rarely
spoke, even to his sons, of the brilliant circles in which he had
been figuring; and when some casual circumstance led to the
passing mention of some splendid connection, there was such
unaffected simplicity in the little vanity of his air, if I may so
call it, that it only served to show that he did appreciate justly,
what his natural good sense would not permit him to value
above its real worth, or to dwell on so as to interfere with the
usual duties and pursuits of his own station and long-formed
tastes. He resumed next morning, just as if nothing had happened, his visits among his parishioners, his care of parish
business, his books and papers, and last, not least, his long
rambles among the quarries near Trowbridge: for never, after
my mother's death, did he return seriously to botany, the
favourite study of his earlier life. Fossils were thenceforth to
him what weeds and flowers had been: he would spend hours
on hours hammer in hand, not much pleased if anyone interrupted him, rarely inviting either my brother or myself to

Q

accompany him, and, in short, solitary as far as he could manage to be so—unless when some little boy or girl of a friend's family pleaded hard to be allowed to attend him, and mimic his labours with a tiny hammer. To children he was ever the same. No word or look of harshness ever drove them from his side, "and I believe," says a friend[24] who knew him well, "many a mother will bless, many days hence, the accident that threw her offspring into the way of his unlaboured and paternal kindness and instruction."

To his proper ministerial duties he returned with equal zeal. "To these," observes the same dear friend of his, "Mr. Crabbe ever attached great importance. He would put off a meditated journey rather than leave a poor parishioner who required his services; and from his knowledge of human nature, he was able, in a remarkable manner, to throw himself into the circumstances of those who needed his help—*no sympathy was like his*; and no man, perhaps, had the inmost feelings of others more frequently laid open to his inspection. He did not, however, enjoy the happiness which many pastors express in being able to benefit their flocks; never was satisfied that he used the best means; complained that men more imbued with a sense of the terrors of the Lord and less with his mercies, succeeded better; and was glad to ask advice for all in whose judgment and experience he confided. Whatever might be the enjoyments of his study, he never allowed any of the numerous petitioners who called in the course of the day to be dismissed by a servant. He saw them all, and often gave them more pecuniary aid than he thought right; and when the duties of a magistrate were afterwards added to those of a clergyman, these multiplied calls scarcely allowed him necessary relaxation."

[24] Miss Hoare.

His then parishioner, Mr. Taylor, says [25] on the same subject:—"His income amounted to about 800*l.* per annum, a large portion of which he spent in acts of charity. He was the common refuge of the unhappy—

'In every family
Alike in every generation dear,
The children's favourite, and the grandsire's friend,
Tried, trusted, and beloved.'

To him it was recommendation enough to be poor and wretched. He was extremely moderate in the exaction of tithes. When told of really poor defaulters, his reply was, 'Let it be— they cannot afford to pay so well as I can to want it—let it be.' His charity was so well known that he was regularly visited by mendicants of all grades. He listened to their long stories of wants and woes, gave them a trifle, and then would say: 'God save you,—I can do no more for you'; but he would sometimes follow them, on reflection, and double or quadruple his gift. He has been known to dive into those obscure scenes of wretchedness and want, where wandering paupers lodge, in order to relieve them. He was, of course, often imposed upon; which discovering, he merely said, 'God forgive them,—I do.'

"He was anxious for the education of the humbler classes. The Sunday-school was a favourite place of resort. When listening to the children, he observed, 'I love to hear the little dears, and now old age has made me a fit companion for them.' He was much beloved by the scholars: on leaving the school he would give them a Bible, with suitable admonition. His health was generally good, though he sometimes suffered from the tic douloureux. Not long before his death he met a

[25] In a short sketch of his life, published at Bath.

poor old woman in the street, whom he had for some time missed at church, and asked her if she had been ill. 'Lord bless you, Sir—no,' was the answer, 'but it is of no use going to *your* church, for I can't hear; you *do* speak so low.'—'Well, well, my good old friend,' said he, slipping half-a-crown into her hand, 'you do quite right in going where you can hear.' "

I may here add, that Mr. Crabbe was a subscriber to most of our great charitable institutions, and, as a member of the British and Foreign Bible Society, was prevailed upon to take the chair at the meetings in Trowbridge; but his aversion to forms and ceremony, and to set speeches, made it a very painful station.

Mr. Crabbe was now (1817 and 1818) busily engaged in finishing the last of his hitherto published works—that which he originally entitled "Remembrances," but which, by Mr. Murray's advice, was produced as "Tales of the Hall." His note-book was at this time ever with him in his walks, and he would every now and then lay down his hammer to insert a new or amended couplet. He fancied that autumn was, on the whole, the most favourable season for him in the composition of poetry; but there was something in the effect of a sudden fall of snow that appeared to stimulate him in a very extraordinary manner. It was during a great snow-storm that, shut up in his room, he wrote almost *currente calamo* his Sir Eustace Grey. Latterly, he worked chiefly at night, after the family had all retired; and in case any one should wish to be informed of such important particulars, he had generally by him a glass of very weak spirits and water, or negus; and at all times indulged largely in snuff, which last habit somewhat interfered, as he grew old, with the effects of his remarkable attention to personal cleanliness and neatness of dress.

Would the reader like to follow my father into his library

—a scene of unparalleled confusion—windows rattling, paint in great request, books in every direction but the right—the table—but no, I cannot find terms to describe it, though the counterpart might be seen, perhaps, not one hundred miles from the study of the justly-famed and beautiful rectory of Bremhill. Once, when we were staying at Trowbridge, in his absence for a few days at Bath, my eldest girl thought she should surprise and please him by putting every book in perfect order, making the best bound the most prominent; but, on his return, thanking her for her good intention, he replaced every volume in its former state; "for," said he, "my dear, grandpapa understands his own confusion better than your order and neatness."

The following is part of a letter to a female friend at Trowbridge, written on the 7th of May, 1819, when Mr. Crabbe was again in London:

"I came to town with a lady who resides near W——, and her husband is an agriculturist upon a large scale; that, I suppose, is the more consequential name for a farmer; but Mr. —— is a reading and studying farmer, and upon another scale than ordinary persons of that class; and Mrs. —— also reads, and knows what is read and talked of. She spoke of most of those of whom other people talk, and, among other things, asked me if I knew Crabbe? I did not act generously, for I evaded the question: and then she told me that she was invited to meet him at dinner at Mr. West's, the painter. I thought it proper to put the lady right; which, however, was a matter of no importance: she went on in the same way; but I, of necessity, withdrew a part of my attention.

"If I could convey to you a good picture of the Academical Dinner, I would try and paint one; but I can only say it was singular and grand. We dined in the great room, where the principal pictures were placed, which covered every part of it. Our number I judge about 180 or 200: we had one royal duke, Sussex; the duke of Wellington; we had four ambassadors (at whose table I was placed, with two English gentlemen, luckily); and many of our nobility. The dinner itself was like all very large dinners; but the toasts, music, and speeches after we had dined, were in a high style. Between the healths were short pieces from a band of performers, who were paid for attendance; and there was an imposing air of dignity during the whole time. I had the pleasure of meeting several friends, but Lord Holland was prevented by a fit of the gout. I was not a little surprised to see my picture by Phillips;[26] for, if any, I expected the other;— and they all said that not only the likeness was strong, but the picture good: and I believe it is so, because Lord Holland is to have it copied, and placed with those in his library. I slept two nights at Holland House, and dined three times before Lady H. was weary of me, and even at last I was treated with marvellous kindness. I shall be lectured at ——; but no matter; we must pay for the honours and emoluments which we gain in this world of struggles. I am going to-day to dine at the Thatched House, being elected a member of the Literary Society. When I have seen my brethren, and paid my subscriptions, I shall better judge whether the honour makes amends for the costs."

In June, 1819, the "Tales of the Hall" were published by Mr. Murray, who, for them and the remaining copyright of all my father's previous poems, gave the munificent sum of 3,000l. The new work had, at least, as general approbation as any that had gone before it; and was not the less liked for its opening views of a higher class of society than he had

[26] Mr. Crabbe had also sat for his portrait to Mr. Pickersgill.

hitherto dealt much in. But I reserve what particulars I have to offer with respect to the subjects of these Tales for notes to its forthcoming republication in the collective edition, of which this little narrative may be considered as the preface. I shall, however, avail myself of the permission to insert in this place a letter lately addressed to Mr. Murray by Mr. Moore, which, among other interesting particulars, gives a curious enough account of some transactions respecting the publication of the new work:

"Sloperton Cottage, January 1, 1834.

"MY DEAR MR. MURRAY,—Had I been aware that your time of publication was so near, the few scattered notices and recollections of Mr. Crabbe, which it is in my power to furnish for his son's memoir, should have been presented in a somewhat less crude and careless shape than, in this hasty reply to your letter, I shall be able to give them.

"It was in the year 1817, if I recollect right that, during a visit of a few weeks to London, I first became acquainted with Mr. Crabbe; and my opportunities of seeing him during that period, at Mr. Rogers's and Holland House, were frequent. The circumstance connected with him at that time, which most dwelt upon my memory, was one in which you yourself were concerned; as it occurred in the course of the negotiations which led to your purchase of the copyright of his poems. Though to Crabbe himself, who had up to this period received but little for his writings, the liberal sum which you offered, namely, 3000l., appeared a mine of wealth, the two friends whom he had employed to negotiate for him, and who, both exquisite judges of literary merit, measured the marketable value of his works by their own admiration of them, thought that a bargain more advantageous might be made, and (as you, probably, now for the first time learn)

applied to another eminent house on the subject. Taking but
too just a measure of the state of public taste at that moment,
the respectable publishers to whom I allude named, as the
utmost which they could afford to give, but a third of the
sum which you had the day before offered. In this predicament
the situation of poor Crabbe was most critical. He had seen
within his reach a prize far beyond his most sanguine hopes,
and was now, by the over-sanguineness of friends, put in
danger of losing it. Change of mind, or a feeling of
umbrage at this reference to other publishers, might, not
unnaturally, it was feared, induce you to decline all further
negotiation; and that such was likely to be the result there appeared every reason to apprehend, as a letter which Crabbe had
addressed to you, saying that he had made up his mind to accept your offer, had not yet received any answer.

"In this crisis it was that Mr. Rogers and myself, anxious
to relieve our poor friend from his suspense, called upon you,
as you must well remember, in Albemarle-Street; and seldom
have I watched a countenance with more solicitude, or heard
words that gave me much more pleasure, than when, on the
subject being mentioned, you said, 'Oh yes—I have heard
from Mr. Crabbe, and look upon the matter as all settled.' I
was rather pressed, I recollect, for time that morning, having
an appointment on some business of my own; but Mr.
Rogers insisted that I should accompany him to Crabbe's
lodgings, and enjoy the pleasure of seeing him relieved from
his suspense. We found him sitting in his room, alone, and
expecting the worst; but soon dissipated all his fears by the
agreeable intelligence which we brought.

"When he received the bills for 3000l., we earnestly advised
that he should, without delay, deposit them in some safe
hands; but no—he must 'take them with him to Trowbridge,
and show them to his son John. They would hardly believe

in his good luck, at home, if they did not see the bills.' On his way down to Trowbridge, a friend at Salisbury, at whose house he rested (Mr. Everett, the banker), seeing that he carried these bills loosely in his waistcoat pocket, requested to be allowed to take charge of them for him, but with equal ill-success. 'There was no fear,' he said, 'of his losing them, and must show them to his son John.'

"It was during the same visit of Mr. Crabbe to London that we enjoyed a very agreeable day together at Mr. Horace Twiss's;—a day remarkable, not only for the presence of this great poet, but for the amusing assemblage of other remarkable characters who were there collected; the dinner guests being, besides the Dowager Countess of Cork and the present Lord and Lady Clarendon, Mr. William Spencer, Kean the actor, Colonel Berkeley, and Lord Petersham. Between these two last-mentioned gentlemen Mr. Crabbe got seated at dinner; and though I was not near enough to hear distinctly their conversation, I could see that he was alternately edified and surprised by the information they were giving him.

"In that same year I had the good luck to be present with him at a dinner in celebration of the memory of Burns, where he was one of a large party (yourself among the number), whom I was the means of collecting for the occasion; and who, by the way, subscribed liberally towards a monument to the Scottish bard, of which we have heard nothing ever since. Another public festival to which I accompanied him was the anniversary of the Wiltshire Society; where, on his health being proposed from the chair by Lord Lansdowne, he returned thanks in a short speech, simply, but collectedly, and with the manner of a man not deficient in the nerve necessary for such displays. In looking over an old newspaper report of that dinner, I find, in a speech by one of the guests, the following passage, which, more for its truth than its eloquence, I here venture to cite: 'Of Mr. Crabbe, the speaker would say, that the *Musa severior* which he worships has had no influence whatever on the kindly dispositions of his heart: but that, while, with the eye of a sage and a poet, he looks penetratingly into the darker region of human nature, he stands surrounded by its most genial light himself.'

"In the summer of the year 1824, I passed a few days in his company at Longleat, the noble seat of the Marquis of Bath; and it was there, as we walked about those delicious gardens, that he, for the first time, told me of an unpublished poem which he had by him, entitled, as I think he then said, the 'Departure and the Return,' and the same, doubtless, which you are now about to give to the world. Among the visitors at Longleat, at that time, was the beautiful Madame ——, a Genoese lady, whose knowledge and love of English literature rendered her admiration of Crabbe's genius doubly flattering. Nor was either the beauty or the praises of the fair Italian thrown away upon the venerable poet; among whose many amiable attributes a due appreciation of the charms of female society was not the least conspicuous. There was, indeed, in his manner to women, a sweetness bordering rather too much upon what the French call *doucereux*, and I remember hearing Miss ——, a lady known as the writer of some of the happiest *jeux d'esprit* of our day, say once of him, in allusion to this excessive courtesy—'the cake is no doubt very good, but there is too much sugar to cut through in getting at it.'

"In reference to his early intercourse with Mr. Burke, Sir James Mackintosh had, more than once, said to me, 'It is incumbent on you, Moore, who are Crabbe's neighbour, not to allow him to leave this world without putting on record, in some shape or other, all that he remembers of Burke.' On mentioning this to Mr. Rogers, when he came down to

Bowood, one summer, to meet Mr. Crabbe, it was agreed between us that we should use our united efforts to sift him upon this subject, and endeavour to collect whatever traces of Beaconsfield might still have remained in his memory. But, beyond a few vague generalities, we could extract nothing from him whatever, and it was plain that, in his memory at least, the conversational powers of the great orator had left but little vestige. The range of subjects, indeed, in which Mr. Crabbe took any interest was, at all times of his life, very limited; and, at the early period, when he became acquainted with Mr. Burke, when the power of poetry was but newly awakening within him, it may easily be conceived that whatever was unconnected with his own absorbing art, or even with his own peculiar province of that art, would leave but a feeble and transient impression upon his mind.

"This indifference to most of the general topics, whether of learning or politics, which diversify the conversation of men of the world, Mr. Crabbe retained through life; and in this peculiarity, I think, lay one of the causes of his comparative inefficiency, as a member of society,—of that impression, so disproportionate to the real powers of his mind, which he produced in ordinary life. Another cause, no doubt, of the inferiority of his conversation to his writings is to be found in that fate which threw him, early in life, into a state of dependent intercourse with persons far superior to him in rank, but immeasurably beneath him in intellect. The courteous policy which would then lead him to keep his conversation down to the level of those he lived with, afterwards grew into a habit which, in the commerce of the world, did injustice to his great powers.

"You have here all that, at this moment, occurs to me, in the way either of recollection or remark, on the subject of our able and venerated friend. The delightful day which Mr.

Rogers and myself passed with him, at Sydenham, you have already, I believe, an account of from my friend, Mr. Campbell, who was our host on the occasion. Mr. Lockhart has, I take for granted, communicated to you the amusing anecdote of Crabbe's interview with the two Scotch lairds—an anecdote which I cherish the more freshly and fondly in my memory, from its having been told me, with his own peculiar humour, by Sir Walter Scott, at Abbotsford. I have, therefore, nothing further left than to assure you how much and truly I am, yours,

"THOMAS MOORE."

During his first and second visits to London, my father spent a good deal of his time beneath the hospitable roof of the late Samuel Hoare, Esquire, on Hampstead Heath. He owed his introduction to this respected family to his friends, Mr. Bowles, and the author of the delightful "Excursions in the West," Mr. Warner; and though Mr. Hoare was an invalid, and little disposed to form new connections, he was so much gratified with Mr. Crabbe's manners and conversation, that their acquaintance soon grew into an affectionate and lasting intimacy.[27] Mr. Crabbe, in subsequent years, made Hampstead his head-quarters on his spring visits, and only repaired from thence occasionally to the brilliant circles of the metro-

---

[27] I quote what follows from a letter which I have recently been favoured with from Mr. Bowles:—"Perhaps it might be stated in your memoir that, at Bath, I first introduced your father to the estimable family of the Hoares of Hampstead; with whom, through his subsequent life, he was so intimate, and who contributed so much of the happiness of all his later days. I wish sincerely that any incident I could recollect might be such as would contribute to the illustration of his mind, and amiable, gentle, affectionate character; but I never noted an expression or incident at the time, and only preserve an impression of his mild manner, his observations, playful but often acute, his high and steady principles of religious and moral obligation, his warm feelings against anything which appeared harsh or unjust, and his undeviating and steady attachments."

polis. Advancing age, failing health, the tortures of tic douloureux, with which he began to be afflicted about 1820, and, I may add, the increasing earnestness of his devotional feelings, rendered him, in his closing years, less and less anxious to mingle much in the scenes of gaiety and fashion.

The following passage of a letter which he received, in April, 1821, from his amiable correspondent at Ballitore, descriptive of his reception at Trowbridge of her friend Leckey, is highly characteristic:

"When my feeble and simple efforts have obtained the approbation of the first moral poet of his time, is it surprising that I should be inflated thereby? Yet thou art too benevolent to intend to turn the brain of a poor old woman, by commendation so valued, though thou has practised on my credulity by a little deception; and, from being always accustomed to matter of fact, I generally take what I hear in a literal sense. A gentlewoman once assured me that the husband of her waiting-woman came to her house stark naked— naked as he was born. I said, 'O dear,' and reflected with pity on the poor man's situation; certainly thinking him mad, as maniacs often throw away their clothes. My neighbour went on:—'His coat was so ragged! his hat so shabby!'—and, to my surprise, I found the man dressed, though in a garb ill-befitting the spouse of a lady's maid. And thou madest me believe thou wert in good case, by saying, 'Am I not a great fat rector?' We said, it was the exuberance of good humour that caused increase of flesh: but a curate, with six hungry children, staggered our belief. Now we know thy son is thy curate, and that thou art light and active in form, with looks irradiated, and accents modulated by genuine kindness of heart. Thus our friend John James Leckey describes thee; for I have seen his long letter to his mother on the subject of his visit, which with his letter to me, has placed thee so before our view, that we all but see and hear thee, frequently going out and coming into the room, with a book in thy hand, and a smile and friendly expression on thy lips—the benevolence which swam in thy eyes, and the cordial shake of both hands with which thou partedst with him—and thou came out with him in the damp night, and sent thy servant with him to the inn, where he should not have lodged, had there been room for him in thy own house."

It was during the last of my father's very active seasons in London (1822), that he had the satisfaction of meeting with Sir Walter Scott; and the baronet, who was evidently much affected on seeing Mr. Crabbe, would not part with him until he had promised to visit him in Scotland the ensuing autumn. But I much regret that the invitation was accepted for that particular occasion; for, as it happened, the late king fixed on the same time for his northern progress; and, instead of finding Sir Walter in his own mansion in the country, when Mr. Crabbe reached Scotland, in August, the family had all repaired to Edinburgh, to be present amidst a scene of bustle and festivity little favourable to the sort of intercourse with a congenial mind, to which he had looked forward with such pleasing anticipations. He took up his residence, however, in Sir Walter's house in North Castle Street, Edinburgh, and was treated by him and all his connections with the greatest kindness, respect, and attention; and though the baronet's time was much occupied with the business of the royal visit, and he had to dine almost daily at his majesty's table, still my father had an opportunity not to be undervalued of seeing what was to him an aspect of society wholly new. The Highlanders, in particular, their language, their dress, and their manners were contemplated with exceeding interest. I am enabled, by the kindness of one of my father's female friends, to offer some extracts from a short Journal, which he kept for her amusement during his stay in the northern metropolis:

"Whilst it is fresh in my memory, I should describe the day which I have just passed, but I do not believe an accurate description to be possible. What avails it to say, for instance, that there met at the sumptuous dinner, in all the costume of the Highlanders, the great chief himself and officers of his company. This expresses not the singularity of appearance and manners—the peculiarities of men, all gentlemen, but remote from our society—leaders of clans—joyous company. Then we had Sir Walter Scott's national songs and ballads, exhibiting all the feelings of clanship. I thought it an honour that Glengarry even took notice of me, for there were those, and gentlemen, too, who considered themselves honoured by following in his train. There were, also, Lord Errol, and the Macleod, and the Frazer, and the Gordon, and the Ferguson; and I conversed at dinner with Lady Glengarry, and did almost believe myself a harper, or bard, rather—for harp I cannot strike—and Sir Walter was the life and soul of the whole. It was a splendid festivity, and I felt I know not how much younger."

The lady to whom he addressed the above journal says, "A few more extracts will, perhaps, be interesting. It is not surprising that, under the guidance of Mr. Lockhart, Mr. Crabbe's walks should have been very interesting, and that all he saw should take an advantageous colouring from such society."

"I went to the palace of Holyrood House, and was much interested;—the rooms, indeed, did not affect me,—the old tapestry was such as I had seen before, and I did not much care about the leather chairs, with three legs each, nor the furniture, except in one room—that where Queen Mary slept. The bed has a canopy very rich, but time-stained. We went into the little room where the Queen and Rizzio sat, when his murderers broke in and cut him down as he struggled to escape: they show certain stains on the floor; and I see no reason why you should not believe them made by his blood, if you can.

"Edinburgh is really a very interesting place,—to me very singular. How can I describe the view from the hill that overlooks the palace—the fine group of buildings which form the castle; the bridges, uniting the two towns; and the beautiful view of the Frith and its islands?

"But Sunday came, and the streets were forsaken; and silence reigned over the whole city. London has a diminished population on that day in her streets; but in Edinburgh it is a total stagnation—a quiet that is in itself devout.

"A long walk through divers streets, lanes, and alleys, up to the Old Town, makes me better acquainted with it; a lane of cobblers struck me particularly; and I could not but remark the civility and urbanity of the Scotch poor; they certainly exceed ours in politeness, arising, probably, from minds more generally cultivated.

"This day I dined with Mr. Mackenzie, the Man of Feeling, as he is commonly called. He has not the manner you would expect from his works; but a rare sportsman, still enjoying the relation of a good day, though only the ghost of the pleasure remains.—What a discriminating and keen man is my friend; and I am disposed to think highly of his son-in-law, Mr. Lockhart—of his heart—his understanding will not be disputed by any one."

At the table of Mr. Lockhart, with whom he commonly

dined when Sir Walter was engaged to the King, he one day sat down with three of the supposed writers or symposiasts of the inimitable "Noctes Ambrosianae"; viz. his host himself—the far-famed Professor Wilson, whom he termed "that extraordinary man"—and the honest Shepherd of Ettrick, who amused him much by calling for a can of ale, while champagne and claret, and other choice wines, were in full circulation. This must have been an evening cheaply purchased by a journey from Trowbridge. On the other hand, he was introduced, by a friend from the south, to the "Scottish Chiefs" of the opposite clan, though brothers in talent and fame—the present Lord Advocate Jeffrey, Mr. John Archibald Murray, Professor Leslie, and some other distinguished characters.

Before he retired at night, he had generally the pleasure of half an hour's confidential conversation with Sir Walter, when he spoke occasionally of the Waverley Novels—though not as compositions of his own, for that was yet a secret—but without reserve upon all other subjects in which they had a common interest. These *were* evenings!

I am enabled to present a few more particulars of my father's visit to Edinburgh, by the kindness of Mr. Lockhart, who has recently favoured me with the following letter:

"London, December 26th, 1833.

"DEAR SIR,—I am sorry to tell you that Sir Walter Scott kept no diary during the time of your father's visit to Scotland, otherwise it would have given me pleasure to make extracts for the use of your memoirs. For myself, although it is true that, in consequence of Sir Walter's being constantly consulted about the details of every procession and festival of that busy fortnight, the pleasing task of showing to Mr. Crabbe the usual *lions* of Edinburgh fell principally to my

R

share, I regret to say that my memory does not supply me with many traces of his conversation. The general impression, however, that he left on my mind was strong, and, I think, indelible: while all the mummeries and carousals of an interval, in which Edinburgh looked very unlike herself, have faded into a vague and dreamlike indistinctness, the image of your father, then first seen, but long before admired and revered in his works, remains as fresh as if the years that have now passed were but so many days.—His noble forehead, his bright beaming eye, without any thing of old age about it—though he was then, I presume, above seventy—his sweet, and, I would say, innocent smile, and the calm mellow tones of his voice—all are reproduced the moment I open any page of his poetry: and how much better have I understood and enjoyed his poetry, since I was able thus to connect with it the living presence of the man!

"The literary persons in company with whom I saw him the most frequently were Sir Walter and Henry Mackenzie; and between two such thorough men of the world as they were, perhaps his *apparent* simplicity of look and manners struck one more than it might have done under different circumstances; but all three harmonised admirably together—Mr. Crabbe's avowed ignorance about Gaels, and clans, and tartans, and everything that was at the moment uppermost in Sir Walter's thoughts, furnishing him with a welcome apology for dilating on such topics with enthusiastic minuteness—while your father's countenance spoke the quiet delight he felt in opening his imagination to what was really a new world—and the venerable 'Man of Feeling,' though a fiery Highlander himself at bottom, had the satisfaction of lying by and listening until some opportunity offered itself of looking in, between the links, perhaps, of some grand chain of poetical imagery, some small comic or sarcastic trait, which

Sir Walter caught up, played with, and, with that art so peculiarly his own, forced into the service of the very impression it seemed meant to disturb. One evening, at Mr. Mackenzie's own house, I particularly remember, among the *noctes cœnæque Deum.*

"Mr. Crabbe had, I presume, read very little about Scotland before that excursion. It appeared to me that he confounded the Inchcolm of the Frith of Forth with the Icolmkill of the Hebrides; but John Kemble, I have heard, did the same. I believe, he really never had known, until then, that a language radically distinct from the English, was still actually spoken within the island. And this recalls a scene of high merriment which occurred the very morning after his arrival. When he came down into the breakfast parlour, Sir Walter had not yet appeared there; and Mr. Crabbe had before him two or three portly personages all in the full Highland garb. These gentlemen, arrayed in a costume so novel, were talking in a language which he did not understand; so he never doubted that they were foreigners. The Celts, on their part, conceived Mr. Crabbe, dressed as he was in rather an old-fashioned style of clerical propriety, with buckles in his shoes, for instance, to be some learned abbé, who had come on a pilgrimage to the shrine of Waverley; and the result was, that when, a little afterwards, Sir Walter and his family entered the room, they found your father and these worthy lairds hammering away, with pain and labour, to make themselves mutually understood in most execrable French. Great was the relief, and potent the laughter, when the host interrupted their colloquy with his plain English 'Good-morning.'

"It surprised me, on taking Mr. Crabbe to see the house of Allan Ramsay on the Castle Hill, to find that he had never heard of Allan's name; or, at all events, was unacquainted with his works. The same evening, however, he perused 'The

Gentle Shepherd,' and he told me next morning, that he had been pleased with it, but added, 'there is a long step between Ramsay and Burns.' He then made Sir Walter read and interpret some of old Dunbar to him; and said, 'I see that the Ayrshire bard had one giant before him.'

"Mr. Crabbe seemed to admire, like other people, the grand natural scenery about Edinburgh; but when I walked with him to the Salisbury Craigs, where the superb view had then a lively foreground of tents and batteries, he appeared to be more interested with the stratification of the rocks about us, than with any other feature in the landscape. As to the city itself, he said he soon got wearied of the New Town, but could amuse himself for ever in the Old one. He was more than once detected rambling after nightfall by himself, among some of the obscurest wynds and closes; and Sir Walter, fearing that, at a time of such confusion, he might get into some scene of trouble, took the precaution of desiring a friendly *caddie* (see Humphry Clinker), from the corner of Castle Street, to follow him the next time he went out alone in the evening.

"Mr. Crabbe repeated his visits several times to the Royal Infirmary of Edinburgh, and expressed great admiration of the manner in which the patients were treated. He also examined pretty minutely the interior of the Bedlam. I went with him both to the Castle and Queen Mary's apartment in Holyrood House; but he did not appear to care much about either. I remember, however, that when the old dame who showed us Darnley's armour and boots complained of the impudence, as she called it, of a preceding visitor, who had discovered these articles to be relics of a much later age, your father warmly entered into her feelings; and said, as we came away, 'this pedantic puppyism was *inhumane*.'

"The first Sunday he was in Edinburgh, my wife and her

sister carried him to hear service in St. George's church, where the most popular of the Presbyterian clergy, the late Dr. Andrew Thomson, then officiated. But he was little gratified either with the aspect of the church, which is large without grandeur, or the style of the ceremonial, which he said was *bald and bad*, or the eloquence of the sermon, which, however, might not be preached by Dr. Thomson himself. Next Sunday he went to the Episcopalian chapel, where Sir Walter Scott's family were in the habit of attending. He said, however, in walking along the streets that day, 'this unusual decorum says not a little for the Scotch system: the silence of these well-dresssed crowds is really grand.' King George the Fourth made the same remark.

"Mr. Crabbe entered so far into the feelings of his host, and of the occasion, as to write a set of verses on the royal visit to Edinburgh; they were printed along with many others, but I have no copy of the collection. (Mr. Murray can easily get one from Edinburgh, in case you wish to include those stanzas in your edition of his poetical works.) He also attended one of the king's levees at Holyrood, where his majesty appeared at once to recognise his person, and received him with attention.

"All my friends who had formed acquaintance with Mr. Crabbe on this occasion appeared ever afterwards to remember him with the same feeling of affectionate respect. Sir Walter Scott and his family parted with him most reluctantly. He had been quite domesticated under their roof, and treated the young people very much as if they had been his own. His unsophisticated, simple, and kind address put every body at ease with him; and, indeed, one would have been too apt to forget what lurked beneath that good-humoured unpretending aspect, but that every now and then he uttered some brief pithy remark, which showed how narrowly he had been scrutinising into whatever might be said or done before him, and called us to remember, with some awe, that we were in the presence of the author of 'The Borough.'

"I recollect that he used to have a lamp and writing materials placed by his bed-side every night; and when Lady Scott told him she wondered the day was not enough for authorship, he answered, 'Dear Lady, I should have lost many a good hit, had I not set down, at once, things that occurred to me in my dreams.'

"I never could help regretting very strongly that Mr. Crabbe did not find Sir Walter at Abbotsford as he had expected to do. The fortnight he passed in Edinburgh was one scene of noise, glare, and bustle—reviews, levees, banquets, and balls—and no person could either see or hear so much of him as might, under other circumstances, have been looked for. Sir Walter, himself, I think, took only one walk with Mr. Crabbe: it was to the ruins of St. Anthony's Chapel, at the foot of Arthur's Seat, which your father wished to see, as connected with part of the Heart of Mid-Lothian. I had the pleasure to accompany them on this occasion; and it was the only one on which I heard your father enter into any details of his own personal history. He told us, that during many months when he was toiling in early life in London, he hardly ever tasted butcher's meat, except on a Sunday, when he dined usually with a tradesman's family, and thought their leg of mutton, baked in the pan, the perfection of luxury. The tears stood in his eyes while he talked of Burke's kindness to him in his distress; and I remember he said, 'The night after I had delivered my letter at his door, I was in such a state of agitation, that I walked Westminster Bridge backwards and forwards until day-light.' Believe me, dear Sir, your very faithful servant,

"J. G. LOCKHART."

Shortly after his return from Scotland, Mr. Crabbe had a peculiarly severe fit of the tic douloureux, to which he thus alludes, in one of his letters to Mrs. Leadbeater:

"I am visited by a painful disorder, which, though it leaves me many intervals of ease and comfort, yet compels me to postpone much of what may be called the business of life; and thus, having many things to do, and a comparatively short time in which they must be done, I too often defer what would be in itself a pleasing duty, and apply myself to what affords a satisfaction, only because it has been fulfilled."

It was this affliction which prevented his complying with a kind invitation to spend the Christmas of 1822 at Belvoir; on which occasion he received the following letter, which I select as indicating the esteem in which he was held, after his removal from Leicestershire, by the whole of the family of Rutland:

"Belvoir Castle, Dec. 16, 1822.

"DEAR SIR,—I was much disappointed to find, from your letter of the 11th instant, that you have been obliged once more to abandon (for the present) the idea of a visit to this place. I feel the more regret at this circumstance, from the cause which you have to decline exposure to the cold weather of winter, and the fatigue of travelling. You have no two friends who wish you more cordially well than the Duchess and myself; and I can truly say that, whenever it may be convenient and pleasant to you to visit the castle, a hearty and sincere welcome will await you. I am, dear sir, &c.,

"RUTLAND."[28]

[28] I extract what follows from a letter with which his Grace honoured me after my father's death:—"It is indeed true that my lamented Duchess vied with myself in sincere admiration of his talents and virtues, and in warm and hearty esteem for your father."

About the same time, having received an intelligible scrawl from my eldest girl, Caroline, who was then in her fourth year, he addressed his letter to the child. Who will require to be told that his coming to Pucklechurch was always looked forward to by the young people as a vision of joy?—

"Trowbridge, 24th Dec., 1822.

"MY DEAR CARRY,—Your very pretty letter gave me a great deal of pleasure; and I choose this, which is my birthday, that in it I may return you my best thanks for your kind remembrance of me; and I will keep your letter laid up in my new Bible, where I shall often see it; and then I shall say, 'This is from my dear little girl at Pucklechurch.' My face is not so painful as it was when I wrote to papa; and I would set out immediately, to see you all, with great pleasure, but I am forced, against my will, to remain at home this week by duty; and that, you know, I must attend to: and then, there is an engagement to a family in this place, Waldron by name, who have friends in Salisbury, and among them a gentleman, who, though he is young, will have grandpapa's company, and grandpapa, being a very old man, takes this for a compliment, and has given his promise, though he is vexed about it, that he will be in Trowbridge at that time; and so he dares not yet fix the day for his visit to his dear Caroline, and her good mamma, and papa, and her little brothers; but he is afraid that papa will not be pleased with this uncertainty; yet I will write to papa the very first hour in which I can say I shall be free to go after my own pleasure; and I do hope that if it cannot be in the next week, it will be early in the following. And so, my dear, you will say to papa and mamma, 'You must forgive poor grandpapa, because he is so puzzled that he does not know what he can do, and so vexed beside, that he cannot do as his wishes and his affection would lead him;

and you know, dear papa and mamma, that he grows to be a very old man, and does not know how to get out of these difficulties, but I am sure that he loves to come to us, and will be here as soon as ever he can.' I hope, my dear Carry, that Master Davidson is well after the waltz, and his lady with whom he danced. I should have liked very much to have seen them. I gave your love to uncle John, and will to your other uncles when I see them: I dare say they all love you; for good little girls, like my Carry, are much beloved. Pray, give my kind respects to Miss Joyces. You are well off in having such ladies to take so much pains with you; and you improve very prettily under their care. I have written a very long letter to my Carry; and I think we suit each other, and shall make fit correspondents: that is, writers of letters, Caroline to grand-papa, and grandpapa to Caroline. God bless my dear little girl. I desire earnestly to see you, and am your very affectionate

"GRANDPAPA."

I close this chapter with a fragment of a letter from his friend, Mr. Norris Clark, of Trowbridge:

"I wish it was in my power to furnish you with anything worth relating of your late father. The fault is in my memory; for, if I could recollect them, hundreds of his conversations would be as valuable as Johnson's, though he never talked for effect. I will mention two which impressed me, as being the first and last I had with him. When I called on him, soon after his arrival, I remarked that his house and garden were pleasant and secluded: he replied that he preferred walking in the streets, and observing the faces of the passers-by, to the finest natural scene. The last time I spoke to him was at our amateur concert; after it concluded, which was with the overture to

Freyschutz, he said, he used to prefer the simple ballad, but he now, by often hearing more scientific music, began to like it best. I have no doubt he had a most critical musical ear, as every one must have perceived who heard him read. I never heard more beautifully correct recitative."

CHAPTER X

1823—1832

The closing Years of Mr. Crabbe's Life—Annual Excursions—Domestic Habits—Visits to Pucklechurch—His last Tour to Clifton, Bristol, &c.—His Illness and Death —His Funeral.

IT NOW remains to sum up this narrative with a few particulars respecting the closing years of Mr. Crabbe's henceforth retired life. Though he went every year to Mr. Hoare's, at Hampstead (the death of the head of that family having rather increased than diminished his attachment for its other members), and each season accompanied them on some healthful excursion to the Isle of Wight, Hastings, Ilfracombe, or Clifton; and though, in their company, he saw occasionally not a little of persons peculiarly interesting to the public, as well as dear to himself—as, for example, Mr. Wilberforce, Mrs. Joanna Baillie, Miss Edgeworth, and Mrs. Siddons—and though, in his passings through town, he generally dined with Mr. Rogers, Lord Holland, and Mr. Murray, and there met, from time to time, his great brothers in art, Wordsworth and Southey—for both of whom he felt a cordial respect and affection—still, his journals, in those latter years, are so briefly drawn up, that, by printing them, I should be giving little more than a list of names. While, at home, he seldom visited much beyond the limits of his parish—the houses of

Mr. Waldron and Mr. Norris Clark being his more familiar haunts; and in his own study he continued, unless when interrupted by his painful disorder, much of the habits and occupations which have already been described, comprising poetry, and various theological essays, besides sermons; of all of which specimens may hereafter be made public. The manuscript volumes he left behind him at his death, not including those of the rough copies of his published works, amount in number to *twenty-one*. The gradual decline of his health, but unshaken vigour of his understanding, will be, perhaps, sufficiently illustrated by the following extracts from his note-books, and his own letters to his friends and family:

"Aldborough, October, 1823.
"Thus once again, my native place, I come
Thee to salute—my earliest, latest home:
Much are we alter'd both, but I behold
In thee a youth renew'd—whilst I am old.
The works of man from dying we may save,
But man himself moves onward to the grave."

To Mrs. Leadbeater.

"Trowbridge, June, 1824.
"I must go to town, and there be stimulated by conversations on the subjects of authorships, and all that relates to the business of the press. I find, too, that I can dedicate more time to this employment in London than in this seat of business, where every body comes at their own time; and, having driven the mind from its purposes, leave a man to waste no small portion of it in miscellaneous reading, and other amusement, such as nursing and construing the incipient meanings that come and go in the face of an infant. My grand-daughter and I begin to be companions; and the seven months and the

seventy years accord very nicely, and will do so, probably (the parties living), for a year or two to come; when, the man becoming weaker and the child stronger, there will come an inequality to disturb the friendship.

"I think something more than two years have passed, since the disease, known by a very formidable name, which I have never consented to adopt, attacked me. It came like momentary shocks of a grievous tooth-ache; and, indeed, I was imprudent enough to have one tooth extracted which appeared to be most affected; but the loss of this guiltless and useful tooth had not one beneficial consequence. For many months the pain came, sometimes on a slight touch, as the application of a towel or a razor, and it sometimes came without any apparent cause, and certainly was at one time alarming, more especially when I heard of operations, as cutting down and scraping the bone, &c.; but these failing, and a mode of treating the disease being found,[1] I lost my fears, and took blue pills and medicines of like kind for a long season, and with good success."

To a Lady at Trowbridge.

"Beccles, May 10, 1825.

"A letter from my son to-day, gives me pain, by its account of your illness: I had hope of better information; and though he writes that there is amendment, yet he confesses it is slow, and your disorder is painful, too. That men of free lives, and in habits of intemperance, should be ill, is to be expected; but we are surprised, as well as grieved, when frequent attacks of this kind are the lot of the temperate, the young, and the careful: still, it is the will of Him who afflicts not his creatures without a cause, which we may not perceive, but must believe; for he

[1] The kind and skilful physician on whose advice my father relied was Dr. Kerrison, of New Burlington Street.

is all wisdom and goodness, and sees the way to our final happiness, when we cannot. In all kinds of affliction, the Christian is consoled by the confiding hope, that such trials, well borne, will work for glory and happiness, as they work in us patience and resignation. In our pains and weakness we approach nearer, and learn to make our supplications to a merciful Being, as to a parent, who, if he doth not withdraw the evil from us, yet gives us strength to endure and be thankful.—I grant there is much that we cannot know nor comprehend in the government of this world; but we know our duty is to submit, because there is enough we can see to make us rest in hope and comfort, though there is much that we cannot understand. We know not why one in the prime of life should suffer long; and, while suffering, should hear of threescore persons, of every age and station, and with minds, some devoted to their God, and others to this world altogether, all in one dreadful moment to be sunk in the ocean, and the stillness of death to surround them. But though this and a number of other things are mysteries to us, they are all open to Him from whom nothing can be hidden. Let us, then, my dear Miss W., have confidence in this, that we are tried, and disciplined, and prepared—for another state of being; and let not our ignorance in what is not revealed, prevent our belief in what is. 'I do not know,' is a very good answer to most of the questions put to us by those who wish for help to unbelief. But why all this? will you ask: first, because I love you very much, and then you will recollect that I have had, of late, very strong admonition to be serious; for though the pain of itself be not dangerous, yet the weakness it brought on, and still brings, persuades me that not many such strokes are needed to demolish a frame which has been seventy years moving, and not always regulated with due caution: but I will not fatigue you any more now, nor, I hope, at any future time. I trust, my dear friend, to see you in good health, cheerful and happy, relying entirely on that great and good Being, whose ways are not ours, neither can we comprehend them; and our very ignorance should teach us perfect reliance on his wisdom and goodness. I had a troubled night, and am thinking of the time when you will kindly send, and sometimes call, to hear, 'how Mr. Crabbe does to-day, and how he rested'; for though we must all take the way of our friend departed, yet mine is the natural first turn; and you will not wonder that restless nights put me in mind of this."

A friend having for the first time seen the "Rejected Addresses," had written with some soreness of the parody on my father's poetry; he thus answers:

"You were more feeling than I was, when you read the excellent parodies of the young men who wrote the 'Rejected Addresses.' There is a little ill-nature—and, I take the liberty of adding, undeserved ill-nature—in their prefatory address; but in their versification, they have done me admirably. They are extraordinary men; but it is easier to imitate style, than to furnish matter."[2]

[2] In the new edition of the "Rejected Addresses", I find a note, part of which is as follows:—"The writer's first interview with the Poet Crabbe, who may be designated Pope in worsted stockings, took place at Wm. Spencer's villa at Petersham, close to what that gentleman called his gold-fish pond, though it was scarcely three feet in diameter, throwing up a *jet-d'eau* like a thread. The venerable bard, seizing both the hands of his satirist, exclaimed, with a good-humoured laugh, 'Ah, my old enemy, how do you do?' In the course of conversation he expressed great astonishment at his popularity in London; adding, 'In my own village they think nothing of me.' The subject happening to be the inroads of time upon beauty, the writer quoted the following lines:—

'Six years had pass'd, and forty ere the six,
When Time began to play his usual tricks:
My locks, once comely in a virgin's sight,
Locks of pure brown, now felt th' encroaching white.
Gradual each day I liked my horses less,
My dinner more—I learnt to play at chess.'

In June, 1825, he thus writes from Mr. Hoare's villa at Hampstead:—

"Hampstead, June, 1825.

"My time passes I cannot tell how pleasantly, when the pain leaves me. To-day I read one of my long stories to my friends, and Mrs. Joanna Baillie and her sister. It was a task; but they encouraged me, and were, or seemed, gratified. I rhyme at Hampstead with a great deal of facility, for nothing interrupts me but kind calls to something pleasant; and though all this makes parting painful, it will, I hope, make me resolute to enter upon my duties diligently when I return.—I am too much indulged. Except a return of pain, and that not severe, I have good health; and if my walks are not so long, they are more frequent. I have seen many things and many people; have seen Mr. Southey and Mr. Wordsworth; have been some days with Mr. Rogers, and at last have been at the Athenæum, and purpose to visit the Royal Institution; and have been to Richmond in a steam-boat; seen, also, the picture galleries, and some other exhibitions: but I passed one Sunday in London with discontent, doing no duty myself nor listening to another; and I hope my uneasiness proceeded not merely from breaking a habit. We had a dinner social and pleasant, if the hours before it had been rightly spent: but I would not willingly pass another Sunday in the same manner. I have my home with my friends here (Mrs. Hoare's), and exchange it with reluctance for the Hummums occasionally. Such is the state of the garden here, in which I walk and read,

'That's very good!' cried the bard; 'whose is it?'—'Your own.'—'Indeed! hah! well, I had quite forgotten it.' " The writer proceeds to insinuate, that this was a piece of affectation on the part of my father. If Mr. Smith had written as many verses, and lived as long, as Mr. Crabbe, he would, I fancy, have been incapable of expressing such a suspicion.

that, in a morning like this, the smell of the flowers is fragrant beyond anything I ever perceived before. It is what I can suppose may be in Persia, or other Oriental countries—a Paradisiacal sweetness.

"I am told that I or my verses, or perhaps both, have abuse in a book of Mr. Colburn's publishing, called 'The Spirit of the Times.' I believe I felt something indignant: but my engraved seal dropped out of the socket and was lost, and I perceived this vexed me much more than the 'spirit' of Mr. Hazlitt."

"Trowbridge, Feb. 3, 1826.

"Your letter, my dear Mrs. Leadbeater, was dated the 9th of the tenth month of last year; just at a time when I was confined in the house of friends, most attentive to me during the progress and termination of a painful disease to which I had been long subject, though I was not at any time before so suddenly and so alarmingly attacked. I had parted from my son, his wife, and child, about ten days before, and judged myself to be in possession of health, strength, and good spirits fitted for my journey—one about 200 miles from this place, and in which I had pleased myself with the anticipation of meeting with relatives dear to me, and many of the friends of my earlier days. I reached London with no other symptom of illness than fatigue; but was indisposed on the second night, and glad to proceed to Hampstead on the third day, where I found my accustomed welcome in the house of two ladies, who have been long endeared to me by acts of unceasing kindness, which I can much better feel than describe. On the second evening after my arrival, Miss Hoare and I went to the place of worship to which she is accustomed, where, just as the service of the day terminated, a sudden and overpowering attack of the disease to which I allude was the commencement of an illness which was troublesome to my friends about three weeks, but, as the pain gradually passed away, was scarcely to be esteemed as a trial to me, or to the resignation and patience which pain should give birth to. I am now—let me be thankful—in a great measure freed from pain, and have, probably, that degree of health, and even exertion, which, at my age, is a blessing rather to be desired than expected; the allotted threescore and ten has passed over me, and I am now in my seventy-second year! thankful, I hope, for much that I have, and, among other things, for the friendship of some very estimable beings. I feel the heaviness and languor of time, and that even in our social visits at this season. I cannot enjoy festivity; with friends long known I can be easy, and even cheerful,—but the pain of exertion, which I think it a duty to make, has its influence over me, and I wonder—be assured that I am perfectly sincere in this—I wonder when young people—and there are such—seem to desire that I should associate with them."

"Pucklechurch, 1826.

"Caroline, now six years old, reads incessantly and insatiably. She has been travelling with John Bunyan's 'Pilgrim,' and enjoyed a pleasure never, perhaps, to be repeated. The veil of religious mystery, that so beautifully covers the outward and visible adventures, is quite enchanting. The dear child was caught reading by her sleeping maid, at five o'clock this morning, impatient—'tis our nature—to end her pleasure."

"Trowbridge, 1827.

"I often find such difficulties in visiting the sick, that I am at a loss what thoughts to suggest to them, or to entertain of them. Home is not better (to the aged), but it is better loved and more desired; for in other places we cannot indulge our humours and tastes so well, nor so well comply with those of our people.

"In the last week was our fair; and I am glad that quiet is restored. When I saw four or five human beings, with painted faces and crazy dresses and gestures, trying to engage and entice the idle spectators to enter their showhouse, I felt the degradation; for it seemed like man reduced from his natural rank in the creation: and yet, probably, they would say,— 'What can we do? We were brought up to it, and we must eat.'

"I think the state of an old but hale man is the most comfortable and least painful of any stage in life; but it is always liable to infirmities: and this is as it should be. It would not be well to be in love with life when so little of it remains."

The two following extracts are from notes written to the same kind friend, on his birthday of 1827, and on that of 1828:

"Parsonage, Dec. 24, 1827.—There can be only one reason for declining your obliging invitation; and that is, the grievous stupidity that grows upon me daily. I have read of a country where they reckon all men after a certain period of life to be no longer fitted for companionship in business or pleasure, and so they put the poor useless beings out of their way. I think I am beyond that time; but as we have no such prudent custom, I will not refuse myself the good you so kindly offer, and you will make due allowance for the stupidity aforesaid."

"Parsonage, Dec. 24, 1828.—This has been a very busy day with me. My kind neighbours have found out that the 24th of this month is my birthday, and I have not only had music in the evening, but small requests all the day long, for 'Sure

the minister will not mind giving us a trifle on his birthday'—
and so they have done me the honour of making a trial; as if
it were a joyful thing for a man to enter into his seventy-sixth
year; and I grant it ought to be. But your time is precious,
and I must not detain you. Mr. ——, I hear, has been with you
to-day. I have never yet been able to fulfil my engagements.
He puzzles me. It is strange, I can but think, for a man of sense
and reflection openly to avow disbelief of a religion that has
satisfied the wisest, converted the most wicked, and consoled
the most afflicted of our fellow-creatures. He says he is happy;
and it may be so. I am sure I should not, having the same
opinions. Certainly, if we wait till all doubts be cleared away,
we shall die doubting. I ought to ask your pardon, and I do.
How I came to be in a grave humour, I know not; for I have
been dancing with my little girl to all kinds of tunes, and, I
dare say, with all kinds of steps, such as old men and children
are likely to exhibit."

In October, 1829, he thus writes to the present biographer:

"I am in truth not well. It is not pain, nor can I tell what it is.
Probably when you reach the year I am arrived at, you will
want no explanation. But I should be a burden to you: the
dear girls and boys would not know what to make of a
grandfather who could not romp nor play with them."

In January, 1830, he thus addresses his grand-daughter:

"You and I both love reading, and it is well for me that I do;
but at your time reading is but one employment, whereas with
me it is almost all. And yet I often ask myself, at the end of
my volumes,—Well! what am I the wiser, what the better, for
this? Reading for amusement only, and, as it is said, merely to

kill time, is not the satisfaction of a reasonable being. At your age, my dear Caroline, I read every book which I could procure. Now, I should wish to procure only such as are worth reading; but I confess I am frequently disappointed."

Dining one day with a party at Pucklechurch, about this period, some one was mentioning a professor of gastronomy, who looked to the time when his art should get to such perfection as to keep people alive for ever. My father said, most emphatically, "God forbid!" He had begun to feel that old age, even without any very severe disease, is not a state to hold tenaciously. Towards the latter end of the last year he had found a perceptible and general decline of the vital powers, without any specific complaint of any consequence; and though there were intervals in which he felt peculiarly renovated, yet, from the autumn of 1828, he could trace a marked, though still very gradual change; or, as he himself called it, a breaking up of the constitution; in which, however, the mind partook not, for there was no symptom of mental decay, except, and that only slightly and partially, in the memory.

But the most remarkable characteristic of his decline was the unabated warmth of his affections. In general, the feelings of old age are somewhat weakened and concentrated under the sense of a precarious life, and of personal deprivation; but his interest in the welfare of others, his sympathy with the sufferings or happiness of his friends, and even in the amusements of children, continued to the last as vivid as ever: and he thought, spoke, and wrote of his departure with such fortitude and cheerful resignation, that I have not that pain in recording his latter days which, under other circumstances, would have made the termination of this memoir a task scarcely to be endured.

A most valued friend of my father describes his decline in terms so affectionate, beautiful, and original, that I have obtained her permission to add this to other passages from the same pen:

"Mr. Crabbe was so much beloved, that the approaches of age were watched by his friends with jealousy, as an enemy undermining their own happiness; and the privations inflicted upon him by its infirmities were peculiarly distressing. There is sometimes an apathy attending advanced life, which makes its accompanying changes less perceptible; but when the dull ear, and dim eye, and lingering step, and trembling hand, are for ever interfering with the enjoyments of a man, who would otherwise delight in the society of the young and active —such a contrast between the body and mind can only be borne with fortitude by those who look hopefully for youth renewed in another state of existence. 'It cannot be supposed,' says the Roman orator, 'that Nature, after having widely distributed to all the preceding periods of life their peculiar and proper enjoyments, should have neglected, like an indolent poet, the last act of the human drama, and left it destitute of suitable advantages':—and yet it would be difficult to point out in what these consist. On the contrary, Nature discovers her destitute state, and manifests it in peevishness and repining, unless a higher principle than Nature takes possession of the mind, and makes it sensible, that, 'though the outward man perish, yet the inward man is renewed day by day.' It was by this principle that Mr. Crabbe was actuated; and he at times gave such proofs of his confidence in the promises of the Gospel, that the spot on which he expressed these hopes with peculiar energy is now looked upon by the friend who conversed with him as holy ground. But he rarely spoke thus; for he had such an humble spirit, so much fear of conveying the impression that he believed himself accepted, that the extent of these enjoyments was known to few. Thus, however, the privations of age and frequent suffering were converted into blessings, and he acknowledged their advantage in weaning him from the world. Considering life as the season of discipline, and looking back to the merciful restraints, and also acknowledging the many encouragements, which he had received from an over-ruling Providence, he was not impatient under the most troublesome and vexatious infirmity, or over-anxious to escape that evil which, if rightly received, might add to the evidence and security of the happiness hereafter. He had a notion, perhaps somewhat whimsical, that we shall be gainers in a future state by the cultivation of the intellect, and always affixed a sense of this nature also to the more important meaning of the word 'talents' in the parable: and this stimulus doubtless increased his avidity for knowledge, at a period when such study was of little use besides the amusement of the present hour."

Preparing to visit Hastings, in September, 1830, with his friends from Hampstead Heath, he says:

"I feel, in looking forward to this journey, as if there was a gulf fixed between us: and yet what are three or four weeks when passed! When anticipated, they appear as if they might be productive of I know not what pleasures and adventures; but when they are gone, we are almost at a loss to recollect any incident that occurred. My preaching days are almost over. On the Sunday evening I feel too much like a labourer who rejoices that his day's work is done, rather than one who reflects how it was performed."

Some friends having offered a visit at the parsonage during his absence on this occasion, he thus wrote to my brother:

"Now, my dear John, do remember that you must make the house what it should be. Do me honour, I pray you, till I can take it upon myself: all that the cellar can afford, or the market, rests with you and your guests, who know very well in what good living consists. I doubt if G—— drinks claret. Mr. Spackman, I think, does; at least he produces it, and to him it should be produced. Now do, my good fellow, go along with me in this matter: you know all I would have, as well as I do myself."

This short extract will exemplify another characteristic. Always generous and liberal, I think he grew more so in the later portion of his life—not less careful, but more bountiful and charitable. He lived scrupulously within the limits of his income, increased by the produce of his literary exertions; but he freely gave away all that he did not want for current expenses. I know not which of his relatives have not received some substantial proofs of this generous spirit.

The following letter from Hastings, dated 28th September, 1830, produced in his parsonage feelings which I shall not attempt to describe:—

To the Rev. John Crabbe.

"MY DEAR SON,—I write (as soon as the post permits) to inform you that I arrived in the evening of yesterday, in nearly the same state as I left you, and full as well as I expected, though a rather alarming accident made me feel unpleasantly for some hours, and its effects in a slight degree remain. I had been out of the coach a very short time, while other passengers were leaving it on their arrival at their places; and, on getting into the coach again, and close beside it, a gig, with two men in it, came on as fast as it could drive, which I neither saw nor heard till I felt a shaft against my side. I fell, of course, and the wheel went over one foot and one arm. Twenty people were ready to assist a stranger, who in a few minutes was sensible that the alarm was all the injury. Benjamin was ready, and my friends took care that I should have all the indulgence that even a man frightened could require. Happily I found them well, and we are all this morning going to one of the churches, where I hope I shall remember that many persons, under like circumstances, have never survived to relate their adventure. I hope to learn very shortly that you are all well: remember me to all with you, and to our friends, westward and elsewhere. Write—briefly if you must, but write. From your affectionate father.

"GEO. CRABBE.

"P.S.—You know my poor. Oram had a shilling on Sunday; but Smith, the bed-ridden woman, Martin, and Gregory, the lame man, you will give to as I would; nay, I must give somewhat more than usual; and if you meet with my other poor people, think of my accident, and give a few additional shillings for me; and I must also find some who want where I am, for my danger was great, and I must be thankful in every way I can."

On the 2nd of the next month he thus writes:

"I do not eat yet with appetite, but am terribly dainty. I walk by the sea and inhale the breeze in the morning, and feel as if I were really hungry; but it is not the true hunger, for, whatever the food, I am soon satisfied, or rather satiated: but all in good time; I have yet been at Hastings but one week. Dear little Georgy! I shall not forget her sympathy: my love to her, and to my two younger dears, not forgetting mamma."

A friend, who was with him in this expedition, thus speaks of him:

"He was able, though with some effort, to join a party to Hastings in the autumn, and passed much of his time on the sea-shore, watching the objects familiar to him in early life. It was on a cold November morning that he took his LAST look at his favourite element, in full glory, the waves foaming and dashing against the shore. He returned, with the friends whom he had been visiting, to town, and spent some weeks with them in its vicinity, enjoying the society to which he was strongly attached, but aware for how short a period those pleasures were to last. Having made a morning call in Cavendish Square, where he had met Mrs. Joanna Baillie, for whom he had a high esteem, and several members of her family, he was affected to tears, on getting into the carriage after taking leave of them, saying, 'I shall never meet this party again.' His affections knew no decline. He was never, apparently, the least tenacious of a reputation for talent; but most deeply sensible of every proof of regard and affection. One day, when absent from home, and suffering from severe illness, he received a letter from Miss Waldron, informing him of the heartfelt interest which many of his parishioners had expressed for his welfare. Holding up this letter, he said, with great emotion, 'Here is something worth living for!' "

I may, perhaps, as well insert in this place a kind letter with which I have lately been honoured by the great Poetess of the Passions:

From Mrs. Joanna Baillie.
"I have often met your excellent father at Mr. Hoare's, and frequently elsewhere; and he was always, when at Hampstead, kind enough to visit my sister and me; but, excepting the good sense and gentle courtesy of his conversation and manners, I can scarcely remember anything to mention in particular. Well as he knew mankind under their least

favourable aspect, he seemed never to forget that they were his brethren, and to love them even when most *unloveable*— if I may be permitted to use the word. I have sometimes been almost provoked by the very charitable allowances which he made for the unworthy, so that it required my knowledge of the great benevolence of his own character, and to receive his sentiments as a follower of Him who was the friend of publicans and sinners, to reconcile me to such lenity. On the other hand, I have sometimes remarked that, when a good or generous action has been much praised, he would say in a low voice, as to himself, something that insinuated a more mingled and worldly cause for it. But this never, as it would have done from any other person, gave the least offence; for you felt quite assured as he uttered it, that it proceeded from a sagacious observance of mankind, and was spoken in sadness, not in the spirit of satire.

"In regard to his courtesy relating to the feelings of others in smaller matters, a circumstance comes to my recollection, in which you will, perhaps, recognise your father. While he was staying with Mrs. Hoare a few years since, I sent him one day the present of a blackcock, and a message with it, that Mr. Crabbe should look at the bird before it was delivered to the cook, or something to that purpose. He looked at the bird as desired, and then went to Mrs. Hoare in some perplexity, to ask whether he ought not to have it stuffed, instead of eating it. She could not, in her own house, tell him that it was simply intended for the larder; and he was at the trouble and expense of having it stuffed, lest I should think proper respect had not been put upon my present. This both vexed and amused me at the time, and was remembered as a pleasing and peculiar trait of his character.

"He was a man fitted to engage the esteem and good-will of all who were fortunate enough to know him well; and I have always considered it as one of the many obligations I owe to the friendship of Mrs. and Miss Hoare, that through them I first became acquainted with this distinguished and amiable poet. Believe me, with all good wishes, &c.

"J. BAILLIE."

I shall add here part of a letter which I have received from another of what I may call my father's *Hampstead* friends— Mr. Duncan, of Bath, well known for the extent and elegance of his accomplishments. He says:

"My first acquaintance with him was at the house of Mr. Hoare, at Hampstead; by whose whole family he appeared to be regarded as a beloved and venerated relation. I was much struck, as I think every one who was ever in his company must have been, by his peculiar suavity, courtesy, and even humility of manner. There was a self-renunciation, a carelessness of attracting admiration, which formed a remarkable contrast with the ambitious style of conversation of some other literati, in whose company I have occasionally seen him. I have often thought that a natural politeness and sensitive regard for the feelings of others occasioned him to reject opportunities of saying smart and pointed things, or of putting his remarks into that epigrammatic, and, perhaps, not always extemporaneous form, which supplies brilliant scraps for collectors of anecdotes. His conversation was easy, fluent, and abundant in correct information; but distinguished chiefly by good sense and good feeling. When the merits of contemporary authors were discussed, his disapprobation was rather to be collected from his unwillingness to dwell on obvious and too prominent faults, than from severity in the exposure of them. But his sympathy with good expression of good feelings, such as he found, for example, in the pages of Scott, roused him to occasional fervour. If he appeared at any time to show a wish that what he said might be remembered, it was when he endeavoured to place in a simple and clear point of view, for the information of a young person, some useful truth, whether historical, physiological, moral, or religious. He had much acquaintance with botany and geology; and, as you know, was a successful collector of local specimens; and as I, and doubtless many others, know, was a liberal imparter of his collected store.

"The peculiar humour which gives brilliancy to his writings, gave a charm to his conversation: but its tendency was to excite pleasurable feeling, by affording indulgence to harmless curiosity by a peep behind the scenes of human nature, rather than to produce a laugh. I remember to have heard a country gentleman relate an instance of his good temper and self-command. They were travelling in a stage-coach from Bath; and as they approached Calne, the squire mentioned the names of certain poets of the neighbourhood; expressed his admiration of your father's earlier works;—but ventured to hint that one of the latter, I forget which, was a failure, and that he would do well to lay his pen aside. 'Sir,' said your father, 'I am quite of your opinion. Artists and poets of all ages have fallen into the same error. Time creeps on so gently, that they never find out that they are growing old!' 'So,' said the squire, 'we talked of Gil Blas and the Archbishop, and soon digressed into talk of parish matters and justice business. I was delighted with my companion, who soon alighted; and I only learned by inquiring of the coachman who had been my fellow-traveller.' I told this to your father, who laughed, remembered the incident, and said, 'the squire, perhaps, was right; but you know I was an incompetent judge upon that subject.'"

I have already mentioned his visits to Pucklechurch. Great

was the pleasure of our household in expecting him, for his liberality left no domestic without an ample remembrance. What listening for the chaise among the children! It is heard rattling through the street—it is in the churchyard—at the door. His pale face is lighted with pleasure—as benevolent, as warm-hearted as in his days of youth and strength; but age has sadly bent his once tall stature, and his hand trembles. What a package of books—what stores for the table—what presents for the nursery! Little tales, as nearly resembling those which had delighted his own infancy as modern systems permit— one quite after his own heart—the German Nursery Stories.[3] After dinner the children assemble round the dessert, and perhaps he reads them the story of the Fisherman, his greatest favourite. How often have I heard him repeat to them the invocation—

> "O, man of the sea, come listen to me,
> For Alice, my wife, the plague of my life,
> Hath sent me to beg a boon of thee."

And he would excite their wonder and delight, with the same evident satisfaction, that I so well remembered in my early days. Of the morose feelings of age, repining for lost pleasures, he knew nothing; for his youth had been virtuous, his middle age intellectual and manly, his decline honourable and honoured. Such minds covet not, envy not, the advantages of youth, but regard them with benevolent satisfaction—perhaps not unmixed with a species of apprehensive pity, for their fiery ordeal is not yet past.

He loved, particularly at last, to converse on early scenes and occurrences; and when we began that theme, it was generally a late hour before we parted. Unfortunately, I

[3] The translation of Grimm's Kinder- und Haus-Märchen.

meditated this record too recently to reap the full advantage. On these reminiscences, even at the date to which my narrative has now come, his spirits have risen, and his countenance has brightened into the very expression which marked his happiest mood in his most vigorous years.

In the morning, even in the roughest weather, he went his way (always preferring to be alone) to some of our quarries of blue lias, abounding in fossils, stopping to cut up any herb not quite common, that grew in his path; and he would return loaded with them. The dirty fossils were placed in our best bed-room, to the great diversion of the female part of the family; the herbs 'stuck in the borders, among my choice flowers, that he might see them when he came again. I never displaced one of them.

When we had friends to meet him, with what ease and cheerfulness would he enter into the sociality of the evening, taking his subject and his tone from those around him; except when he was under the too frequently recurring pain, and then he was sometimes obliged to retire. Few aged persons so readily acquired an attachment to strangers; he was ever ready to think warmly of every one who treated him with kindness. There was no acrimony in him; and to the end he had that accommodating mind in conversation which often marks the young, but which is rarely found at the age of threescore and ten.

We dreaded his departure. It was justly remarked by one of his nieces, that he left a feeling of more melancholy vacancy when he quitted a house than any other person,—even than those whose presence afforded more positive pleasure. "I hope," said she, one day, very earnestly, "that my uncle will not come into Suffolk this year; for I shall dread his going away all the time he is with us." He generally left the young people all in tears—feeling strongly, and not having the power to conceal it. The stooping form, the trembling step, the tone and manner of his farewell, especially for the last few years, so hurried, so foreboding, so affectionate, overcame us all.

My brother has the following observations on his perseverance in his clerical duties:—"With my father's active mind and rooted habits—for he did not omit the duty on one Sunday for nearly forty years—it would have been distressing to him to have ceased to officiate; but the pain to which he was subject, was frequently very severe; and when attacked during the service, he was obliged to stop and press his hand hard to his face, and then his pale countenance became flushed. Under these paroxysms, his congregation evidently felt much for him; and he often hesitated whether he had not better give it up altogether. I was accustomed to join him in the vestry-room, after reading the prayers; and whilst sitting by the fire, waiting till the organ had ceased, I well recollect the tone of voice, firm and yet depressed, in which he would say, 'Well!—one Sunday more'; or, 'a few Sundays more, but not many.' I was astonished, however, to observe how much his spirits and strength were always renovated by an absence from home. He continued to officiate till the last two Sundays before his decease."

In the midst of one of the radical tumults of this period, he thus wrote to Mr. Phillips, the eminent Academician, whose portrait of him had been recently re-engraved:

"Amid the roar of cannon, and that of a tumultuous populace, assembled to show their joy, and to demand shows of the same kind from those who reside among them, I retire for a few minutes, to reply to your favour: and this must be my apology if I do not thank you as I ought, for the kindness you express, and your purpose to oblige me in my wishes to possess a few copies of the engraving, of which I heard such a highly-approving account, by my friend Mr. Dawson Turner, of Yarmouth, a gentleman upon whose taste I can rely; nor ought I to omit to mention that of his lady, who herself designs in a superior manner, and is an excellent judge of all works of the kind. If I were sure of having a room to retire to on the morrow, with a whole window in it, I believe I should postpone my acknowledgment of your letter; but there is no setting bounds to the exertions of a crowd, in a place like this, when once they entertain the idea, be it right or wrong, that you are not of their opinion."

On the 19th of January, 1831, he thus writes to Mr. Henchman Crowfoot, of Beccles, the relative of his son John's wife, and for whom he had a strong partiality:

"19th January, 1831.

"A long journey, as that would be into Suffolk, I contemplate with mixed feelings of hope and apprehension. After a freedom of several months' duration, I have once more to endure the almost continual attacks of the pain over which I boasted a victory, that, alas! is by no means complete. Again I have recourse to steel, and again feel relief; but I am nearly convinced that travelling in stage-coaches, however good the roads, has a tendency to awaken this kind of disease, which (I speak reverendly) is not dead, but sleepeth. Yet I should rejoice to revisit Beccles, where every one is kind to me, and where every object I view has the appearance of friendship and welcome. Beccles is the home of past years, and I could not walk through the streets as a stranger. It is not so at Aldborough: there a sadness mixes with all I see or hear; not a man is living whom I knew in my early portion of life; my contemporaries are gone, and their successors are unknown to me and I to them. Yet, in my last visit, my niece and I passed an old man, and she said, 'There is one you should know; you played together as boys, and he looks as if he wanted to tell you so.' Of course, I stopped on my way and Zekiel Thorpe and I became once more acquainted. This is sadly tedious to you: but you need not be told that old men love to dwell upon their Recollections: and that, I suppose, is one reason for the many volumes published under that name.—Recollections of gentlemen who tell us what they please, and amuse us, in their old age, with the follies of their youth!

"I beg to be remembered to and by Mrs. Crowfoot, Sen., my ——— what shall I call the relationship? We are the father and mother of our son and daughter, but in what legal affinity I cannot determine; but I hope we may discuss that question, if it be necessary, at Trowbridge. And now, finally—in which way we close our sermons—once more accept my thanks, and those of my son and daughter. We have this day dined magnificently on your turkey, and drank our wine with remembrances to our friends in Suffolk? We are all—if I except my too frequently recurring pain—in good health; and—the indisposition of Mrs. George Crabbe excepted—so are the Gloucestershire part of my family: *mine*, I repeat with some pride and with more pleasure. I should much like an hour's conversation, *inter nos*, without participation, without interruption; and I am fully persuaded that you would not reject it."

The following is from a letter dated in the April of the same year—the last of his life:

"Comparing myself with myself, I have felt the weakening effect of time more within the last six months than I ever experienced before. I do not know that I am weaker than numbers are at my age, but I am sure that there is great difference between me at this time, and *me* (if I may so say) at Hastings last year. I cannot walk, no, not half the distance; and then—(one more complaint, and I have done)—I cannot read, but for a short time at once: and now I would ask myself, What would I do at Pucklechurch? if my feet fail me when I walk, my sight when I read—why, I should be a perpetual incumbrance? You will say, What, then, do you do at Trowbridge? There, you know, I have a number of small and often recurring duties, and I play with my fossils; but still I am always purposing to come to you when I can."

Again in May:

"I am still weak, and just, as I suppose, like other old declining people, without any particular diseases. But in the latter part of the day I become much renovated. Mr. Waldron and I talked of a London journey last evening, till I began to persuade myself I was capable of the undertaking. A little serious consideration when I left him, and especially this morning's feelings, put to flight all such young man's fancies."

Towards the close of this year he again visited his friends, his kind and attached friends, of Hampstead, at their residence at Clifton; and this visit occurring at the memorable time of the Bristol riots, I will subjoin some extracts from his letters from thence—the last we ever received:

"Clifton, October 24.—Assure our dear Caroline,[4] that I feel pleasure in the thought of sitting in any room she assigns me; there to employ myself in my own way, without being troubled or interrupted by any one's business, as at Trowbridge, even by my own. You can scarcely believe how the

[4] His daughter-in-law.

love and enjoyment of quiet grows upon me. One of my great indulgencies is to feel myself alone, but to know, and perhaps hear, that a whole family, little ones and great, are within a few paces of me, and that I can see them when I please—this is a grandpapa's luxury, Miss Caroline!

"I have to thank my friends for one of the most beautiful as well as comfortable rooms you could desire. I look from my window upon the Avon and its wooded and rocky bounds— the trees yet green. A vessel is sailing down, and here comes a steamer (Irish, I suppose). I have in view the end of the Cliff to the right, and on my left a wide and varied prospect over Bristol, as far as the eye can reach, and at present the novelty makes it very interesting. Clifton was always a favourite place with me. I have more strength and more spirits since my arrival at this place, and do not despair of giving a good account of my excursion on my return.

"I believe there is a fund of good sense as well as moral feeling in the people of this country; and if ministers proceed steadily, give up some points, and be firm in essentials, there will be a union of sentiment on this great subject of reform by and by; at least, the good and well-meaning will drop their minor differences and be united.

"So you have been reading my almost forgotten stories— Lady Barbara and Ellen! I protest to you their origin is lost to me, and I must read them myself before I can apply your remarks. But I am glad you have mentioned the subject, because I have to observe that there are, in my recess at home, where they have been long undisturbed, another series of such stories—in number and quantity sufficient for an octavo volume; and as I suppose they are much like the former in execution, and sufficiently different in events and characters, they may hereafter, in peaceable times, be worth something to you; and the more, because I shall, whatever is mortal of me, be at rest in the chancel of Trowbridge church; for the works of authors departed are generally received with some favour, partly as they are old acquaintances, and in part because there can be no more of them."

This letter was our first intimation that my father had any more poems quite prepared for the press;—little did we at that moment dream that we should never have an opportunity of telling him, that since we knew of their existence, he might as well indulge us with the pleasure of hearing them read by himself. On the 26th of the same October he thus wrote to me:

"I have been with Mrs. Hoare at Bristol, where all appears still: should any thing arise to alarm, you may rely upon our care to avoid danger. Sir Charles Wetherell, to be sure, is not popular, nor is the Bishop, but I trust that both will be safe from violence—abuse they will not mind. The Bishop seems a good-humoured man, and, except by the populace, is greatly admired.—I am sorry to part with my friends, whom I cannot reasonably expect to meet often,—or, more reasonably yet, whom I ought to look upon as here taking our final leave; but, happily, our ignorance of our time is in this our comfort,—that let friends part at any period of their lives, hope will whisper, 'We shall meet again.' "

Happily, he knew not that this *was* their last meeting. In his next letter he speaks of the memorable riots of Bristol—the most alarming of the sort since those recorded in his own London diary, of 1780—and which he had evidently anticipated.

"Bristol, I suppose, never, in the most turbulent times of old, witnessed such outrage. Queen's Square is but half standing; half is smoking ruin. As you may be apprehensive for my safety, it is right to let you know that my friends and I are undisturbed, except by our fears for the progress of this mob-government, which is already somewhat broken into parties, who wander stupidly about, or sleep wherever they fall wearied with their work and their indulgence. The military are now in considerable force, and many men are sworn in as constables: many volunteers are met in Clifton churchyard, with white round one arm, to distinguish them; some with guns, and the rest with bludgeons. The Mayor's house has been destroyed,—the Bishop's palace plundered, but whether burnt or not I do not know. This morning, a party of soldiers attacked the crowd in the Square; some lives were lost, and the mob dispersed, whether to meet again is doubtful. It has been a dreadful time, but we may reasonably hope it is now over. People are frightened certainly—and no wonder, for it is evident these poor wretches would plunder to the extent of their power. Attempts were made to burn the cathedral, but failed. Many lives were lost. To attempt any other subject now would be fruitless. We can think, speak, and write only of our fears, hopes, or troubles. I would have gone to Bristol to-day, but Mrs. Hoare was unwilling that I should. She thought, and perhaps rightly, that clergymen were marked objects. I therefore only went about half way, and of course could learn but little. All now is quiet and well."

Leaving his most valued friends in the beginning of November, my father came to Pucklechurch, so improved in health and strength, that his description of himself would have been deemed the effect of mere *ennui*, except by those who know the variableness of age—the temporary strength—the permanent weakness. He preached at both my churches the following Sunday, in a voice so firm and loud, and in a manner so impressive, that I was congratulated on the power he manifested at that advanced stage of life, and was much comforted with the indications of a long protracted decline. I said, "Why, Sir, I will venture a good sum that you will be assisting me ten years hence."—"Ten weeks," was his answer —and that was almost literally the period when he ceased to assist any one. He left us after a fortnight, and returned to Trowbridge. On the 7th of January he wrote:

"I do not like drowsiness—mine is an old man's natural infirmity, and that same old man creeps upon me more and more. I cannot walk him away: he gets old on the memory and my poor little accounts never come right. Let me nevertheless be thankful: I have very little pain. 'Tis true from a stiffness in my mouth, I read prayers before we take our breakfast with some difficulty; but that being over, I feel very little incommoded for the rest of the day. We are all in health, for I will not call my lassitude, and stupidity by the name of illness. Like Lear, I am a poor old man and foolish, but happily I have no daughter who vexes me."

In the course of this month, I paid him a visit, and stayed with him three or four days; and if I had been satisfied with the indications of his improved health when at Pucklechurch, I was most agreeably surprised to find him still stronger and in better spirits than I had witnessed for the last three years. He had become perceptibly stouter in that short interval; he took his meals with a keen appetite, and walked in a more upright position; and there were no counter-tokens to excite our suspicions. It is true, he observed that he did not like the increase of flesh; but this was said in that light cheerful manner, which imported no serious fears. On the 29th, I received a letter from my brother, stating that he had caught a sharp cold, accompanied with oppression in the chest and pain in the forehead, for which he had been bled. He added, that my father felt relieved, and that he would write again immediately; but on the following morning, while I was expecting an account of his amendment, a chaise drove to the door, which my brother had sent me to save time. In fact, all hope of recovery was already over.

I had once before seen him, as I have already described, under nearly similar circumstances, when, if he was not in extreme danger, he evidently thought he was. He had then said, "Unless some great change takes place, I cannot recover," and had ordered my mother's grave to be kept open to receive him. I asked myself, Will he bear the shock now as firmly as he did then? I feared he would not; because he must be aware that such a change as had then ensued was next to impossible under the present disorder at the age of seventy-seven; and because, whenever he had parted with any of us for the last four or five years, he had been much affected, evidently from the thought that it might be the last meeting. I greatly feared, therefore, that his spirits would be woefully depressed—that the love of life might remain in all its force, and that the dread of death might be strong and distressing. I now state with feelings of indescribable thankfulness, that I had been foreboding a weight of evil that was not; and that we had only to lament his *bodily* sufferings and our incalculable loss.

During the days that preceded his departure, we had not one painful feeling arising from the state of his *mind*. That was more firm than I ever remembered under any circumstances. He knew there was no chance of his recovery, and yet he talked at intervals of his death, and of certain consequent arrangements with a strong complacent voice;

and bade us all adieu without the least faltering of the tongue
or moisture of the eye. The awfulness of death, apprehended
by his capacious mind, must have had a tendency to absorb
other feelings; yet was he calm and unappalled;—and intervals
of oblivion, under the appearance of sleep, softened his
sufferings and administered an opiate to his faculties. One of
his characteristics,—exuberance of thought, seemed sometimes
even when pleased, as if it oppressed him; and in this last
illness, when he was awake, his mind worked with astonishing rapidity. It was not delirium; for on our recalling his
attention to present objects, he would speak with perfect
rationality; but, when uninterrupted, the greater portion of
his waking hours were passed in rapid soliloquies on a variety
of subjects, the chain of which, from his imperfect utterance
(when he did not exert himself), we were unable to follow.
We seldom interrupted the course that nature was taking, or
brought him to the effort of connected discourse, except to
learn how we could assist or relieve him. But as in no instance
(except in a final lapse of memory) did we discover the least
irrationality—so there was no despondency; on the contrary,
the cheerful expressions which he had been accustomed to use,
were heard from time to time; nay, even that elevation of the
inner side of the eyebrows, which occasionally accompanied
some humorous observation in the days of his health, occurred once or twice after every hope of life was over. But,
if we were thankful for his firmness of mind, we had to
lament the strength of his constitution. I was not aware how
powerful it was till tried by this disease. I said, "It is your
great strength which causes this suffering." He replied, "But
it is a great price to pay for it."

On one essential subject it would be wrong to be silent.
I have stated, that the most important of all considerations had
had an *increasing* influence over his mind. The growth had

been ripening with his age, and was especially perceptible in his later years. With regard to the ordinances of religion, he was always manifestly pained if, when absent from home on a Sunday, he had been induced to neglect either the morning or evening services: in his private devotions, as his household can testify, he was most exemplary and earnest up to the period of his attack; yet at that time, when fear often causes the first real prayer to be uttered, *then* did he, as it were, confine himself to the inward workings of his pious and resigned spirit, occasionally, however, betrayed by aspirations most applicable to his circumstances. Among the intelligible fragments that can never be forgotten, were frequent exclamations of, "My time is short; it is well to be prepared for death." "Lucy,"—this was the affectionate servant that attended along with his sons,—"dear Lucy, be earnest in prayer! May you see your children's children." From time to time he expressed great fear that we were all over-exerting ourselves in sitting up at night with him; but the last night he said, "Have patience with me—it will soon be over.—Stay with me, Lucy, till I am dead, and then let others take care of me." This night was most distressing. The changes of posture sometimes necessary, gave him extreme pain, and he said, "This is shocking." Then again he became exhausted, or his mind wandered in a troubled sleep. Awaking a little refreshed, he held out his hand to us, saying—as if he felt it might be the last opportunity, "God bless you—be good, and come to me!" Even then, though we were all overpowered, and lost all self-command, he continued firm. His countenance now began to vary and alter. Once, however, we had the satisfaction of seeing it lighted up with an indescribable expression of joy, as he appeared to be looking at something before him, and uttered these words, "That blessed book!"

After another considerable interval of apparent insensibility, he awoke, and said, in a tone so melancholy that it rang in my ears for weeks after, "I thought it had been all over," with such an emphasis on the *all*! Afterwards he said, "I cannot see you now." When I said, "We shall soon follow," he answered, "Yes, yes!" I mentioned his exemplary fortitude; but he appeared unwilling to have any good ascribed to himself.

When the incessant presents and enquiries of his friends in the town were mentioned, he said, "What a trouble I am to them all!" And in the course of the night, these most consolatory words were distinctly heard, "All is well at last!" Soon after, he said, imperfectly, "You must make an entertainment"; meaning for his kind Trowbridge friends after his departure. These were the last intelligible words I heard. Lucy, who could scarcely be persuaded to leave him, day or night, and was close by him when he died, says that the last words he uttered were, "God bless you—God bless you!"

About one o'clock he became apparently torpid; and I left him with my brother, requesting to be called instantly, in case of the least returning sensibility,—but it never returned. As my brother was watching his countenance at seven o'clock in the morning a rattling in the throat was heard once, and twice, but the third or fourth time all was over.

The shutters of the shops in the town were half closed, as soon as his death was known. On the day of his funeral, ninety-two of the principal inhabitants, including all the dissenting ministers, assembling of their own accord in the school-room, followed him to the grave. The shops on this day were again closed; the streets crowded; the three galleries and the organ-loft were hung with black cloth, as well as the pulpit and chancel. The choir was in mourning—the other inhabitants of the town were in their seats and in mourning—the church was full—the effect appalling. The terrible solemnity seems yet recent while I write. The leader of the choir selected the following beautiful anthem:

"When the ear heard him, then it blessed him;
And when the eye saw him, it gave witness of him.
He delivered the poor that cried, the fatherless, and him
    that had none to help him:
Kindness and meekness and comfort were in his tongue."

The worthy master of the Free and Sunday school at Trowbridge, Mr. Nightingale, on the Sunday after his funeral, delivered an impressive address to the numerous children under his care, on the death of their aged and affectionate minister. It was printed, and contains the following passage: " 'Poor Mr. Crabbe,' said a little girl, the other day very simply, *'poor Mr. Crabbe will never go up in pulpit any more with his white head.'* No! my children, that hoary head—found, as may yours and mine be found!—in the ways of righteousness and peace, is gone to rest; but his memory is embalmed in the house of our God. Sacred is the honoured dust that sleeps beside yonder altar. Is there one of you who has not experienced his kindness?—who has not seen his eyes beam with pleasure to hear you repeat 'Thy Kingdom come: Thy will be done'? Religiously keep the Bibles he gave you; and when you read these words of your Saviour—'I go to prepare a place for you—and when I come, I will receive you to myself'—think of your affectionate minister, and that these were his dying words— 'Be good and come to me.' "

Soon after his funeral, some of the principal parishioners met, in order to form a committee, to erect a monument over his grave in the chancel: and when his family begged to contribute to the generous undertaking, it was not permitted

"They desired," it was observed by their respected chairman,[5] "to testify their regard to him as a friend and a minister." And, I trust, his children's children will be taught to honour those who, by their deep sense of his worth, have given so strong a token of their own worthiness.

The subscriptions to his monument being sufficiently large to sanction the commission of the work to the hands of Mr. Baillie, he finished it in July, and it was placed in the church, August, 1833. The eminent artist himself generously contributed the marble.

A figure admirably represents the dying poet casting his eyes on the sacred volume; two celestial beings are looking on, as if awaiting his departure: on the last page of this volume is the short and beautiful inscription, judiciously expressed in his own native tongue.

It is the custom to close a biographical work with a summary of character. I must leave the reader of these pages to supply this for himself. I conclude with simply transcribing a few verses—ascribed to an eminent pen,[6]—which appeared in print shortly after my dear and venerable father's departure:

"Farewell, dear CRABBE! thou meekest of mankind,
With heart all fervour, and all strength of mind.
With tenderest sympathy for others' woes,
Fearless, all guile and malice to expose:
Steadfast of purpose in pursuit of right,
To drag forth dark hypocrisy to light,
To brand th' oppressor, and to shame the proud,
To shield the righteous from the slanderous crowd;

[5] Mr. Waldron, his young friend and adviser, now like himself numbered with the departed. He died, universally beloved and lamented, April, 1833, a year and two months after my father.

[6] John Duncan, Esq., of New College, Oxford.

To error lenient and to frailty mild,
Repentance ever was thy welcome child:
In every state, as husband, parent, friend,
Scholar, or bard, thou couldst the Christian blend.
Thy verse from Nature's face each feature drew,
Each lovely charm, each mole and wrinkle too.
No dreamy incidents of wild romance,
With whirling shadows, wilder'd minds entrance;
But plain realities the mind engage,
With pictured warnings through each polished page.
Hogarth of Song! be this thy perfect praise:—
Truth prompted, and Truth purified thy lays;
The God of Truth has given thy verse and thee
Truth's holy palm—His Immortality."

SACRED TO THE MEMORY

OF

THE REV. GEORGE CRABBE, LL.B.,

WHO DIED FEBRUARY THE THIRD, 1832,
IN THE SEVENTY-EIGHTH YEAR OF HIS AGE, AND THE
NINETEENTH OF HIS SERVICES AS RECTOR
OF THIS PARISH.

BORN IN HUMBLE LIFE, HE MADE HIMSELF WHAT HE WAS.
BY THE FORCE OF HIS GENIUS,
HE BROKE THROUGH THE OBSCURITY OF HIS BIRTH
YET NEVER CEASED TO FEEL FOR THE
LESS FORTUNATE;

ENTERING (AS HIS WORKS CAN TESTIFY) INTO
THE SORROWS AND DEPRIVATIONS
OF THE POOREST OF HIS PARISHIONERS;
AND SO DISCHARGING THE DUTIES OF HIS STATION AS
A MINISTER AND A MAGISTRATE,
AS TO ACQUIRE THE RESPECT AND ESTEEM
OF ALL HIS NEIGHBOURS.

AS A WRITER, HE IS WELL DESCRIBED BY A GREAT
CONTEMPORARY AS
"NATURE'S STERNEST PAINTER, YET HER BEST."